# AN ANGLE ON
# THE WORLD

# AN ANGLE ON THE WORLD

*Dispatches and Diversions from the*
New Yorker *and Beyond*

# BILL BARICH

Skyhorse Publishing

Skyhorse Publishing books may be purchased in bulk at special discounts for sales promotion, corporate gifts, fund-raising, or educational purposes. Special editions can also be created to specifications. For details, contact the Special Sales Department, Skyhorse Publishing, 307 West 36th Street, 11th Floor, New York, NY 10018 or info@skyhorsepublishing.com.

Skyhorse® and Skyhorse Publishing® are registered trademarks of Skyhorse Publishing, Inc.®, a Delaware corporation.

Visit our website at www.skyhorsepublishing.com.

10 9 8 7 6 5 4 3 2 1

Library of Congress Cataloging-in-Publication Data is available on file.

Cover design by Anthony Morais
Cover photograph courtesy of QT Luong/terragalleria.com

Print ISBN: 978-1-5107-0833-4
Ebook ISBN: 978-1-5107-0834-1

Printed in the United States of America

For Imelda

# Table of Contents

# Introduction

I once had a schoolteacher who joked that I was the most curious boy she'd ever met. She meant that in the dictionary sense of "eager to learn or know something" rather than "strange, unusual," or so I choose to believe, although I may have been guilty on both counts. Whatever the case, I've spent much of my writing life indulging that curiosity, throwing myself into situations and subcultures to gain an education and acquire my own angle on the world. The dispatches collected here arose from that desire. All but one first appeared in the *New Yorker*, where my editors gave me the support and encouragement to tackle such in-depth reports.

The dispatches have a common thread. They all explore stories that the press had ignored or reported on in a desultory way, at least in my view. For years I'd been reading about the Troubles in Northern Ireland, for instance, but the focus was always on the sensational aspects of the conflict. I had no idea what Belfast looked like or how the people of the city conducted their daily affairs, so I decided to spend three weeks there. My hope was to capture what Norman Mailer described as "the feel of the phenomenon," or a palpable sensation of living in Ulster.

To keep from repeating the usual clichés, I avoided politicians, official sources, and other journalists. Instead I talked with greengrocers, butchers, newsagents, and so on, including a barber who swore he'd never visit San Francisco, my hometown at the time, because he was scared of earthquakes, proving that fear is relative. I walked from my hotel near Queens University through the Catholic Falls and the Protestant Shankill, and heard from the locals how the paramilitaries operate and the price they extract from the citizens they supposedly protect. It soon became clear who reaped the biggest benefits from the sectarian divide.

"Board-and-Care" addressed the plight of the homeless in San Francisco. A great many suffered from a mental disorder. Government programs to help out were sadly lacking, so I looked elsewhere for a possible solution. A psychiatrist friend, an activist in the field, steered me to Chateau Agape, a Queen Anne Victorian in the Mission District, where twenty-seven chronic adult paranoid schizophrenics lived together in relative harmony.

The chateau struck me as a cost-effective model for what could and should be done in a caring society. Its owners, the Loopers, were heroes in my eyes, and so, too, was Manuel Velasquez ("The Crazy Life"), who labored to prevent teenage gang members in Los Angeles County from dying young in turf or drug wars.

The disheartening mess along our border with Mexico hasn't improved much since I wrote "La Frontera." When I first arrived in San Ysidro, California, directly opposite Tijuana, I expected a tightly controlled perimeter as in the movies, but instead I witnessed an elaborate, never-ending game of cat-and-mouse. The border patrol was understaffed and overwhelmed, and its agents were almost powerless. So little has changed I'd only have to include the Trump factor and the vigilante patrols to bring the story up-to-date. As long as there's work on offer, the migrants will continue to risk a crossing.

"The Victim's Wake" came about when an editor at *Outside* asked if I'd like to cover a murder trial in the Caribbean, in St. Vincent and the Grenadines, where a wealthy American couple stood accused of killing a water taxi operator named Jolly Joseph. If a jury found them guilty, they might hang from the gallows. I sat in the dusty old courtroom and listened as bewigged barristers argued the case, while islanders in their Sunday best observed and delivered a whispered commentary, trying not to laugh or applaud.

The pieces I've grouped together as diversions offer lighter fare. I'd probably never have met Jerry Garcia, if the *New Yorker* under Tina Brown hadn't doted on celebrities. When David Milch invited me to work on his HBO horse racing show *Luck*, sadly short-lived, I got a master class in screenwriting from a genius of the form and lots of laughs in the bargain. The trips I made to Barbados and Culebra were courtesy of *Islands*. The essays on Italy, my Peace Corps days in Nigeria, and the Haight-Ashbury add up to a fragmentary portrait of my often-confused youth, when the dream of being a writer seemed too farfetched to ever be realized.

*An Angle On the World* is meant to be a bedside book, one to dip into at random and at leisure. Hopefully, the reader will find much to enjoy and only a little to provoke. Even when investigating the most difficult subjects, I've attempted to be as optimistic as common sense would allow. Looking back, as Satchel Paige advised us never to do, I'm pleased to see that I've made an adventure of my writing life and remain deeply grateful to all those who helped that miracle to happen.

# One: Dispatches

# Board and Care:
# San Francisco

Chateau Agape, San Francisco, seven o'clock on a February morning. The air smells of bacon frying, coffee percolating. With a spatula, Leroy Looper eases an egg off a stove-top grill and onto a plate, then hands it to a woman who wears an old raincoat for a robe. She's holding tightly to the collar, clinging to it for security. From a plastic tray, Leroy gives her two Mellaril pills and smiles at her in approval, pleased to see that her hair is neatly combed and her eyes are bright. Only yesterday, the woman was confused and frightened, unwilling to eat or to speak, and Leroy's wife, Kathy, had to coax some nourishment into her by offering cups of hot chocolate.

"You look real nice today, Carla," Leroy says to her, in a rich, preacherly voice, and this simple bit of praise seems to lift her off her feet. Meanwhile, he takes another egg from a cardboard carton and lets it rest for a moment on his palm. Against his skin, it resembles an oblong marble. He is a very big man of sixty-two, built on the scale of a retired pro-football tackle, and when he walks through the Tenderloin, a tough downtown district

15

where he runs a hotel and works as a neighborhood organizer, the pimps and dealers scatter. A former addict himself, he spent twelve years of his youth strung out on heroin, bouncing from prison to prison, but he kicked his habit for good.

Leroy cracks the egg and sets it to sizzling. He lays out more bacon strips—cheerful, humming to himself—and starts another pot of coffee, and the seductive aromas drift up a broad mahogany staircase to rooms on the second and third floors. The Chateau, a rambling Queen Anne Victorian mansion, is a board-and-care home for the mentally disabled, and all but one of twenty-seven men and women who share it with the Loopers are chronic schizophrenics. A secretary, a practical nurse, a rock musician—in a few minutes, they begin to roll into the dining room, half awake and in need of caffeine. They range in age from nineteen to fifty-two. Often in the past they've had to be hospitalized, some in locked facilities, but here they usually function well, creating an atmosphere of mutual support, a therapeutic community.

From an urn I help myself to hot water for tea, and I ask one of the boarders, whose name is Anatole, if I can join him at his table. "By all means," he says, gesturing grandly with an arm. In the weeks I've been visiting, we've become friends. We shoot pool in the basement, or sit around and discuss global affairs, solving—with amazing ease—many of the world's problems. Anatole has a quick wit, and the handsome, grizzled, toothless face of a prospector. His longish black hair is flecked with gray, and when he served in the Army, near Frankfurt, the Frauleins told him he was a double for Elvis. He, too, is looking good, having recently and reluctantly agreed to increase his daily dose of Stelazine, an anti-psychotic. Like most mental patients, he wants to be free of drugs and doctors, free of craziness, but at least he's sleeping better now, not staying up most of the night, wired and rapping.

When I first came to the Chateau, in late January, Anatole was hostile toward me, suspicious of my motives, informing me in his regal way that the only good writer around was Tom Brokaw of NBC. He resented the idea that I might be studying him, reducing his life to the stuff of research, so I had to be very clear about what I was doing. I explained that I'd got curious about the nationwide crisis in housing the mentally ill. In every major urban area of the United States, the streets were thick with disturbed people living in squalor, and I wondered if, in the absence of hospital beds, there was truly no place for them to go.

The number of mental institutions in the country has dropped radically since the nineteen-fifties. In California, privately owned, state-licensed board-and-cares are the primary long-term shelters for individuals with chronic illnesses. When I began to look into them, I met a local psychiatrist, Mel Blaustein, an expert in the field. He took me to two homes he visits weekly, acting as a medical adviser. (There are seventy-three board-and-cares in San Francisco, with seven hundred and five beds.) The homes I saw were small and run-down, set on busy, dismal blocks in poor neighborhoods, and the patients in them were sullen, giddy, or without affect, dozing in chairs, drinking beer, or watching endless hours of TV.

In terms of quality, Dr. Blaustein said, the homes were about average for the system, providing clean rooms, regular meals, monitoring of medication, and some supervision—an acceptable alternative, certainly, to forcing people to camp in alleys. Yet he believed it was possible for a board-and-care to be much more than just a holding tank, so he brought me to the Chateau, where the Loopers, with no special training or financial aid, were investing a tired concept with fresh energy.

All this I explained to Anatole (I have changed his name as well as the names of the other residents), and he nodded gravely, using his radar—a sixth sense some schizophrenics seem to have for determining the truth—to see if I was being honest. Apparently, I passed the test, because afterward he started seeking my company, laughing, teasing me, telling me jokes.

"I might be doing some writing myself pretty soon," he informs me this morning, rolling a cigarette from a pouch of Bugler, one of the sixty or eighty he'll smoke today.

"What will you write about?" I ask.

"Oh, something important, probably." He pauses for effect. "You know, like the Jurassic Age."

Light pours through the curved windows of the dining room. It's a balmy day, and in the garden roses are blooming, flaring up in reds and strong yellows. Again I am impressed by the beauty of the Chateau. Built in 1881 by a lumber tycoon, it was a mansion in ruin when the Loopers bought it, but they have gradually restored it and turned it into an architectural landmark. With bright white paint, a widow's walk, and an eccentric Turkish cupola, it stands out from the other houses on Guerrero Street, and often makes passersby stop to wonder what's going on inside. Sometimes at the Chateau, I feel as if I were on a fine old sailing ship. That comes in part from its size and in part from its period flavor. In every room, there are valuable antiques—brass beds, lamps with marble bases, armoires, gilt mirrors from the Barbary Coast.

The decor is even more remarkable when you consider that Kathy Looper scavenged every piece from a thrift shop or a garage sale, and refinished it. Now in her early forties, she is a short, sturdy, supremely dedicated woman of Greek ancestry, who wears glasses and bold colors, and hates to think that anything on earth might be going to waste. She was educated at Catholic schools in San Francisco and met Leroy in 1969, while she was still in college. "He was the first guy I ever dated," she told me once, giggling, her hands on her hips. "Yeah! Can you believe it?"

I notice that Anatole is involved in the morning paper. He has been reading a lot lately, hoping to reconstruct the areas of his brain he feels are damaged, so I leave him alone, walk down a hallway to the front door, and bump into three of the Looper children—a girl and two of the boys—on their way to school. Residents are also milling around, collecting themselves, preparing to go to day centers or to volunteer jobs. I pass Dorothy and Jane, and then I pass Georgie, a gentle, long-nosed Russian in a neat shirt and tie. Years ago, Georgie underwent electroshock treatment at Napa State Hospital. "And you know what?" he whispered to me the other day, fiercely proud. "I still remember how it felt!"

19

He grins as I stroll by, and picks up the thread of our ongoing conversation. "You like your meat rare, right?" he asks.

"That's right, Georgie."

A broader grin. "Just throw it on the barbecue and take it off, right?"

"Right again."

Very happy now. "Did your father have a temper?"

"When I was a kid. Not so much anymore."

With a wicked sort of glee, he says, "Did he give you lickings?"

"A spanking once in a while," I say.

Georgie quits talking and processes the data, storing it in a memory file he keeps on me. Always, he begins on a casual note and then grows more intimate, probing. He works by making comparisons, holding up another's life against his own, so that a measure is taken, something is gained. You should have been a tailor, Georgie, I think, stepping onto the front porch. Out in the yard, a resident named Darnell is uncoiling a hose, getting ready to water some pansies in tubs. A recent arrival, he is a shy young black man in a yellow knit cap. He waves to me. The sky above him, all around him, is a delicate, almost transparent blue.

\* \* \*

When Leroy Looper was a boy growing up in Washington, D.C., his father sometimes drank too much and beat him. He beat Leroy's mother as well, and whenever he knocked out a tooth of hers he replaced it with a gold one. But in Leroy's eyes the gold was less an apology than a form of insurance, something to be yanked out and pawned during the next bender; and at the age of seven, to keep from getting hit, he ran away from home. He earned some pocket money by shining shoes, begging for pennies, and selling copies of the *Afro-American* newspaper in bars and fancy hotels. His own name turned up in its "Missing Persons" column once, but he ignored the message, having already fallen in love with the streets.

Often when he was hungry, he would go to his Aunt Carrie's house, in Glick Alley, behind the old Howard Theatre. The alley was a hive of action, thick with numbers runners, bootleggers, prostitutes, and entertainers down on their luck. Leroy soon got caught up in the flow of crime, nabbed a woman's purse, and was sent to a reform school for a year—the year he was eight. The discipline there was strict. If you misbehaved, you were rapped on the knuckles with a ruler or were made to kneel for hours on concrete, under a blazing sun. Major offenders were stripped to the waist, tied to a rack, and lashed with a bullwhip.

On his release, Leroy vowed to avoid trouble, but he began cutting classes and roaming again, and, once more, when he was eleven, he foolishly stole a purse. The judge thought he must be a little crazy to repeat himself, so she sent him to an institution forty miles from the District that offered some psychiatric counselling. It had acres of land, and the security was not so tight. Leroy taught himself to box, played horseshoes and baseball, and steered clear of gangs. He had one very good teacher, Mr. Orange, who was Jewish and had been denied jobs at better schools because of his religion. Mr. Orange gave him books to read and started him on a course of self-education. At times, Leroy swore that he could feel his mind expanding; and as he walked over the vast property he dreamed about escaping.

One night, after cadging some food, he and two friends slipped out a window. He felt rapturous at first, blending into the woods, but it was also dark and cold, and after a while the boys couldn't tell one star from another and wandered aimlessly in circles until the guards captured them.

As punishment, Leroy was banished for three weeks to the Hole—a rank, bare, confining room in the cellar of the institution. Undaunted, he kept trying to get away, and on his third attempt he came upon a devious, little-travelled route that took him through orchards and cornfields and then to a railroad track that led him to the city. He was sixteen and had been away from home for five years, but his father still had no use for him. Instead of giving him comfort or advice, the old man reported him to the police, and he and Leroy had a vicious fight before Leroy bolted out the door.

For a few months, he hung out in District pool halls, supporting himself by hustling suckers at eight ball and rotation. After Pearl Harbor was bombed, other men from the area enlisted in the Army, but Leroy felt no particular allegiance to the country that had jailed him as a child, and he decided instead to travel and gain some experience. He packed a knapsack and hoboed around the East Coast, working as a waiter, a bellhop, a welder, and a cook. When he couldn't find a straight job, he indulged in petty cons, running a Murphy Game with a pal and sending unwary johns (they'd paid in advance) up the stairs of a nowhere apartment building for a tryst with the voluptuous but nonexistent Miss Murphy.

While Leroy was snoozing in a Manhattan cafeteria one afternoon in 1947, luxuriously unemployed, he struck up a friendship with a blues singer, Jimmy (Babyface) Lewis, who toured with an all-girl band, the Sweethearts of Rhythm. They got on so well that Jimmy hired him as his valet, and Leroy started travelling with the boss, making time with various Sweethearts, dressing in high style, and meeting people like Duke Ellington and Lionel Hampton at parties. An accommodating type, he kept a stash of marijuana on hand and sold it to band members and hangers-on, always holding back a little for himself, but he became incautious in his dealing and sold a few reefers to an undercover cop, earning a three-year term on Rikers Island.

There, in 1947, courtesy of a fellow-inmate, he got his first taste of heroin. It gave him a wonderful insulated feeling of relief, and once he was back outside he chased after it desperately.

An excuse, a blessing, a sickness, a seducer—to Leroy, heroin was all those things and more, and to buy it he dipped deeper into crime, pulling robberies and embarking on a familiar downward spiral to oblivion. The drug had such a grip on him that he might never have quit if he hadn't almost died of an overdose, waking one miserable Harlem dawn to find himself stuffed in an apartment closet with the rigid, ice-cold body of another junkie.

That was enough, finally, to drive him into a New York hospital for a difficult course of treatment and therapy, which involved facing his childhood, his terrors, all the good and not so good reasons for his addiction. When he returned to Harlem, in the mid-nineteen-sixties—drug-free but with no firm plans for the future—he saw that the place was not the hallucinatory night town he'd remembered from his years on dope. While he'd been nodding off, a regular Rip van Winkle, Harlem had changed in positive, unanticipated ways.

Young blacks and whites were canvassing on behalf of civil rights, and Leroy joined them as an organizer for the Harlem Action Group, mainly because it was a paying job. But he was quickly seized by the spirit, thrilled to hear his secret grievances articulated in public. His life took on purpose and direction, and all his natural sympathies were aroused. He discovered that he had a talent for leadership, like his heroes Malcolm X and Frederick Douglass, and he put it to use by arranging marches and rent strikes. He also opened a cleaning business, giving work to many of his neighbors in the community.

In 1966, after a trip to Africa encouraged his militancy, he returned to New York and began counseling drug abusers in state prisons. He was so effective that a wealthy benefactor gave him fifty thousand dollars to open a drug-treatment center of his own. He rented a building on 145th Street and called it Reality House. Many clients were waiting for him, because the word was out that he'd been through it all himself. He had mastered every trick in the doper's repertoire, and he got scoundrels to cooperate by telling them the truth: heroin is a superior high until it kills you. And, he warned, there would be no immediate rewards for recovering— you bought back some health and self-respect, but they were likely to be grabbed from you the minute you left the center.

Although the message was honest, Leroy did not enjoy delivering it. In a short time, overburdened, he was disillusioned with the rehab game, asking himself hard questions. For instance, why bother to treat someone if you're only going to discharge him into the same poverty and neglect that contributed to—maybe even caused—his addiction? Moreover, he was feeling restless, uncomfortable with his new status and success—he had recently married a black woman he'd met in Harlem, and had become a father—and eager for another challenge. So, like many other pilgrims of the period, he headed for California.

Leroy arrived in San Francisco in 1968, nearly broke, a year after the Summer of Love, when psychedelics were giving way to hard drugs. He had promised to join a friend in a black-oriented clothing company, New Breed, but instead, drawn to a scene he recognized and identified with, he sought out a vacant storefront in the Fillmore district and started Reality House West. The conditions there were awful—a leaky roof, one toilet, sacks of beans and rice for food—but he seemed to thrive on adversity: he was wholly in his element, willing to feud with Huey P. Newton and his Black Panthers over turf.

Devoted to his new center, he put in twelve- and fourteen-hour days and scrambled to make ends meet. Always short of cash to pay his staff, he encouraged volunteers, and one morning a prim young white woman in high heels and lipstick landed unexpectedly on his doorstep. It was Kathy, and she announced that she wanted to do some work with addicts, because a student strike had shut down San Francisco State College and she was supposed to earn credits off campus.

Looking down at her from a point about eighteen inches above the top of her head, Leroy gave her the full force of his skepticism, thinking she was yet another Lady Bountiful dispatched from the Kingdom of Good Intentions. He was wrong. Kathy's family was not well-to-do, and her intentions, however plainly stated, were pure.

Her father, an engineer for the Southern Pacific railroad, had had a bad heart, and had died while Kathy and her younger sister were still girls, leaving them in the care of their mother— an old-fashioned, old-country woman, who was born in 1905. A strict adherent of the Greek Orthodox faith, she had far less interest in revolutionary politics than in Archbishop Makarios; and, being uneducated, she supported the family by running a cottage industry in the basement, preparing phyllo dough and selling it to the city's better restaurants. After school and on weekends, Kathy would help her stretch the dough, pulling it out in long, taffylike strands.

Because of her rigorous upbringing, Kathy took to the harsh labor at Reality House. Without complaint, she mopped floors, scrubbed the bathroom, and walked the sickest junkies through their tremors. She'd always sympathized with the suffering of outcasts; in fact, she was haunted by an episode from her teens, when she had gone downtown to Union Square in a new suit she'd made for herself, believing she looked elegant enough to cross a class barrier and shop at I. Magnin. But as she approached its revolving door a crippled, horrendously disfigured man came at her out of a crowd, asking for help, and she fled from him. At night, in dreams, his pleading face still came back to her.

Kathy had been pursuing a degree in international relations, but after six months at Reality House this seemed silly. She traded her dresses for jeans and sweatshirts, and learned to swear, braid hair into cornrows, and raise a fist in salute. At home, her mother prayed for her, accusing her of betraying the family and giving up her education; and that pushed her closer to Leroy and his cause. He had two sons now, Malik and Esan (both Swahili names), yet his marriage had fallen apart, and he was relying on Kathy for support. She was strong, capable, and energetic, and she stood by him as Reality House entered a period of crisis that threatened it with collapse: the financial situation was grave; there was more heroin and cocaine around than ever; and Leroy's arguments with the Black Panthers had got so heated that he was carrying a gun.

It took a few years to sort out the problems. By then, Leroy and Kathy had married, and were living in an ordinary town house in suburban South San Francisco. They had managed to keep Reality House together (they're still running it, as a nonprofit corporation), and now, thanks to grant money from the city and the state, it was healthy enough to provide them with a joint income of about two thousand dollars a month. Leroy had made peace with Huey Newton and had begun studying for an equivalency degree in psychology at Antioch West college and writing his autobiography.

At the age of fifty-one, he was mellowing. Although he was rueful about the pain he'd caused others, he tried not to dwell on the past. He still liked to read, and knew a bit of Shakespeare and Homer, and more of the Bible and Dale Carnegie. What

gave him greater pleasure than anything else was a new ability to demonstrate openly his affection for his new wife and his
children—Malik and Esan and a boy and a girl he'd had by Kathy.
The boy, an infant, was known as Camlo, after a Gypsy god; and
for Camlo's older sister Kathy had chosen the name Agape, the
ancient Greek word for love.

* * *

A mid afternoon at the Chateau, and the dining room smells
of pork roast in plum sauce. A pair of cockatiels carry on in
their cage, while one of four miniature poodles the Loopers own
makes a loud yipping noise. A resident named Duane and his
friend Bud come in, back from a day center, their faces pink from
walking in the sun. Bud used to be a sailor. Duane plays electric
guitar, writes rock music, and once had a three-state hit ("My
Bayou Baby") on an independent label out of Atlanta. The song,
which he performed on the record, has a Roy Orbison flavor—
that spooky Southern feel of gators, swamps, and voodoo.

Ever since Duane was a boy in a backwoods Florida town,
he has been hearing what he calls "suicidal voices" in his head.
The voices put him in a hospital for the first time when he was
twelve, and at their most strident they tell him he's utterly worth-
less and urge him to do everybody a favor by killing himself. He
tried this once, in 1983, shortly after he moved to San Francisco
in the hope of furthering his career. Over the Christmas holidays, a friend left him alone in the apartment they were sharing,
and he became delusional and overwhelmed and drank a can of

plastic-wood solvent. Fortunately, he recovered with his throat and stomach intact, and after he got some counseling at a halfway house he took a room at the Chateau. He has never again done anything self-destructive.

Even though the voices are still with him ("They're real faint now," he says), Duane is often in good spirits. Today, joking around, he's wearing a painter's cap he found in a giveaway box in the neighborhood. He gets a big kick out of it, regarding it as a weird gloss on the whole notion of hats, but the truth is that he doesn't have many decent clothes, nor do most of the other residents. Rodrigo, who's meticulous, wanting to pin down permanently every thought, word, and emotion, felt compelled to explain this to me last week. He wore a wildly patterned but almost colorless sports coat, a remnant of somebody's Caribbean vacation. "Touch this," he said, extending an arm. The shiny material was as thin as tracing paper. "It's hard to be in fashion when you have to shop at the Salvation Army," Rodrigo said.

The irony of such wardrobes is that they sometimes make residents look crazier than they are. This can also be true of antipsychotic drugs. Even as they control hallucinations and stabilize mood, they can cause impotence, dizziness, blurred vision, a cottony mouth, and drowsiness. They may make one constipated or give one diarrhea. Occasionally, they add a herky-jerky edge to a person's gait, or cause his legs to bounce or jiggle. (Residents call this the Prolixin Stomp.) About twenty per cent of those who use such drugs for long periods develop tardive dyskinesia, a sometimes irreversible condition characterized by involuntary facial contortions and darting movements of the mouth, tongue, and jaw.

Yet the sad fact is that nobody at the house functions well without meds. The Loopers will let a resident go off drugs at any time, as long as Mel Blaustein approves, but such experiments have almost always ended badly, with a gradual return to psychosis as the chemicals dissipate from the bloodstream. (That can take as much as six months.)

The dining room is the social hub of the Chateau. If you sit at a table, you invite company, so I am not surprised when Rodrigo pulls up a chair. In a polite, earnest way, he asks if I think smoking is a sin—this has been his major preoccupation lately. Worried about both his soul and his health, he has decided to cut down on tobacco, and save some money as well, by smoking only butts; he collects them from ashtrays and deposits them, little treasures, in a blue plastic file-card box.

With his close-cropped graying hair, Rodrigo reminds me of a dashing movie bandit. (In turn, he says I resemble his seventh-grade chemistry teacher.) He comes from a big family and has some Cree Indian blood. Only one of his five siblings talks to him regularly; he catches up on the others at weddings and funerals. Devoutly religious, he dabs holy water on his brow when he's "cranked up," and keeps a tattered prayer book in his back pocket. As a teenager, he had a bizarre psychotic break during which he left home in a delirium and wandered into the countryside, dazed, frothing at the mouth, speaking in tongues. A farmer rescued him at last and phoned his parents, and he was taken by ambulance to Langley Porter Institute, at the University of California, where he had shock treatments. They cured him, he claims, with some help from *The Mike Douglas Show*, which he watched in amusement every afternoon.

When I first heard such stories, I didn't know what to make of them. They reflect the organic weight of schizophrenia—how it drags one down and leaves one defenseless against the onrushing power of the world. Nothing stays in its compartment: the brain admits every perception, and beauty can flip-flop into ugliness in a matter of seconds. What a relief, then, for Rodrigo to come to himself in a clean hospital room, cared for in privacy and released from his demons. It's easy to picture him between crisp white sheets, calm and peaceful, his temples shaved, laughing along with the guests on TV. The image is as vivid to me as one he actually describes—a cold, beaded can of Rainier ale that the farmer gave him to quench his thirst.

"I can still remember the taste," he'll say, dreamy-eyed, smacking his lips as people do when they drink from a stream high in the mountains.

Anatole goes by on his way to the basement with a load of laundry. His clothes are a record of his past. He has faded suits from his days as an insurance underwriter, jeans and flannel shirts from an outdoorsy phase, and a Moroccan robe, as intricate as a tapestry, that he used to wear to parades and events of civic magnitude. He told me once that his brain collapsed on May 12, 1964. When I pressed him for details, he said sarcastically, "What do you mean, 'details'? It just exploded!" Still awed by the cataclysm, he keeps sifting through it for clues, straddling a gulf between what he was and what he has become, and his awareness of his degeneration, together with his battle to halt it, lends him a tragic, noble air.

Probably Anatole is the most convivial person at the Chateau, but in the beginning whenever we had a chat he had trouble concentrating. He'd bite his lip and work to modify his erratic patterns of thinking, trying to smooth out all the peaks and valleys. He seemed like a cowboy roping in strays. The task was neither simple nor bleak for him—merely a challenge—and now it goes more quickly each time. But other residents have spent so little of their lives in ordinary human relationships that they've lost the gift of language—a primary means of self-definition and protection. After a minute or two of conversing, they forget the subject, stumble over broken sentences, or just fall silent. Often they blame their medication, or suggest, with typical paranoid vigor, that they've been poisoned, doped, or sabotaged.

This afternoon is a payday, so everyone is a little tense, waiting for Leroy or Kathy to appear with a stack of envelopes containing their Supplemental Security Income, or S.S.I., checks. A share of the money, three hundred and forty dollars, comes from the federal government, and each state adds something on top. California is the most generous, and that attracts patients from all over the country. "I love it out here," a resident from Alabama said to me once. "It's warm, it hardly ever rains, and I'm a lot better off financially than I was in Tuscaloosa."

As I cross the dining room to get a glass of water, Georgie intercepts me, his neck craned, swooping in from a great height. "You're a Virgo, right?" he asks.

"That's right, Georgie."

"Who do you think killed President Kennedy?"

"Lee Harvey Oswald."

"I hate violence," Georgie says. In the kitchen, Susan Brier, the manager of the Chateau, is basting the pork roast. Emanations of plum come at me, along with whiffs of garlic and sage. (In most board-and-cares, the menu runs to hot dogs, peanut butter, and canned spaghetti.) Susan offers me a chocolate-chip cookie fresh from the oven. A former philosophy major, she dropped out of college in the late nineteen-fifties to be a beatnik, and her attitudes and ideas remain unconventional. She has worked at the house for seven years, putting in four ten-hour days every week. In addition to cooking dinner, she does some administrative chores, and she supervises everything in the Loopers' absence.

Around four o'clock, Leroy makes an entrance with the envelopes. "Darnell!" he booms. "Ruth! Paul!" The checks, a monthly disability stipend, are for six hundred and thirty-two dollars, and almost everybody gets one. To qualify for S.S.I., you must be unable to hold a job, and you must have a doctor who'll attest to the severity of your impairment. It is important, too, to have been hospitalized at least once; the average here is five times. S.S.I. may seem to be an uncomplicated subsidy, but it isn't. Once your name goes on the roll, you've admitted your failure to live independently and acquired another badge that marks you as crazy.

It can be as difficult to get off S.S.I. as it is to get on. One month in a licensed California board-and-care costs a state-set fee of five hundred and fifty-eight dollars, so after Rodrigo pays the Loopers he'll have seventy-four dollars to last him until his next check. He puts on his colorless coat and heads for the corner market, where he has to settle a thirteen-dollar tab for highly priced toiletries and cans of soda. Ruth tells me she's going to treat herself to sushi, and Paul—a plump, brilliant New Yorker with the glowing eyes of a Talmudic scholar—says he's going to a Chinese restaurant for a four-course meal.

I ask Anatole if he has any plans to celebrate, but he says he doubts it—he's a bit tired. On other paydays, he has eaten lobster at Fisherman's Wharf, had a half-dozen pizzas delivered to the Chateau, or gone on long taxi rides to no particular destination—an emperor, briefly, of all he surveys.

\* \* \*

Every weekday morning after breakfast, the Loopers, who are seldom idle, drive their old station wagon to Eddy Street, in the Tenderloin, where they run a hundred-and fifty-nine-room residential hotel called the Cadillac. On a windy March day, I join them in their office—a cluttered room behind the front desk furnished with antiques Kathy has reclaimed from the hotel basement. The pieces are all in California Mission style and date from the turn of the century, when the Cadillac had a staff of thirty maids and catered to the elite. Its tenants now are people on welfare, alcoholics drying out, elderly pensioners, ex-cons, and a handful of ambulatory mental patients whose doctors have certified that they are not likely to commit suicide or arson. When I walk in, Kathy is doing some bookkeeping and Leroy is talking on the phone.

"Mmm-hmm," he says, holding the receiver a few inches from his ear. "Well, we do thank you for the offer, but we just can't use two hundred hamburgers for the banquet. We got this cooking school in North Beach, they're going to fix us a nice, *sit-down* dinner .... I understand that. It's very generous of you." Raising his eyes toward the heavens, Leroy whispers to us, "Man wants me to serve his burgers at a banquet Mayor Dianne Feinstein's coming to. You feed a politician franchise food, she'll never do you any favors."

The Cadillac is Leroy's power base. He's a boss in the district, and he has an assortment of titles—chairman of the Tenderloin Crime Abatement Committee, chairman of San Francisco Alive's Tenderloin Cleanup Committee, and chairman of the Tenderloin Community Fund. I asked him once about the last title, and he laughed, and said, "The developers who build down here have to contribute to our community programs, and *I* get to hand that money out." When Leroy looks out a hotel window, he doesn't always register the details of Eddy Street. Instead, he sees the same archetypal inner-city strip he roamed as a boy. Same pitfalls, same temptations.

Leroy's activities in the Tenderloin—all voluntary—are a logical extension of the kind of public-service work he began back in Harlem. A local philanthropist who knew about the work offered to sell the Cadillac to Reality House West on a no-money-down basis in 1977, as a private venture in urban renewal, and after Leroy discussed the offer with Kathy he closed the deal with a handshake and threw himself into a campaign to revive the place. He had it cleaned, painted, redecorated, and fumigated, killing off several generations of roaches. The hotel is now a handsome beige monument in a landscape of decay, and its rooms, which rent for about two hundred dollars a month, are safe and secure.

Buying the Cadillac gave the Loopers some economic leverage, and Kathy was glad about this, since she was bored with the suburbs and wanted to move to a more spacious house in town. So she began shopping around in San Francisco and soon discovered that everything on the market was either too small or too cute or too ugly. Then one night in 1977, by chance, she drove home through the Mission—a mostly Hispanic district then, where, in those days, property was still affordable— and saw a ramshackle Victorian mansion that appealed to her immensely. A superstitious person, she felt that it was destined to be hers, and in the morning she learned from a realtor that the place was indeed for sale.

The asking price was a lofty three hundred and twenty-five thousand dollars, but in ritzier areas that bought you only a gingerbread shoebox; and there was also a low-interest assumable loan available. At the same time, the mansion had problems, both structural and ethical. The foundation was shot, termites had eaten away many acres of wood, and the owner housed about a dozen boarders, all chronic mental patients, who would have to be evicted before anybody could take possession. This owner, an elderly woman, apparently had a romantic turn of mind. Imagining that her house bore a resemblance to the stately ones in Bordeaux, she had named it Chateau Laura.

In light of the problems, Kathy considered her options. A trip to the library taught her that since the nineteen-sixties, when anti-psychotic drugs were first widely prescribed, and patients—supposedly more tractable, and more capable of living independently—were released from hospitals into the community, board-and-care homes like the Chateau had become the principal long-term shelters for people with chronic mental illness. In California, as in New York, beds in public hospitals were so scarce that you had to be a 5150—the police code for someone who is dangerous to himself or others—just to get one. Although Kathy knew that schizophrenics could be difficult to handle, she began to wonder if perhaps she and Leroy should keep the boarders. (An owner of a home can earn a profit, but to do so honestly, without scrimping, is hard. Since 1977, forty-one homes in the city have closed, partly because of rising taxes and insurance rates.) After all, they had lots of experience with junkies, who were not exactly pussycats; and, besides, they could use the extra cash to meet their monthly mortgage payments.

The Loopers took over the mansion in 1978 and decided to rename it for one of their children. Chateau Camlo? Chateau Malik? No—Chateau Agape. "We had no idea what we were getting into!" Leroy cries as he paces around the office.

"No idea!" Kathy may be half his size, but she matches him in volume. "You know what? The Department of Public Works had condemned that house in 1952, and we had to correct all the violations. There were buckets on every floor to catch the rain, and we had to rewire and replumb. We sealed off part of the basement, because of the termites. What else? Oh, yeah. Community Care Licensing, over in Emeryville. They didn't want to give us a board-and-care license. They made us install all these special features, like an intercom. You know how often we use it? Never. Plus they were concerned about Leroy's background."

"My 'background,'" Leroy mutters, in disdain.

"And they were worried about our kids, what they should or shouldn't be exposed to. 'Hey, man!' I told them." Kathy jabs a thumb into her chest. "'I'm their mother. I make those decisions!' So they backed down on that issue. Then the older boys, they went on strike. They didn't want to move. They were *happy* in the suburbs, living out there like little Yuppies.

"Finally, they gave in, but they hated the Chateau at first. It embarrassed them—it was so old. They called it the Mystery House."

"You can't blame 'em," Leroy says. "Some of our neighbors thought the house was haunted. Paperboy, he was afraid to come around. It took us six months to get a paper delivered."

"Anyhow, once we had our license we had to start coping with our boarders," Kathy says. "And we were not ready for it. We didn't know a thing about mental illness."

Leroy shakes his head in amazement. "We had some strange people in there. This one fellow, he'd had about half of a transgender operation, and he didn't have enough money for the other half. He had a big old beard, and he'd put on lipstick and eye shadow and sit around in a silk dress that was falling off him. A couple of other people, they drank all the time. We brought in a doctor, he looked 'em over and said, 'Hell, they're so sick they might as well be drunk.'

"Because that's how it is in some board-and-cares, you understand? Only, we didn't know it then. We were honestly shocked. We just felt so sorry for everybody—and the sorrier we felt, the worse they got. I mean, we had people decompensating all over the place! Every five minutes or so, we were phoning the police. Somebody was always riding off to the hospital in an ambulance. You know what that costs? A bed in psych emergency? About six hundred dollars a night and taxpayers get stuck with the tab.

"It's criminal, really. Some schizophrenics, they hate to bother with their toenails and we had a podiatrist who'd come by, spend a minute clipping, and send these huge bills to Medi-Cal. Then, you've got your psychiatrists therapizing and formulating, and half the time they tell you something different from what you've seen with your own eyes. Things were getting out of control! We had to do something, so we quit feeling sorry for everybody and tried to be crystal clear about who we were and what our purpose was. And you know what? When we began to change, the house began to change."

\* \* \*

There's a big party at the Chateau. The Loopers are hosting a soiree for Art Agnos, a Democratic assemblyman who has a good record on mental-health issues and is running for mayor, hoping to succeed Dianne Feinstein. Kathy has laid out a home-made buffet of dolmas and spanakopita, and scads of social workers, politicians, and mental-health professionals—perhaps two hundred of them—are piling food on paper plates and filling cups with fruity punch. Leroy is in his element, circling the crowd, clapping backs, and gathering in anybody who comes within fifteen feet of him—dipping, with his long arms, into a swarming sea.

"Hello, Reverend!" he shouts to a friend, a Baptist minister.

"Well, hello, Leroy!"

"Agnos for Mayor, hear?"

"All right, then."

I watch Ruth walk by, leading some guests on a tour of the upstairs rooms. She has been doing this all evening, and she's exhausted, dragging from the effort of fielding so many questions. Why do people talk so much? Other residents are pinning name tags on lapels, or pretending to be invisible and making one stab after another at the food. Off in a corner, Anatole sits by himself, looking glum. He has shaved for the occasion, though not very skillfully, and I can't help feeling that he wishes he could be off in an apartment of his own somewhere. But when he last lived alone, in a seedy downtown dive, he pretended to be an F.B.I. man to fend off the sharks who prey on the mentally ill; and that was worse, he claims, than giving up his privacy.

On my way to the buffet, I stop and ask him what he thinks of the candidate.

"Oh, Agnos has some fine ideas!" he exclaims. And then he adds with no intent to be satiric, "Course, I've heard a lot of them before."

I take some cheese and bread from the table, and then join Paul by the kitchen counter. He is unusually animated, and I remark on this. "It's because I feel safe in crowds," he confides, leaning closer and joking about his waistline. He has a soft, round, slope-shouldered body. The only child of Polish Jews, survivors of a concentration camp, he graduated near the top of his class at Bronx Science in New York—this was about twenty years ago—and was set to attend college, but he swallowed a bottleful of aspirin that summer and landed in Bellevue instead. Awkward in public and terrified in private, he didn't think he was capable of transforming himself into the person everyone imagined he could be.

Once, Paul told me about a hiking trip he'd made to the Housatonic River when he was in his early twenties and, as he put it, "still struggling to create an identity." He described the trees and the water, the mild air and the green earth, all in crystalline detail, and there emerged out of his description a portrait of the self he was craving—easygoing, at one with nature, free. But when he was home again he found everything the same, and fell victim to obsessions, including an irrepressible attachment to anything Irish. I asked if he ever heard voices, like Duane. No, he said, but painful electric currents would sometimes shoot through him, as if he were being poked with a cattle prod.

This past Sunday, at the weekly house meeting, Paul was a hero. While everybody was sitting in the dining room and listening to a litany of ordinary grievances (a broken door lock, a faucet in need of fixing), a distraught woman of middle age, Bea, rose to address us. She was as haughty as a Back Bay matron and could have been speaking from a rostrum in the sky. Swaying from side to side, almost dancing, she said, "I am sorry to have to mention this, but people here have been stealing from me since last November."

Anthony Smith, the assistant house manager, remained calm. A quiet, intelligent black man, as large in most dimensions as Leroy, he is an artist in his free time, and works in many mediums. "What have you lost?" he asked.

"I don't care to discuss specifics."

"Have you reported the thefts to the Loopers?"

Bea sways. "That has nothing to do with it."

A ripple went through the room, a wave of discomfort. Bea's paranoia, however unjustified, reached out and touched the paranoia latent in everyone else. Residents were squirming in their chairs, but then Paul stood up to respond. His attitude was uncritical, even supportive. He referred to his own "drab, acquisitive personality" and admitted that he sometimes became so fond of his possessions that he panicked if he couldn't find something right away. Then, with conciliatory humor, he reminded Bea that those at the Chateau were inclined to be—well, *suspicious*, and that this suspicion had to be guarded against.

He was so tactful that his words seemed to put the house back in order, restoring a subtle balance, along with clarity. Defused, Bea quit swaying, but she did not offer an apology. She has since left to live for free in a Catholic Charities shelter. I saw her on Mission Street just recently, barefoot, chattering to herself.

The women at the Chateau, nine of them, have a tougher time with schizophrenia than the men, primarily because their condition is more severe. In general, only the most difficult female patients wind up in board-and-cares; as a rule, a family will go a long way to protect and harbor a daughter, a sister, or a mother before admitting defeat. The women are less manageable, more prone to mood swings and wild displays of emotion. They may experience their isolation more acutely, for they seem to have a greater longing to connect with what's outside them. Only one man at the house has ever lived with a woman, but a number of the women have been married, or still are, and a few have children. Often the younger women give off a sharp charge of sexual energy, but it dissipates fast, like an idea that can't be held on to.

By eight o'clock, the party is concluding. The last guests depart, carrying off sandwiches and pastries, and through a debris of napkins and crushed crepe-paper streamers move two Looper kids, Camlo and Agape, helping their mother clean up.

Camlo, who is ten now, has a round, expressive face and—like his sister—skin the color of cafe au lait. If it bothers him to live at the Chateau, he doesn't show it. He frequently searches out Anatole for a game of Scrabble, just as Malik and Esan used to do when they were his age. He is interested in space travel, and dreams of being an astronaut, while Agape, at fifteen, thinks she may want to be a doctor, maybe even a psychiatrist. She is a scholarship student at University High School, long-legged, enthusiastic, and a basketball star. To grow up in an ordinary house, she said to me once, would be merely ordinary.

\* \* \*

Among the first changes the Loopers made in 1978 when they felt the Chateau slipping out of control was to draw a sharp line between their lives and the lives of their boarders. From the start, they have occupied a big, high-ceilinged room, like a grand Victorian parlor, at the back of the house, down a hallway from the kitchen, and at first people kept dropping in at odd hours to report, for instance, that there was arsenic in the city's water supply. "From now on, we're only here if it's real," Leroy told the residents, laying down the law to preserve his own sanity, and this came as a shock to everyone, because, as clients of the mental-health system, they were used to being treated like irresponsible adolescents. The suggestion that they were mature enough to respect the Loopers' privacy and also to distinguish *between* fact and fiction granted them a humanity they were often denied.

Then, the Loopers posted a strict set of house rules. No alcohol or street drugs would be allowed on the premises, and there would be no more fistfights or shoving matches to resolve disputes. Anyone who wanted to smoke had to do it downstairs or out in the garden, because Kathy was tired of worrying about the Chateau burning to the ground. At eleven o'clock every night, Leroy locked the front door, and anyone who stayed out later than that without permission was welcome to sleep in the bushes. The Loopers also became more selective about accepting referrals, refusing to admit anybody who had a history of substance abuse. (On the streets, left to their own devices, mental patients often fall into the trap of medicating themselves with anything that's handy.) The message in all this was clear: schizophrenia is an illness, not an excuse for bad behavior.

For whatever reason, the residents seemed to improve. They were not so listless, and began to take pride in how they looked. But it troubled Leroy and Kathy that they still passed their days in limbo, lounging around and staring into space. So they insisted, despite complaints, that everybody attend a day-treatment center during the week. These centers are sociable places, offering classes in such things as music and handicrafts, along with some counselling; and though they don't really prepare a client to live independently, they do force people to interact, to speak and be conscious—an accomplishment if you've been doing nothing but smoking Camels and watching "Wheel of Fortune" for the last three years.

Leroy was impressed by how positively his boarders responded to an increase in structure. He had seen the same thing happen among inmates in prison. Men who were overwhelmed on the outside, surly and lost, longing for discipline, functioned perfectly well behind bars, in a community where the rules were simple and explicit. And he noticed, too, an odd psychological similarity between schizophrenics and the heroin addicts he'd been working with for so long: they both tended to get so involved in their game that the game wound up playing them.

It was like the course that alcoholism takes, Leroy thought. A person drinks for fun and then out of routine and finally from desperation, having no other way to cope with his loose time or his emotions. Say you're a teen-ager, isolated, shy, gangly, probably confused about sex, and you hear voices in your head, and have feelings and perceptions that don't fit with those of others all around you. Eventually, you go to a doctor, and he gives a name to your condition—and this is a great relief, because it presents you with a mask to hide behind. At first, you can put it on at will, using it to your advantage, but slowly you begin to blend with it, and in time you and the mask are one.

That's what Leroy saw at the Chateau—schizophrenics who were addicted to "crazy" patterns of thought and action, and had to break their addiction before they could go on to the next phase of recovery. Yet at the same time he understood that schizophrenia was a debilitating organic disease, rooted in biology. Both he and Kathy were aware of the anguish in the house—how much labor it took some boarders just to tie their shoes and put on a shirt. Although the Chateau was a more orderly place, some residents still made trips to the hospital, and the Loopers were upset at being unable to detect the signs that preceded such episodes. Then, one day, their worst nightmare came true: with no warning, a man climbed onto a neighbor's roof and jumped to his death.

Early in 1979, the Loopers were introduced to Mel Blaustein, and they invited him to be their consulting psychiatrist. Blaustein was in his mid-thirties, a trim, fast-moving transplant from New York, who still had a trace of Brooklyn accent and sometimes carried a copy of *The Ring*, boxing's Bible, on his clipboard as he made his rounds. This was appropriate, for he had a triage approach to board-and-care medicine.

Only a few doctors in the Bay Area were willing to deal with such poor (and demanding) patients. Blaustein himself had got into the field by chance, in 1976, after being mustered out of the Army in Oakland. A physician friend told him he could earn seventeen dollars in Medi-Cal money by giving a shot of Prolixin to an old woman in a home, and he was glad to get the cash, since his private practice was new and undersubscribed. But he found, too, that he enjoyed the work, which had an appealing immediacy; and he felt a professional obligation to serve those in need.

On his first visit to the Chateau, Blaustein was awed by its extravagance, and by the scope of the Loopers' efforts. From his research he knew that the average board-and-care operator was a single person over the age of fifty, often female and widowed, usually black or Filipino, who had some health-care training, took in about eight people, and did not rely on the income for a livelihood. (San Francisco is too expensive, liberal-minded, and bureaucratically complex to support an owner whose sole intent is larceny.) Having been to many such homes, he had come to expect the patients in them to be apathetic, and he marvelled at how healthy, vigorous, and engaging the Loopers' residents were. It wasn't that other owners were insensitive, he decided, but that they didn't have the political sophistication of Leroy and Kathy, or their tenacity.

In Blaustein's opinion, the Chateau was an evolving model of what a home *could* be, and he worked to make it stronger. Twice a week, he stopped by—once to see patients and once to talk with the Loopers and their staff. He had them buy a logbook and record any instances of bizarre behavior—"getting hot," he called it. This taught them to recognize the warning signs they had been missing. A loss of appetite, a temper tantrum, a sudden desire for a blue Corvette—any one of these might be a tip that a person was coming unglued. With his wife, a nutritionist, Blaustein revamped the menu, limiting coffee (and heady jolts of caffeine) to breakfast; and always he carried a pager, so he could be reached in an emergency.

Over the next two years, 1980 and 1981, Blaustein collected data at the house. The Loopers took in forty-seven referrals in that period, about half of whom came to them directly from a hospital. There were thirty-six men and eleven women, and they were mostly in their early thirties. Some had been jailed for acts of violence; eighteen had a documented attempt at suicide in their files. Blaustein assumed that with such a volatile population an ambulance would have to be parked by the curb, but just twelve residents were hospitalized during the study period—for an average stay of seven days—and they were all highly dysfunctional schizophrenics, who would have done worse on their own. The savings to the city and the state had to be enormous.

As the atmosphere at the Chateau became less frantic, the Loopers had more time to fix up the building. They got a grant to strip off the exterior paint, which was a dull mustard color, and overlay the old wood with a new coat of white. Inside, they ripped away wallpaper, buffed floors, waxed bannisters, and hung an elegant glass chandelier in the foyer. Some evenings when they walked in from the Cadillac, they could actually feel a calm, as if every overheated brain in the house had arrived at a moment of peace. For Kathy, this meant more hours in the garden, planting seedlings and bulbs. Leroy did not have a real hobby (though he had started collecting German beer mugs), but every now and then, when things were going well, he'd give Dr. Blaustein a call, and together they'd sneak out in the evening to attend a boxing match.

\* \* \*

The Loopers' quarters, in late afternoon. Their room measures about forty by sixty feet—it's the size of a large studio apartment—and it has a fireplace and big windows and a certain homey clutter, from the overflow of Kathy's many projects. Nearly half the room is taken up with overstuffed chairs and couches, which are usually covered with sheets and arranged around a coffee table. A mahogany-frame bed dominates the other half, and on it Leroy is currently stretched out, barefoot, dozing, indulging in a ritual pre-dinner nap—company or no company.

Leroy's years in prison altered the way he relates to space, scaled down all his needs. In a cell, he says, you look for beauty in a patch of light. It's different for Kathy, though. If she were redesigning the Chateau, she'd put her family on the second floor, so they could all be together. As it is, her children are deployed around the house—the two older boys upstairs, Agape in a room off the kitchen, and Camlo in a big, converted ground floor closet. Also, Kathy is cramped in here, among all the antiques and collectibles that she absolutely must have for her emotional well-being; it offends her that some of them disappear behind others—the piles of Mario Lanza 78s behind the boxes of carnival glass, say, or the rolled-up rugs and tapestries behind the two anatomically correct statues of nymphs shouldering urns.

Right now, Kathy is searching for her yellow slicker and her red rubber boots. She wants to wear them to an invitation-only premiere of August Wilson's "Fences" that the Loopers are attending tonight.

"They asked all the blacks in town, right, Leroy?" she says, digging through a pile of old curtains on the floor.

"Uh-uh," Leroy replies, a forearm shielding his eyes. "Only the cosmopolitan ones."

Another woman left the house this week. On the day she got her S.S.I. check, a man who had been a patient in the mental-health system picked her up on the street, made some extreme promises, and escorted her home and bragged that she was going to live with him. He was a pimpy-looking dude in tight rhinestone-studded pants, clearly after her money. To discourage any violence, Leroy decided to do some cooking, even though it was almost midnight. In the kitchen, he took a cleaver, glared at the pimp, and loudly chopped an onion—*whack, whack, whack!*

Meanwhile, Kathy darted up the back stairs and asked the woman if she was sure about her choice, suggesting that it might just possibly be a mistake.

"Oh, I'm sure!" the woman said, in a high, squeaky voice, her hands clasped at her bosom. "It's going to be lovely! We'll be so happy together!" Three days later, she was sick and broke, occupying a bed in San Francisco General Hospital.

"That's how confusing this business is," Leroy says when I mention the incident. "When to interfere, when not to interfere."

"The hospital wanted us to take her back." Kathy is rooting around in a freestanding cupboard by the old RCA Victrola. "But we wouldn't."

"Because she hasn't learned anything yet. She won't admit she's got anything wrong with her."

"The only person we ever took back was Anatole."

"Well, Anatole, he's different. He's Anatole." Leroy yawns. "We got all kinds of crisises around here. Did you talk to Ed about his troubles at the day center?"

Ed is a former carpenter in his twenties, and he has dark circles under his eyes and the long blond Buffalo Bill hair of a cowboy hippie. Until a year ago, he had his own construction firm in Marin County, but the stress of competing for work got to him, and he lost all his money, fell ill, and had to be hospitalized.

Because he has recovered fairly well, stabilizing on Haldol, his counsellor at the center—a young person with little experience—arranged for him to enter a vocational-rehab program to be trained as a clerk. That was fine with Ed, since he likes to type and file, and believes he could manage to stay cool if he had a quiet job at, say, a post office. But he has just found out that he'll ultimately be placed in a nongovernmental job that pays a minimum wage, and he's angry. He'll be thrust into the same sort of poverty that contributed to his breakdown.

"Those counsellors, they're doing the best they can," Leroy says. "But you got to take that as a center for socialization, not education."

"They go overboard, Leroy!" Kathy pushes aside a wicker rocker in need of recaning. "What looks good on a report isn't always good for a client. How about Paul? He's got this counsellor who wants him to switch from his day program to the Jewish Community Center, cut down on his meds, move to a hotel, and make a bunch of new friends." Appalled, she counts on her fingers. "One, two, three, *four* major changes! Even a sane person would have a problem with that."

It isn't always easy for the Loopers to maintain their optimism. Inevitably, they lose people to the disease, and to quirks in the system. But they have their victories, too—Duane, for instance, who is in such good shape that he is planning to visit his mother in Georgia. When he first moved into the Chateau, after his suicide attempt, he was still so sick that he would sneak off every three months without telling anybody, and then do something weird to get into a hospital. Leroy and Kathy sat him down and explained that he was violating a trust, concealing his emotional problems from them; if he wanted to stay in the house, he had to be more open and in touch. Since then, Duane has struggled successfully to stay out of the emergency wards, and has been improving by the day.

At last, Kathy finds her slicker. Buried under many unidentifiable things, it is wrinkled like a relief map. She asks Agape to throw it into the dryer and goes off to take a bath. With another yawn, Leroy bends over, puts on shoes and socks, and rises from the bed in what amounts to stages.

"If this show's no good, I'll fall asleep in my seat," he says, with a laugh. "That's my way of being a critic, you understand?"

He slips into a shirt and sweater, and then adds a huge medallion on a chain. The size of a small clock, it bears a Wedgwood image of Sagittarius, the Archer, his birth sign. He runs a hand through his hair, humming, as he does at breakfast, and sits on a couch across from me. After all these years, he has a guileless face, and when his features are in repose I see reflected in them a look that is weary but not without hope.

In a friendly way, marking time until Kathy is ready, he tells me about a conference for board-and-care operators they went to last weekend, where a medical researcher presented some of the current evidence in support of a biological basis for schizophrenia. "It's important research," he says, "because, the thing is, it might move us out from under our guilt. Mental illness, it's still a taboo in this society. Instead of blaming parents for everything, I'd like to see them more involved. Because we need help, understand? There's no money around for mental health—no money at all."

For research on schizophrenia, the federal government spends fourteen dollars a year per patient, compared with three hundred dollars per cancer patient. "People here at the Chateau, they didn't do this to themselves. They're victims, really—of their background, their chemistry. Some of them, they'll never be able to work, or live alone. The smallest favor you do for them, they're grateful. Because they've been kicked around the block. And that's not right. They are sweet, sweet people."

Kathy returns to the room, the tips of her hair still wet from the bath. "How do I look?" she asks, with a pirouette. In a pink blouse, green slacks, and the red boots, she looks a little blinding. When I first met the Loopers, I thought of Kathy as everybody's aunt and Leroy as nobody's uncle. But that's only half the truth. They are the sort of married couple who complement each other, forming a unit larger than the sum of its parts. What is it that sustains them? Aside from their commitment, it's a belief that they're earning a fair reward for their work—a house they love, a house they couldn't have owned under any other circumstances, a house that is the realization of their dreams.

* * *

An April afternoon, mild and breezy. With a shopping bag containing a toothbrush and some clothes, I arrive at the Chateau to spend the night. Georgie's sitting in the foyer, one leg crossed over the other. I always think he'll forget who I am, but he never does. I'm a part of his world now—an object in it, a tree or stone—probably forever. "You weigh about a hundred and fifty pounds, right?" he asks.

I nod.

He says, "Are you a Catholic?"

I shake my head.

Georgie looks perplexed. "How come? You've got a Yugoslav name."

"My father's family was Catholic," I say. "But he married a Lutheran."

"Was your father strict?"

"You know the answer, Georgie."

A small voice. "He ever hit you with a razor strop?"

"Never. Did yours?"

"Nope." The famous Georgie grin. "But I got lickings from the nuns at school."

Next is Rodrigo, whose battle with smoking goes on. He's very curious about what might be in my shopping bag, so I let him have a look. It isn't that he wants to pry; it's the permission that excites him, the possibility we're about to share a secret. He examines my toothbrush carefully, and seems glad to learn that I, too, wear underwear. Rodrigo doesn't care much for mysteries. One of his own secrets is that he needs to be constantly reassured.

Kathy comes into the dining room and shows me the form I'd fill out if I were actually checking in. It is as complex as a legal contract, and spells out all the general and health services I'd be due: seventeen dollars a day for three meals, a snack, bedside care during minor illnesses, and transportation to and from medical and dental appointments. When I've finished reading, she leads me to Room No. 4, at the top of the stairs, on the second floor. It's got two beds, but I'll be alone. The beds are oak with carved posts, and there are two oak bureaus, a lamp with a marble base, an Oriental rug, and four French prints depicting scenes from the life of a courtly woman.

Dinner is at five. I eat with Darnell and Anatole. Darnell is too shy to speak very much, but Anatole makes up for him. "I hope you don't mind if I eat my dessert along with my entree," he says, alternating forkfuls of meat loaf and Jell-O. Sometimes he gives a nervous little laugh, high in his throat. As he warms to my company, his eyes begin to sparkle. I can see the mischief in him, a dormant muscle he's starting to flex. He's remembering things, how one moves from Topic A to Topic B, and after every successful leap across the chasm he pauses briefly, as if to brush the dust from his trousers and wait for applause.

When we turn in our plates at the kitchen counter, somebody suggests a game of pool. It isn't easy to round up players, since chronic schizophrenics are nothing if not set in their ways. But after some negotiation Duane, Bud, Anatole, and I descend into the basement, a cramped space with the feel of a suburban recreation room. Women come down here occasionally, but at their own risk. Although there's a rule forbidding sex between residents, when sex happens it's likely to happen here. (Leroy: "I make the rules, but I'm no policeman.") Every nonessential item the Loopers own also lands in the basement, including Kathy's high-school yearbooks, more than three hundred used record albums, and some paintings on black velvet.

By accident, I knock an album off a shelf with my cue. It breaks. I stare at the pieces. There lies Mantovani in full high-fidelity sound, a relic from 1955. "Just so it isn't anything by Mary Wells," Anatole says, chalking up. We're partners in eight ball. Anatole played a lot of pool in the Army. He shoots right-handed first; then he shoots left-handed. He shoots with his stick behind his back. After he sinks all but one of our balls, he sinks a ball that belongs to our opponents. Obviously, he's bored. He appears to be rebelling against the laws of physics—they simply don't hold his interest. Soon he's looking for new configurations. "Ever seen the seven and the three lined up like that?" he asks before drilling the cue ball directly into a pocket.

"You missed," I tell him.

He leans toward me confidentially."I don't care much for competition," he whispers.

After three games, we go back upstairs, and everybody wanders off to be alone and have a smoke. It's a relief for the others after so much interaction. I check the kitchen clock. Can it really be only eight? I feel the weight of empty hours. About a third of the residents have already gone to bed, sleeping through the doldrums. I don't know quite what to do with myself, so I make a cup of tea. Thoughts drift idly through my head. What about a walk? "Anybody for a walk?" I ask. Anatole says, "Definitely! A walk—wonderful idea!"

Ed decides to join us, after deliberating for almost a quarter hour. His dilemma over a job has him swinging back and forth on every question. One minute he's angry, and the next he's reconciled. On Guerrero Street, he lashes out at stupid drivers in their idiotic cars. For Anatole, such things hardly exist. The sidewalk is just an extension of the foyer he ordinarily paces, and he ambles along rolling a cigarette and scattering tobacco from his pouch. He's wearing old bedroom slippers without any socks. In the six years he's lived at the Chateau, this has become his neighborhood; though he talks incessantly of moving out, he's more comfortable here than anywhere else on earth.

We stop at a corner market. The merchant, an Arab, shouts, "Hello, Anatole!" It's surprising how easily the community around the house has accepted its residents. They are welcome in shops, in restaurants and bars. Some of them even do odd jobs for store owners, stacking cans and sweeping floors, earning a dollar or two. This store has an electric eye, a beam of light that causes a buzzing if you cross it, and Anatole is standing in the beam. "Anatole! You make too much buzz!"

"Oh, sorry." A chuckle. "I was looking at the girl on that *Playboy* magazine."

Home again, we spread out some food on a dining-room table. Soda, potato chips, pretzels. Ruth leaves the kitchen, where she has been scrubbing the stove, and helps herself. Rodrigo and Ed eat something, too, overgrateful for crumbs. A woman named Alice passes by in her pajamas—she's not hungry. Tomorrow, she starts doing volunteer work with stroke victims, and she's nervous. A native of Maine, she has a bachelor's degree in psychology, but after graduation she worked for five years packing Hummel figurines in boxes at a factory, and then it occurred to her that she really ought to be leading a world revolution. She laughs now when she tells the story. "I think I'm getting better," she says. "So I must be getting better, right?"

Around eleven o'clock, Leroy marches through the hall and locks the front door. Like the shopkeeper's electric eye, he's there but not there. Around him, he has created a force field whose message is "Do not disturb." At five-thirty tomorrow morning, he'll be up cooking breakfast.

I'm tired, too, but I want to watch the late news on TV. "The news?" Anatole says when I mention it. "Sure, I'll watch it with you. Really, that's a good idea. I don't watch much television, you know. It's a little below my intelligence level. There's too much violence, and it gives me nightmares. Of course, some of the comedic shows aren't too bad if you can program your mind to be between eighteen and twenty-five. I do that sometimes. If I have a favorite show at all, I guess it's *Jeopardy.*"

The TV room, on the second floor, is vacant. I switch on the set and turn up the volume, but it's hard to pay attention, because Anatole is more interesting than anything onscreen. What talk he generates! It's like a combination of jazz and improvisational theatre, where every word is a note, and every note is a trigger. He's in sync, catches every reference, finds another reference buried in it, and links that to an exotic dancer he once tried to date, or to something he read about the Tasaday tribe of the Philippines. There's no distinction between conscious and unconscious, between self and other. I'd swear that he's giving off heat, a regular dynamo, but in the midst of being enraptured I have to remind myself of something that Dr. Blaustein once told me. "Don't be romantic," he said. "This is a terrible disease."

Midnight. "Anatole," I say, stretching. "I'm going to bed."

He walks me to my room. I hear the scuff of his slippers, the wheeze of his lungs. At No. 4, I say, "Well, good night." But no: we must shake hands. First with the right, then with the left. His hands feel soft, almost boneless.

I close the door. The sound of the latch brings with it a sense of separation. In the morning, I'll be back in my own house, while here Anarole will wake slowly and repeat his routine, doing so in the face of obstacles, without complaint. He will be kind, decent, and unfailingly generous; he'll even make jokes. Given his burden, this seems to me an act of heroism, like Paul's speech or Duane's efforts to stay out of the hospital, and it ought to be viewed in that light. Along with the others at the

Chateau, he should be praised for managing his disease in the best possible way, inventing a life for himself out of the wreckage and debris.

From my window I look out at the dark hump of Mt. Sutro rising above apartments to the west. Once, Leroy described the Chateau to me as "a living, breathing entity," and as I listen to the creak of the floor and the soft rustle of the breeze I understand what he meant. The mattress on my bed is firm, the sheets are clean, and there is a bright patchwork quilt Kathy must have rescued from somewhere. Everyone deserves this much, really—a quiet, comfortable room in a house where care is worn into the wood, and an atmosphere of trust prevails. How would Leroy put it? "Forget your expectations. Deal with what's in front of you. Let people be what they *can* be."

*The New Yorker*, 1987

# La Frontera:
# The Mexican Border

The most heavily travelled border in the world is a strip of scrubby California desert that runs for fifteen miles between the United States and Mexico, starting at the Pacific Ocean and ending at a thriving yet isolated spot called Otay Mesa. A chainlink fence follows the border for much of its course, but it is torn in many places and trampled in many others, and in some places it has fallen down.

Where the fence is still standing, you find litter on both sides of it which migrant workers have left behind—beer and soda cans, cigarette packs, diapers, syringes, candy wrappers, and comic-book *novelas* that feature cautionary tales about the perils of a trip to *El Norte*. These *novelas* tell of dishonest employers, horrible living conditions, and the corruptive power of American dollars. In their most dramatic stories, families come apart, brothers murder brothers, and lovers' hearts are broken beyond mending. The stories offer a liberal blend of truth and fiction, but that is an accurate reflection of the border, where nothing is absolute.

Between the ocean and the mesa, the only town of any size is San Ysidro, California, just across from Tijuana. About forty-three million people pass through its legal port of entry every year, in vehicles, on bicycles, and on foot, but nobody knows for certain how many undocumented migrants slip over *la frontera*. An educated guess would be about five thousand every day. They come primarily from Mexico and Central America, and they carry their most precious belongings with them in knapsacks or plastic supermarket bags.

The Border Patrol, in its San Diego Sector—a territory roughly as big as Connecticut—catches about a third of them, logging almost fifteen hundred arrests every twenty-four hours, but the others drift on to Los Angeles or San Francisco or Sacramento, or to farms in the Central Valley, staying with relatives and friends while they look for work. If they fail to be hired anywhere, they go farther north, to Oregon and Washington, ready to pick fruit or to gut salmon in a packinghouse, willing to do anything to earn their keep.

Like many border towns, San Ysidro is conducive to paranoia. Set in the midst of sagebrush and dry, brown mountains covered with chaparral, it has the harmless look of an ordinary suburb, but this is deceptive and does not hold up under close inspection. For instance, there is a blood bank on the edge of its largest mall, and all day you can watch donors come out the door with balls of cotton pressed to their forearms, bound for a shopping spree at a nearby K mart before going home to Tijuana.

The sky above San Ysidro is often full of ravens and buzzards, and skulls of small animals turn up in its playgrounds.

Its population is mostly Hispanic, but more and more Anglos—retired folks, and those who commute to San Diego—are buying property in the tile-roofed housing tracts that are devouring the last farms and ranches, and they get very angry when some migrants dash through their back yards, trampling the shrubbery and pausing to drink from garden hoses.

The Border Patrol is supposed to control the flow of uninvited foreigners into the States. In California, as in Texas, its stations are understaffed and underfunded, and are asked to perform a nearly impossible task. In the San Diego Sector, agents must police all of San Diego County, as well as substantial parts of Orange and Riverside Counties, scouring not only the canyons and the backwoods but also the teeming barrios in cities, where the newly arrived frequently seek shelter.

Although the sector captures more migrants than any other sector in the country—more than four hundred and seventy thousand in the last fiscal year, almost half the United States total—this record does little for the morale of the agents, since there is no real penalty imposed on those who are apprehended, unless they have some contraband or resist arrest. Mexicans are given a brief interview, then returned to Tijuana, sometimes so quickly that they get caught crossing again on the same night.

The law isn't the only obstacle that the Border Patrol faces in dispatching its duty. It used to be easy for agents to spot new arrivals because they dressed like field hands and looked dirty and frightened, but now they disguise themselves in clothes fresh off the rack, relying on bluejeans, Reeboks, and L.A. Dodgers caps for protective coloration. The business of providing goods and services to migrants has grown enormously, forming a closed economy worth millions, and they have an elaborate network of support, which often involves extended families and functions in the manner of an underground railroad.

Then, too, migrants are always testing agents by devising new tricks for sneaking into California. On a hot summer day, they like to put on bathing suits and wander up the coast, or they dive from a boat and swim to shore. They wade through raw sewage in the Tijuana River and slip into Imperial Beach, just north of San Ysidro. They jam themselves into car trunks and into boxcars, and they ride across the border spread-eagled on top of freight trains. The boldest ones merely sprint through the backed-up traffic at the port of entry, defying the Border Patrol to chase them.

Once migrants get by this first line of defense, they can relax and blend into the crowd of legal Hispanics in San Ysidro. They treat the town as a sort of flea market, making connections and buying stateside necessities, usually on the sly. If they require fake documents—anything from birth certificates to green cards—they seek out a dealer in such papers and begin negotiations. A high-quality document might cost more than a thousand dollars. Only an expert can detect that it's a forgery, while a so-called "fifty-footer" looks bad even at that distance and can be bought without much haggling.

If migrants have some pesos to be laundered, they speak to the fellows hanging around the pay phones by the United States Customs gate. Those phones, supplied by half a dozen different companies, are the conduit through which a fortune in drug profits—from the sale of cocaine, marijuana, and methamphetamines—is annually rerouted. The men who smuggle in migrants use the phones, too, arranging transportation for their customers. The smugglers are known as *coyotes*, on account of their predatory habits, and they flourish on the border, where expediency is the rule of thumb.

In San Ysidro, there are also safe houses, where, for a price, a migrant can hole up for a while. The safe houses look like the houses around them, but everybody on a given block can point them out. As it happens, secrecy tends to play a very limited role in illegal immigration. Anyone who wants to see how openly migrants cross the border, even in broad daylight, can take a drive on Dairy Mart Road, which winds from the outskirts of town through beanfields, pastures, and fallow land scattered with junked farm machinery. On any morning or afternoon, in any season, you'll have to brake to a halt as people streak by in front of your car, speeding from one hiding place to another. For the most part, they are young men in their late teens and early twenties, and they never seem the slightest bit afraid. They emerge from arroyos, from stands of bamboo and pampas grass, from copses of trees, and from vacant buildings. One morning as I cruised on Dairy Mart Road, I counted twenty-two people in a two-hour period.

The action at night is even more spectacular, and it occurs on a much larger scale. At dusk, you hear sirens and whistles all over San Ysidro, as if several robberies were in progress, and then comes the chopping sound of helicopter blades slashing up the sky. Step outside your motel room and you notice beams

65

from above shining down on a Carl's Jr. restaurant, on kids in baseball uniforms and elderly folks out for an evening stroll. Sometimes a beam illuminates a drainage ditch, and a human form scampers away, like a rabbit rousted from its burrow. It's disconcerting to find normal life going on in what appears to be a suburban war zone. If you walk to a weedy field near the blood bank, you can look toward the concrete levee of the Tijuana River, where, in the glare of I.N.S. floodlights and in full view of the Border Patrol, more than five hundred people will be congregated in little bands, waiting for an opportune moment to begin their journey to the United States.

\* \* \*

All around Tijuana, there are settlements that cater to the needs of people about to cross, and La Libertad, in Canyon Zapata, is one of them. Its most famous entrepreneur is a big, good-natured woman who goes by the name of Manuela. Manuela's friends like to joke that she is a witch, whose supernatural business acumen has permitted her to become well-to-do, at least by the diminished standards of rural Mexico.

She has built up a profitable cafe trade by feeding meals to those who leave for San Ysidro from the base of the canyon, where the ground is so perfectly level that the migrants call it "the soccer field." Hundreds of footpaths are worn into it, fanning out in all directions, and every crack and crevice is stuffed with garbage, which scrawny dogs keep pawing through. Rusty, windowless cars and trucks dot the horizon, because occasionally migrants try driving to the States instead of walking, and they abandon their vehicles if they're foiled by the Border Patrol or by the many potholes, gulleys, and ravines on the way to California.

Manuela is about thirty-five years old. She has bright brown eyes in a handsome face. Her body is compact and fleshy, and she enjoys gossip and has an earthy sense of humor that makes men want to pinch her. Manuela does not actively discourage the men. Sometimes when she cooks she wears a T-shirt that says, in English, "Poverty Sucks," but she hasn't been poor since she started her business, ten years ago.

There were no houses in La Libertad then, but now Manuela owns one on the canyon rim, sharing it with eighteen others, including her nine children, her husband, her two brothers, and an assortment of cousins. The house isn't fancy. It's constructed of plywood and concrete blocks, and has a plastic tarp over a leaky roof. In winter, when a cold wind blows in from the ocean, Manuela's youngest boy, Javier, who is eight, collects cardboard to cram into the walls for insulation.

For Manuela, the working day begins at noon, when she and a few of her children haul her cooking equipment from the house to the canyon. Pots, pans, bottles of peanut oil, tortillas wrapped in paper, tomatoes and onions for salsa, pickled jalapenos, strips of marinated beef—the whole cargo gets carried down in arms and on backs, along with some firewood and some cases of soda and beer. Manuela always sets up in the same place, where she has a wooden picnic table and a blackened oil drum. She starts a fire in the drum and puts an equally blackened grill on top of it. She uses this to roast chickens, make quesadillas, heat beans and tortillas, and sear the beef for *carne asada.*

In addition to food Manuela sells cigarettes, mostly black-market Raleighs. She keeps painstaking records in her account books, and they show that she earns about two hundred dollars a month—as much, she says proudly, as a documented maid in San Diego, or the girls at the *maquiladoras,* or twin plants, on Otay Mesa.

Other food venders operate stands in the canyon, but they don't have Manuela's expertise, or her reputation for cleanliness. She does things skillfully, exploiting every opportunity. This is also true of her attitude toward border life. She approaches it as if it were a contest meant to challenge her intelligence, and she takes pleasure in her victories. Like many other Mexican women without the proper documents, she has managed to be in California "accidentally" while she was nine months pregnant, and two of her boys were born in San Diego County and became instant Americans. (Any Mexican can request a border-crossing card that allows day trips to the States. It costs the United States about a hundred and eighty-five dollars to process each one.) Her husband, a plumber, has papers and often works in San Ysidro, but he and Manuela would never think of living in the States, even if they could afford it. They have no desire to become Americans—they just want a little piece of America's wealth.

About three hours before dark, people assemble on the soccer field, arriving singly or in pairs, in family groups or in loose-knit associations formed on the road. There are always more men than women. Sometimes there are children—infants, toddlers, newborns in pink and blue blankets, nursing at a mother's breast. Almost everyone is neatly dressed, and those who aren't spruce themselves up by buying shirts and trousers from two women who have piles of clothing heaped on folding tables. Many of the migrants have crossed the border before. They speak a bit of English, have the confident air of seasoned travellers, and impart tips to the less experienced. The younger men may have their hair cut in the slick, youth-gang style of East L.A.—flat on the top and long at the sides, or clipped close to the skull with a tiny pigtail at the back. Hip young women have tight pants and spiral perms, and may be wearing heels and makeup.

In the crowd, too, there will be a few criminals, who are concealing small packets of cocaine or heroin on their persons. (Large shipments of drugs go through the port of entry in trucks—hidden, say, in a load of sawdust or broken glass.) The criminals may have knives strapped to their legs, or revolvers tucked into the waistbands of their trousers, but in spite of their presence the atmosphere in the canyon is casual. Children kick balls around and play tag while adults eat tacos and sometimes polish off shots of tequila at a tequila vender's stand. Roosters crow, and chickens scratch at the dirt. Snippets of recorded music may filter out from a shack above—accordions, drums, guitars, trumpets. The feeling in the canyon is communal, much like at a county fair, with crossing the border the ultimate game of chance.

The only people who appear to be anxious are the Central Americans. They have already crossed the border *into* Mexico illegally, and they are fearful that the Mexican border patrol may sweep through La Libertad and toss them into a Tijuana jail, where they are often beaten up before being sent home. The Central Americans are also tired and are probably suffering from some minor illness. They have travelled a great distance to reach the soccer field (in many instances, more than two thousand miles, through jungles, swamps, and highlands), escaping sometimes from war and oppression but more frequently from outmoded agricultural practices that have stripped their homelands bare and made subsistence farming impossible. Nicaraguans, Guatemalans, Salvadorans, Hondurans—they worry that someone is out to harm them, while they simultaneously cast about, in a shy way, for help.

Because of their uncertainty, Central Americans generally employ a *coyote*. They pay between five hundred and seven hundred dollars to be smuggled into the United States, whereas a Mexican seldom pays more than three hundred dollars. The money is paid half in advance and half on completion of the journey, so that the customers will have a slight measure of control over their guides, whose unscrupulousness is legendary. *Coyotes* will lead a migrant across, stick him in a safe house, and then refuse to release him until his relatives in the United States cough up a ransom. This could be construed as kidnapping, but *coyotes* think of themselves as above the law.

In their book of etiquette, the health and safety of their *pollitos*, or chicks, comes last. They'll desert them under pressure from the Border Patrol, perhaps leaving them locked inside a van, where, sick from the stench of sweat and urine, the chicks run the risk of suffocation. In the hierarchy of illegal immigration, *coyotes* occupy an odd niche between the vaguely heroic and the decidedly villainous, and this gives them a mythic stature on which they capitalize, outfitting themselves in fancy sweatshirts and high-top sneakers in the Air Jordan mode.

As an alternative to hiring a *coyote,* it is possible to latch onto a border veteran who'll take pity on you and let you tag along, charging a reasonable fee. One afternoon at La Libertad, I met a young Mexican man, Omar, who regularly makes a little ready cash this way. He was about to return to the United States with five new friends, having completed a girl-chasing expedition to Tijuana.

At the age of twenty-one, Omar knew the border intimately. He had crossed it for the first time at fourteen, going to Yakima, Washington, to join his parents, who worked the orchards there. He had hoped for a factory job, but he wound up picking apples, and he was still picking them every summer. In his Hard Rock Cafe sweatshirt, sipping from a cold Tecate, he looked supremely undaunted by the mission ahead and might have been preparing himself for a trip to the corner store. His car was parked on a street in San Ysidro. It had California plates, and so, he felt, was not likely to be stopped by inquisitive agents.

The route Omar planned to follow zigzagged up and down hills, traversing rough country that offered ideal habitat for scorpions, lizards, tarantulas, and rattlesnakes. If you hiked it by day, it wasn't too intimidating, he said, but after dark you could get lost, or take a fall, or trip on a root or over a boulder and sprain your ankle. On summer nights, the heat could be horrendous, and people became dehydrated and suffered from exhaustion. There were also bandits who ambushed migrants, knocking them over the head with a stick and stealing their grubstake. (They often have lots of money with them, since they deal strictly in cash.) If the Border Patrol wasn't out in force, it took about half an hour to reach San Ysidro, but if agents were in the canyon you could get pinned down for a long time, curled under a bush in a fetal ball. This didn't happen much, though, because the canyon was hard duty, and agents preferred to avoid it if they could.

For people who don't have the stamina for such a crossing, there are places on the border where success depends on other factors—cunning, bravado, even speed of foot. To cross from the Tijuana River levee, for example, a a migrant needs only good timing and a little luck. San Ysidro is about five hundred yards away, and though the Border Patrol tries to clog the buffer zone with agents in jeeps and on all-terrain motorcycles, the men can't grab everyone running past. Instead, it's a matter of random selection.

At the levee, immigration has the look of a futuristic sporting event that might have been dreamed up for a cable TV network. Many Tijuanans drop by just to entertain themselves and be part of the scene. There is always a hint of danger, mainly because of all the drug dealers and junkies. Teen-agers in heavy-metal T-shirts, high from sniffing glue, strut around listening to old Led Zep tapes on their boom boxes, and every now and then one of them takes off for the States in a goofy glide.

If you walk west from the levee for about a mile, you come to a wooded hillside where migrants also meet. It is a much more tranquil place, except on chilly evenings, when people uproot and burn the surrounding vegetation to keep warm. Technically, they're on American soil when they do this, having crawled through holes in the border fence, but if agents make a move toward them they jump back into Mexico.

A fellow called Miguel told me this one evening while he was eating his dinner, a ham sandwich he'd bought from a vender. The vender, too, was talkative. He reminisced about his years in Santa Ana, California, where he had worked in construction until he got strung out on cocaine. His life was much simpler now, he said. Some weeks, he made as much as seventy dollars selling his wares on and around the levee, keeping the sandwiches and drinks in an Igloo cooler that his wife toted around, even though she was pregnant and had already suffered two miscarriages.

Miguel was slender and sensitive. He had a gap between his front teeth, and he fretted that, at thirty-seven, he was beginning to lose his looks. A roofer by trade, he had hooked up with two Guatemalans from Coban, first-timers, and was taking them across, planning to leave that night at eleven o'clock, when the Border Patrol changed shifts and everyone was distracted. Miguel spoke English with a German accent. An American Army colonel from Wisconsin—an archeology buff who'd stopped in Miguel's village to study the ruins—had taught it to him long ago. The colonel had urged Miguel to visit him in the Midwest, but Miguel was too busy exploring the United States, living in Los Angeles, Palmdale, Chicago, Phoenix, Tucson, and Houston. He had been caught only once, in New Orleans. It was his dream to make it to San Francisco someday.

In Canyon Zapata, there are usually about a hundred people on the soccer field at twilight. That's when Manuela begins to put away her supplies and utensils. She is concerned that somebody might try to rob her, and often she lingers at her table until one of her brothers comes to escort her out. While she douses her fire, the *coyotes* brief their customers, sketching maps on the ground and sending scouts to check on the whereabouts of agents. As night approaches, people move tentatively forward— ten steps, a pause, then ten more steps, as if they were inching themselves into a body of water. In a few minutes, they will have vanished from sight, and Manuela will be back in her house, cooking dinner for her family. The next day will be the same for her. Every day is the same for Manuela—except Sunday, when she observes the Sabbath by staying at home and attending to her Bible studies.

\* \* \*

One of the busiest Border Patrol stations in the San Diego Sector is Brown Field, on Otay Mesa. Named for an airport nearby, the station resembles a small-town firehouse in need of paint and refurbishing. The agents assigned to Brown Field frequently have the demeanor of firemen, in fact, because their work is routine, with long, dull periods during which they perform a repetitive chore—apprehending migrants and returning them to Mexico. Their ranks are composed of Army *vets,* former cops, wanna-be cops, and many ordinary guys who are athletic, don't mind wearing a uniform, and enjoy working outdoors. When agents complain, it isn't about government policy but, rather, about how badly they're paid and how their wives must struggle to make ends meet. Boredom is their worst enemy, and sometimes they combat it by competing to see who can bring in the most prisoners in a day, a week, or a month.

From Brown Field Station an agent can look across a highway to the part of Otay Mesa that drops off to the southwest, toward Tijuana. The mesa is huge, and most of it is still raw desert, but it won't be for long. Its history follows a common pattern of land and water grabs in Southern California, where the model for real-estate transactions appears to be the deal that John Huston pulled off in "Chinatown"—diverting the rivers of the West to L.A. Just before the turn of the century, the mesa had a saloon and a racetrack, but they died a natural death, and some settlers from Germany began dry-farming barley.

Irrigation water became available in the Otay area around 1950, and the farmers diversified and put in vegetable crops and citrus orchards, like those in Imperial Valley, to the north. They couldn't beat the prices of Mexican growers, though, and the mesa languished until the late nineteen-sixties, when a combine of speculators bought up property and lobbied to have the local zoning changed from agricultural to industrial and commercial.

The obvious appeal of the mesa was its strategic position, directly across the border from what American business interests refer to as Mexico's "inexhaustible pool of cheap labor." It was such thinking that helped to create an agreement in 1942 that, as a war-emergency measure, allowed farm workers to enter the States legally, so they could harvest crops that might otherwise have rotted in the fields. The agreement saved California farmers from terrible losses, but it also reinforced a notion already prevalent among rural Mexicans that there would always be work up north. (So many Mexicans came in as *braceros* that in 1954 the government, in an initiative called Operation Wetback, ordered them to leave the country or face being deported. According to government records, more than a million Mexicans left, but no one knows how many returned.) California agriculture still depends on "cheap labor," and so do the *maquiladoras* springing up on Otay Mesa—one plant in Tijuana, for tedious piecework, and one in the United States, for the final assembly of products, and for corporate offices.

Among corporations that operate *maquiladoras,* the underlying assumption is that poor Mexicans will be delighted with humdrum jobs that pay a fraction of what an American worker would earn for doing the same thing, but this hasn't proved to be true. The turnover rate at most plants is very high, and so is the rate of absenteeism, with employees often going home for the weekend and not returning until the following Wednesday.

Industry journals address these problems in an oblique way, suggesting, for instance, that "task oriented" Americans have trouble understanding "relationship oriented" Hispanics, but it is more usual for the advice columns to provide cross-cultural tips, such as when to give a co-worker *el abrazo,* the friendly Latin hug—on holidays, of course, but also at funerals and at "any other moment of happiness or sadness." The journals are not as forthcoming about the environmental impact of *maquiladoras,* although *Twin Plant News* did report in a recent issue that American corporations had been caught dumping about half a million tons of toxic waste at "clandestine 'toxic cemeteries'" all along the border.

It can be instructive to visit both sides of Otay Mesa. On the American side, you see bright new industrial parks bearing triumphant corporate logos—Sony, Sanyo, Hughes Aircraft. The Golden Arches are in place. Truckloads of desert-hardy trees and shrubs go by, destined to form the instant landscaping on Maquiladora Street or Pacific Rim Boulevard. Everything's clean.

Drive through the Otay Mesa port of entry, and you're in another world. (The port, which opened in 1985, purportedly to ease the traffic at San Ysidro, has been a tremendous boon to development.) The buildings in the Zona Industrial are drab, the roads are miserably paved, and the air reeks of chemicals and diesel fumes. Most *maquila* workers are young women from the interior, and on their lunch break they leave the plants to eat at carts and flirt with men. This appears to be a moment of happiness, but it fades as soon as the women, whose wages of fifty dollars a week barely cover their housing and transportation costs, must go back inside.

The *maquiladoras* pose no difficulties for the Border Patrol. They have stringent hiring policies, and almost all the employees live in and around Tijuana. At Brown Field Station, the foremost duty of agents remains the capture of migrants. They use a variety of high-tech gear to assist them, and it adds a considerably to the annual budget of the I.N.S. There are electronic sensors buried on the border, and whenever anybody passes by one a blip flashes on a computer screen at headquarters. There is an infrared telescope that rests on a pickup truck, and it is deployed at a different spot each night, somewhere between San Ysidro and the mesa. When you look through it, you can pick out people moving in the dark. They're an eerie green against the dull-red glow of fields and earth. The agent manning the scope pinpoints the location of migrants on a grid and relays it, and then a copter may be called in to throw a search beam on the spot.

In spite of the high-tech equipment, most Border Patrol tracking is done on foot or in a vehicle, often a Chevy Blazer painted a sort of grayish camouflage color. The Blazers are sometimes so dented they look as if they'd been driven off a cliff, and some of them actually have been, because agents seldom pursue migrants over established roads. Instead, they have to motor through mud, marshes, sand, and loose gravel.

As for the mesa, it is as hard as a cast-iron skillet, even after a rain, and a ride across it at top speed is a serious challenge to the human spine. The shock absorbers in most of the Border Partrol's vehicles are ancient, and you bounce around so vigorously that you may bang your head on the roof. Agents also sustain injuries while they're running, jumping fences, and wrestling with migrants. *Coyotes* do them damage by pitching rocks and chunks of concrete at them from fleeing vans. One agent got hit in an ear and went deaf. Another agent took such a solid crack to his forehead that it exposed the frontal lobe of his brain.

These "rockings" are a major nuisance. In the San Diego Sector, the Border Patrol spends about forty thousand dollars a year replacing its vehicles' windshields and side windows. At the same time, however, agents are spared other types of violence, which is a bit strange, given the potentially explosive climate on the border. There are theories to explain this. One theory has it that most migrants are simple folk, who wouldn't know which end of a weapon to hold if you stuck it in their hands. Another theory has it that the criminals who do have weapons control their impulse toward violence, because they don't want to incur the wrath of the United States government and upset the subtle balances of a system that works so beautifully to their advantage.

\* \* \*

Joe Nunez is assigned to Brown Field Station, and in his eleven years as an agent he has been involved in only one threatening incident when a migrant pulled a knife and tried to stab Nunez's partner. Nunez gets excited when he tells about battling for the knife (which, it turned out, was made of wood), but he is really an easygoing type, who likes a beer and a barbecue and doesn't let himself become hung up on the most salient metaphysical issue of this job—that is, whether or not the chaos at the border is intentional.

Sometimes it troubles Joe that the job isn't more stimulating, and he thinks about transferring to an investigative unit in L.A., because the thrills at Brown Field are few and far between. Nunez caught some Chinese once, and once he caught some Yugoslavs, but then O.T.M.s (migrants who are Other Than Mexican) are common in the San Diego Sector: in fiscal year 1988, its agents arrested (among others) three hundred and forty-seven Colombians, two hundred and sixty-six Brazilians, fifty-three South Koreans, twenty Indians, sixteen Turks, eleven Filipinos, seven Canadians, three Israelis, and one person apiece from Nigeria, Somalia, Gambia, Algeria, and France.

One night, when the moon was almost full, Nunez let me ride with him on patrol. In minutes, he noticed five people at the edge of the highway, moving stealthily forward. He shut off the Blazer's headlights, downshifted into first, and crept up on them. They were so preoccupied with the speeding cars and the unfamiliar turf that they didn't see him until he was about ten yards away. Then one of them shouted, and they all spun on their heels and ran, but when Nunez ordered them to halt they complied, slumping to their knees and putting their hands on their heads, as if they had practiced the drill. There were three migrant men, a migrant woman, and a *coyote,* all in their early twenties. Nunez called for a Border Patrol van to collect them. Then he frisked everyone and found a handkerchief tied to one man's leg, hidden under his trousers. The man reacted as if the handkerchief held precious gems. In it were ten crumpled dollar bills.

The mood of the apprehended was sombre. They seemed to be kicking themselves for getting caught. When hundreds were crossing the mesa, why had fate selected them to be pulled aside? Nunez made small talk with them, speaking in Spanish. This was always an awkward time—the dead time before a van arrived—and during it all pretense fell away, and the weirdness of the situation became manifest. Some agents joked about it, while others scolded their captives for breaking the law. Some agents knew what it was like to be poor and so were sympathetic, while others concealed their emotions behind the symbols of office. There were agents who were inquisitive, and there were agents who were rude and made racist remarks.

As for Nunez, he was gentle, polite, and perhaps a bit embarrassed, since everybody knew that the arrest was just a momentary hitch—an inconvenience on the order of a traffic ticket—in a journey that would soon continue.

"Where are you from?" Nunez asked.

The oldest-looking man answered. He kept glancing menacingly at the *coyote,* as if he wanted to strangle him. "Oaxaca," he said. Oaxaca is home to Mixtec and Zapotec Indians. It is sixteen hundred miles to the south, and its hills are so eroded that a corn crop, which has always been a staple of the Indians, can scarcely be grown there anymore.

"Why are you crossing?"

The man shrugged. "To work," he said.

*Trabajar—to* work. All night, whenever Nunez asked "Why are you crossing?" the word was repeated. People wanted to work, and they didn't care what the work was like. They would do stoop labor, wrecking their backs and their knees picking strawberries or artichokes, and they would prune vineyards and orchards that had been sprayed with pesticides. They would swab floors, bathe infants, scrub pots and pans, and breathe in formaldehyde vapors in factories where particleboard was made. They would sell bags of oranges from traffic islands in Santa Monica, and they would hammer dents from bumpers at auto-body shops in Glendale. Contractors would employ them to dig ditches for foundations. They would agree to remove asbestos from around heating ducts and scrape lead-based paint from walls. They would pour hot tar for roofs, handle beakers in meth labs, mow lawns, deliver circulars, clean sewers—anything at all.

The van came, and the Oaxacans climbed into it. They'd have to ride around until it was filled to capacity—about seventeen passengers—and then they would be processed at Brown Field Station. They could be detained for a maximum of seventy-two hours, although it was probable that they would be gone before morning. For a while after arresting them, Nunez had no luck. He spotted only "onesies" and "twosies," and because they were far away he didn't bother to go after them. He did chase four men down a hill, but they "bushed up" on him, vanishing into the mesquite scrub. He spent fifteen minutes tailing a suspicious car and keeping in contact with a fellow-agent, who finally stopped the driver and reported that he was "a Japanese gentleman with a valid passport."

And then Nunez was distracted. Somebody was walking toward him at a brisk clip, reversing the usual order of things. The man approached the Blazer, took off his knit cap, and grinned broadly, as if he'd bumped into an old pal. When Nunez asked for his documents, he fumbled in a pocket, struck himself in the forehead with the palm of a hand—iay, *caramba!*—and said that he had left them at his uncle's house in San Ysidro.

The story delighted him out of all proportion to its merits. It was clear he'd been drinking. Drunks were always wandering across the mesa, often just because another drunk in a *pulque* shop had dared them to, and they wasted everyone's time. The man tried a few more excuses, but he could not invent one that pleased Nunez, and at last he collapsed into a rueful posture of acceptance and sat down to wait for a van.

The night dragged on. There were more arrests, but they were ordinary. Then, at about eleven o'clock, Nunez received a radio call informing him that a big bunch of Salvadorans, as many as twenty of them, were being rounded up. That made him sigh. Central Americans required a lot of paperwork, and he'd have to put in about forty-five minutes with each of them. His shift would stretch into the wee hours. The Salvadorans would ask for political asylum, whether or not they were genuine refugees, and by the time a court date was set they would be working somewhere—and if they weren't working they wouldn't show up in court.

Such job-related frustrations subject agents to constant stress and may cause them to burn out. Some have marital problems, some have problems with booze, and some, who lack Nunez's equanimity, get headaches from patrolling the mesa in the dark and realizing that they often have no idea where Mexico ends and California begins.

* * *

In the last ten years, more and more Oaxacans have crossed into San Diego County, leaving behind one of the poorest and most fractious states in Mexico. There are five hundred and seventy villages in Oaxaca, all dating from the pre-Conquest period, and all fiercely independent. The villages have their own rules and laws, which take precedence over the country's civil codes. And sometimes an extended family within a village will have its own subset of rules and laws, which contradict all the other rules and laws. Disputes are part of everyday life in Oaxaca. Some of them have been raging since the time of Cortes. They center on communal land rights, and lead to altercations, fistfights, and small-scale battles. Tradition matters deeply to Mixtecs and Zapotecs, and, in the face of grinding poverty, it is becoming traditional for the men of both tribes to look for work on American farms, where their friends and relatives have worked in the past.

The farms around San Diego are disappearing rapidly, though, and the men often arrive to find condos where the beans and tomatoes used to be. Yet some farms with a history of hiring Oaxacans are still around, such as one in Carlsbad, where some Mixtecs work. It is a big spread, surrounded by suburban developments, and it has a hundred acres planted to strawberries. The Mixtecs earn three dollars and sixty-five cents an hour to hoe the fields and harvest the fruit, but there isn't always work, and they may have a week or two of inactivity. They aren't as disconcerted by this as Americans might be, since they're accustomed to hardship and know how to make it through a slack period. They behave as they might in their home village, staying close to camp and using their free time to relax, playing cards for pennies and nickels or chatting in the sunshine.

The Mixtecs live in camps out of economic necessity, fear, and ignorance, and also for the comfort of being near their own people. The apartment rents in Carlsbad are way beyond their reach, and, besides, the Mixtecs are saving money to take back to Oaxaca.

If they have any English at all, it will be limited to "yes" and "no" and "O.K.," and when they go out in the streets they get confused and are afraid—or don't know how—to ask questions. Many of them have documents, but they are still uneasy, and believe that they might be deported at any moment. They never bank any of the cash they make, storing it instead in their underwear, their bedrolls, or the ballcaps they love to wear. Thieves descend on them sometimes, including youth-gang members looking for a score. The growers in the county use private security forces to patrol their farms and keep out trespassers, and the guards are responsible for protecting the workers, too, whether or not the workers have asked for protection.

The Mixtec camp in Carlsbad is home to about sixty men. It's built in a dry creekbed below the fenced strawberry fields, in a grove of oaks, bay laurels, and pungent eucalyptus trees. The men live in shacks made of scavenged lumber and cardboard. Some of the shacks have been around for a decade. The Mixtecs are short, but they can seldom enter the doorway of one of their shacks without bending over.

If a man in camp has a mattress, he is doing well. A man with a mattress, a chair, some bedding, and a framed religious picture might be considered rich. There are no toilets available, and no electricity or running water, so trash and excrement lie about, despite the Mixtecs' attempts to be tidy. They buy most of their groceries from a quilt truck they call a *fayuca*, or a "roach wagon," paying too much for canned goods and worrying that they'll get sick because they're not eating fresh vegetables. For sundries, they go to a woman, Dona Elvira, who keeps a shop in a tract house up the road. She lets Mixtecs use her telephone in an emergency. At night, they sit outdoors on her patio and watch programs on a black-and-white TV.

For most of the year, the Mixtecs don't mind the camp, but when winter comes they suffer. They have kerosene lanterns and candles to light their shacks, but they knock them over and start fires. Sometimes they try to heat a shack with charcoal briquettes, or with kindling. They stuff magazines and newspapers into the walls for insulation, much as people do at La Libertad, holding the material in place with thumbtacks or chicken wire. On the day I visited, I saw a U.S. government publication for immigrants jammed between some plastic and some cardboard, with the pages turned to a paragraph that began, "The United States has fifty states. Rhode Island is the smallest state." A Mixtec was standing nearby, and when I asked him, in English, about Rhode Island, he nodded, smiled, and said, "Yes, O.K."

My guide at the camp was Roberto Martinez, the regional director of the American Friends Service Committee, whose offices are in San Diego's Logan Heights barrio, around the corner from some safe houses. For the last few years, Martinez has involved himself in the lives of migrants, both legal and illegal, and has been keeping a record of various abuses committed against them by the Border Patrol, the San Diego police, and vigilantes.

There are dozens of migrant camps in the county, and Martinez knows them all and drops by on a regular basis to hand out donated blankets, sweaters, and food. He likes this aspect of his job, because it gets him out into the fresh air. In his opinion, the Mixtecs' camp isn't a particularly bad one. At other camps, men live in "spider holes," digging a pit and then covering the top with leaves and branches. The Border Patrol rarely raids any camps, nor do any of the county agencies. Martinez isn't sure why this is so.

The Mixtecs were taking it easy that morning. They'd just finished planting some strawberries and now had to wait for the weeds to grow. They were doing their laundry in buckets of water carried down from Dona Elvira's, and hanging the wash on tree limbs to dry. They had a rusty basketball hoop nailed to a tree, but they couldn't play because their ball was punctured and flat.

The Mixtecs ranged in age from about sixteen to about sixty, and they had inky hair and were dressed in very clean clothes, given the circumstances. They seemed to have only two emotions: extreme pleasure or extreme misery. They smiled in an open, unaffected, and generous way, but they're also capable of falling into a funk and going wild, especially if they've been drinking. There was no alcohol in the camp and no women, either, but prostitutes have been known to pay calls. All the men wore cheap digital watches, and nine out of ten wore ballcaps that said, across the crown, such things as "SWAT" and "OLD FART" and "CALIFORNIA HIGHWAY PATROL."

Martinez asked if they were all from the same Oaxacan village, and they nodded and said, "*Sí, mismo pueblo.*" Then he asked if they had papers. They nodded again, but not with as much enthusiasm, and a couple of them remembered chores they had to do and vanished into shacks.

It was Martinez's guess that about three-quarters of the men were in the country legally. Since Congress passed the Immigration Reform and Control Act (IRCA), in 1986, there are more documented workers in the States than ever before, and most of the workers at any farm will be legal—although at harvest time everyone works, papers or no papers. (In businesses other than agriculture, the rate of compliance is much lower.) IRCA hasn't been an unqualified success, however. Some employers use it to discriminate: they refuse to hire Hispanics by insisting that their documents look fake. Or an employer may hire somebody with forged papers, let him work for two weeks, and call in the Border Patrol the day before payday. And there are many crooked lawyers who bilk migrants, charging them five hundred dollars to fill out forms that require only a birth date, a signature, and the remittance of a ten-dollar bill.

In many respects, the most ticklish consequence of IRCA is that it has made a previously invisible phenomenon visible. There have always been plenty of migrant workers in San Diego County, but they have tended to be undocumented and to stay in hiding. A man with papers feels free to roam about, so you now see many more migrants on the streets.

Even the Mixtecs venture into Carlsbad if they run low on money. They walk a few miles to a 7-11 and stand in front of it, flagging motorists in the hope that someone will offer them a day job. If nothing happens by noon or so, they lose their ambition and may lounge around for the rest of the afternoon, as if they were in the *zocalo* in Oaxaca. They sit on curbs or lean against cars and tease one another, and when a pretty woman goes by they lift their eyes and comment appreciatively. If they get sleepy, they take a nap. If they have to pee, they step behind a bush. They don't realize they might be causing offense, or that their very presence might be frightening shoppers away.

These groups of documented migrants can be found in any city in Southern California. The men often segregate themselves by nationality—the Guatemalans on one side of a block and Nicaraguans on the other. Mexicans draw very fine distinctions, with Jaliscans, say, here and Zacatecans there. The groups can be big—up to three hundred—and also rambunctious, and as their size increases so do the protests against them. Irate homeowners phone the Border Patrol and ask that the foreigners be removed. That puts the Border Patrol in a sort of double bind, which the agents recognize but, as public servants, are compelled not to mention; that is, the migrants wouldn't be standing on corners if some people in Vista and Oceanside and Carlsbad and Encinitas weren't hiring and paying them—in cash, off the books, and way below union scale, without deducting any taxes for Uncle Sam. So the agents explain to callers that the men, though demonstrably foreign, are only exercising their right to assemble.

In the old days, the Border Patrol ran sweeps to deal with such complaints. Agents came by in a van, grabbed all the Hispanics in sight, and sifted through them later at the station, apologizing to the few legally documented aliens who happened to crop up. They can't do that anymore. A wrongful arrest brings charges of harassment and may result in a civil-rights suit. Agents in a suburb like El Cajon, northeast of San Diego, must be very cautious about whom they arrest, and how the arrest is conducted, even though they're under pressure from citizens to be more forceful. Throughout the county, there's been a subtle change in the way Mexicans and Central Americans are perceived. Formerly, when an agent hauled in a migrant, he might be met with disapproving glances, as if he were bullying a poor person. Now an arrest outside a convenience store is likely to be greeted with applause.

At the El Cajon Station, agents are concerned about a rise in acts of discrimination, and even violence, against migrant workers. They believe that a backlash has set in. This backlash takes many forms, some open and some covert. It can have an absurdist streak, as it does at Fairbanks Ranch, a wealthy subdivision. Workers loiter by the ranch gates, looking to trim hedges or shovel manure, and periodically some neighborhood matrons give them litter bags of their own, so they won't throw their trash on the grass. Or it can be mean-spirited and life-threatening, as it was at the Carlsbad Country Store, where, two years ago, a butcher and a baker kidnapped a loitering Mexican, bound him with tape, put a paper bag over his head, and left him in a field. The kidnappers' claim that they were making a citizen's arrest for trespassing did not hold up in court.

\* \* \*

In the suburb of Del Mar, in San Diego County, there is a Oaxacan camp right off a two-lane road, across from Evergreen Nursery, where most of the men work. The men here are Mixtecs—about twenty-five in all—but their shacks are cruder than the ones in Carlsbad, more battered and wind-pierced, filthier. The Mixtecs live on brushy land without any shade trees, and the camp smells of decaying garbage, not eucalyptus or bay laurel. In the brush you find crushed beer cans and empty wine bottles. The shacks are thick with dust, because bulldozers are levelling the earth nearby, preparing it for a new housing tract. That means that the Mixtecs will soon have to move, although no one knows where.

It is strange to stand in the camp and look over your shoulder at the bulldozers and, beyond them, the orderly lines of pink and rose-colored condos stretching toward the ocean. In fact, if you're tired or a little disoriented—if you've been crossing the border yourself—you can forget exactly which country you are in. At quitting time, when the Mixtecs return from work, one begins strumming a guitar, while a woman—the only one around—goes from shack to shack borrowing ingredients to make a *caldo de res* for her lover. Her feet are bare, and she wears a new cotton dress that clings to her body. The man with the guitar sighs and wishes aloud that he had a chicken to eat, or at least some tequila to drink.

Samuel Solano shares a shack at the camp with three others from his home village, sleeping on a cheap sleeping bag that pours out cotton stuffing. He has shoulder-length hair and a full beard, and if you tell him, as a joke, that he looks like a hippie he enjoys it very much. He works only three days a week at the nursery, because he doesn't yet have documents. He has applied for them, though, and carries around a creased and dirty envelope that contains photocopies of some formal letters pertaining to his request.

His wife, also a Mixtec, is across the border in Ensenada, less than a hundred miles away, with their four children, and, in season, she picks tomatoes. Samuel wants to visit his family, but he doesn't dare cross over, because he isn't sure he could get back in. The risk is too big, he says, scratching at his beard, so he plans to wait for his documents to arrive. That might happen in the new year, he thinks. Then he will go south for a while, until it's time to leave his wife and head north once again.

*The New Yorker*, 1990

# The Victim's Wake: Murder in the Caribbean

In the Caribbean, there's an old saying that Americans come to the tropics to misbehave. Whacked out on the rum and the sun, they do things they'd never do at home, but few tourists have ever gotten into as much trouble as Jim and Penny Fletcher, a wealthy yachting couple from Huntington, West Virginia, whose run through the islands landed them in prison. The Fletchers found themselves accused of murdering a water-taxi operator, Jerome "Jolly" Joseph, on the little island of Bequia, part of St. Vincent and the Grenadines, a former British colony. They were denied bail and held in bleak, dungeonlike cells for about nine months while they waited for a trial date. If convicted, they would be sentenced to death and hang from the gallows.

When the trial began, I flew down to attend it. I'd been intrigued by the Fletcher case from the start. It had all the elements of an outdoor film noir—drink, drugs, sex, sailing, and betrayal—plus a whodunit at its core. I had no idea whether the accused were guilty or innocent. Had they really pulled the trigger, or were they—as they claimed—merely unfortunate victims who'd made some powerful enemies on Bequia?

Jim Fletcher's family had hired an attorney to massage the State Department in Washington and spin the media, and there'd been so many charges of corruption and mistreatment that it was impossible to decipher the truth. The people who live in St. Vincent and the Grenadines—or SVG, as it's known—were in shock. The tiny country consists of 32 islands and cays stretching almost to Venezuela, and its residents had never been touched by a problem of such magnitude, or forced to wonder about the nature of justice—or, for that matter, tourism and its own power to corrupt.

Kingstown, the nation's capital, is a densely populated city of about 17,000, where only a few buildings are taller than a coconut tree. The airport can't handle big commercial jets, so I arrived from San Juan on a turboprop and stared in hypnotic fascination at the vast expanse of sapphire-blue water below and muttered the usual prayers. In an hour or so, St. Vincent came into view, green, mountainous, and rugged, with a semidormant volcano at its northern tip. In the nineteenth century, British sugar plantations dominated the landscape, but now the chief cash crops are bananas, coconuts, arrowroot, and high-grade marijuana.

At the airport, a light breeze was blowing. There were just a dozen or so passengers on the plane, and we walked into a busy terminal together and lined up at a couple of simple tables, where two customs officers stamped our passports. Outside, taxis were parked at the curb, and I cast my lot with a cabbie called Slim. He wasn't slim, not at all, but he laughed and explained that everyone in town had a jokey nickname, including the prime minister, James "Son" Mitchell, who'd been in office almost since independence in 1979.

Slim showed me around before taking me to my hotel. It was a Saturday, and the downtown streets were thronged and noisy. Hundreds of shoppers pulsed through a huge central market at the edge of the sea. Because of the English connection, I'd expected Kingstown to be somewhat stiff and formal, with the locals and the tourists keeping a polite distance, but instead the atmosphere was raucous and freewheeling. Tinny radios blasted reggae music at maximum volume, while children chased one another through a maze of wooden stalls and rowdy traders bargained with their customers. Skinny dogs nosed about in the open gutters, and a handful of rum sots slept off their fevers in the shade.

For decades, the island has been the breadbasket of the eastern Caribbean, and when yachting types stop at all, it's only for a day or two to lay in provisions and have a few drinks at Basil's bar before sailing on to the Grenadines, where the beaches are far more beautiful and the anchorages rival any in the world. When the Fletchers boarded the *Carefree*, their 47-foot yacht, for a sailing idyll they hoped would last several years, the Grenadines was one of their prime destinations.

Slim, like most Vincies, was well versed in the particulars of the Fletcher case and wanted to know if I had anything to do with it.

"I'm here to write about it," I told him.

"That woman did the crime!" he said with authority, leaning on his horn to scatter some chickens in the road. "The husband, he's just a drunk. But Penny Fletcher—I tell you, mon, she did the crime!"

"You think so?"

"Oh, yeah. Even before comin' here, she had problems in St. Lucia for wavin' around a gun. On Bequia, she was runnin' about and saying she wants to shoot a nigger!"

I hadn't seen the word "nigger" in any of the newspapers I'd read, though some reports alleged that Penny had wanted to shoot "a black man." Otherwise, Slim's version jibed with what I already knew. Jolly Joseph had indeed been shot; his body was discovered floating in Admiralty Bay, off Bequia. He'd been missing for two days, and the Fletchers were among his last known contacts. His skin was peeling off, and small fish had eaten away his eyelids, nose, and lips. A single .22 bullet was lodged between his ribs, having pierced his lungs, his aorta, and his heart.

"The police never found a murder weapon, did they?" I asked.

He shook his head. "But the Fletchers had a .22, mon. They sayin' a deckhand stole it from 'em, but probably they threw it overboard. That's a big ocean out there. Can swallow a lot of things."

Slim made it clear he didn't judge all Americans by Jim and Penny's supposed antics, but he was still angry with the U.S. government. Recently, American drug-squad helicopters had come in and sprayed the marijuana fields, and what had SVG gotten in exchange? Exactly nothing!

"Then those Fletchers bring us all this negative publicity," Slim continued, in disgust. "*Nightline* and everything."

The stateside publicity, including a locally infamous episode of *Nightline*, had certainly been negative, with SVG portrayed as an evil, backward country that tourists should avoid, while Jim and Penny were depicted as the objects of a witchhunt who'd been jailed on flimsy circumstantial evidence. The validity of such charges was still at issue, but nobody denied that the Fletchers had suffered in Kingstown. At the men's prison, Jim shared a 16-by-20-foot cell with 17 other inmates. On a diet of rice, beans, bread, tea, and scraps of meat, he had lost some 30 pounds and claimed that he might be dying, while Penny suffered from malnutrition and complained about the scuttling rats that kept her awake at night.

"You think they're guilty?" I asked.

"I tell you, that woman did the crime."

"Will a jury here convict them?"

"No, I don't think it," Slim said flatly. "They Americans, you know?"

The Grand View Beach Hotel, where I'd booked a room, occupied a bluff called Villa Point outside Kingstown. The main building had once been a cotton-drying house on a colonial estate, and it had lovely, airy rooms and was done everywhere in the lush colors you see in Winslow Homer's island watercolors, the greens and blues of the sea and the bright reds and oranges of tropical flowers. Here, too, the Fletchers turned out to be the chief topic of conversation. The desk clerk mentioned them shyly, and I chatted about the case later with Tony "Miler" Sardine, who owns the hotel with his wife, Heather. Tony had been born and raised on St. Vincent and echoed Slim's distress about all the bad press.

"That prison isn't any worse than the others in the eastern Caribbean," he told me, adding that the guards were so lenient that they sometimes let the inmates slip into the Lyric Cinema across the street to catch a movie. The problem, of course, was that Jim and Penny Fletcher were rich tourists, not poor Vincies— the annual per capita income in SVG is about $2,100—and they weren't accustomed to such hardship.

In fact, it was a quirk of fate that they'd done any time at all. They might have been free and clear of Kingstown before Christmas if a bizarre set of events hadn't prevented them from buying their way out of their cells. It happened that another murder had occurred in the islands shortly after the Fletchers were jailed at the end of October 1996. In early November, two intruders allegedly slipped onto a South African yacht anchored in Cumberland Bay, a remote spot on the leeward side of St. Vincent, and hacked to death Lorraine Heath, a tourist from Durban, with their machetes.

Her husband, Alan, who summoned the police and suffered some superficial cuts, was the only eyewitness. Robbery was presumed to be the motive, but nothing appeared to be missing. Heath was outraged when the officers detained him for about three weeks while they investigated. He would later state that Hans Matadial, a well-connected lawyer in the city, finally approached him with a deal. If he'd pay $25,000 in legal fees, he would be released, and Heath complied.

Word of Heath's narrow escape reached Jim Fletcher in prison, and he informed Arturo Diaz, an attorney of his from Puerto Rico, the U.S. jurisdiction closest to SVG, that he'd pay as much as $100,000 for his and Penny's freedom. Diaz claims to have made the necessary initial arrangements with an unnamed "fixer" when the deal collapsed. "Things were very hot, hot, hot," Diaz recounted on the *Nightline* program. He suggested that his fixer had developed cold feet.

But it was actually Alan Heath who'd queered the deal. Home again in Durban, he had embarked on a one-man crusade to advertise the perceived horrors of St. Vincent and had scared off everybody, according to Diaz. The $25,000 was a bribe, Heath insisted—not "legal fees"—and he swore that the money had gone to Randolph Toussaint, the commissioner of police. (Toussaint denied it and has since resigned.) SVG was corrupt and had no justice system, Heath said on television, and his accusations made headlines everywhere.

I had traveled enough in poor countries not to be shocked by the thought of corruption in Kingstown. Corruption exists at every level of every society, but it's one thing to be a critic of your own people and another to be poked in the eye by foreign critics on worldwide TV. SVG was so new to the global village that hardly anybody could find it on a map, and now there were correspondents tramping around with cameras and notepads to capture its supposed vileness. Prime Minister Mitchell was understandably furious and offended. Heath had been set free, he said, simply because the police lacked the evidence to hold him any longer. But the destructive publicity snowballed anyway, and tourism began to decline.

At any rate, Sir James had a mess on his hands with the Joseph murder. In the wake of the Heath allegations, SVG was about to be tried along with the Fletchers, and the country's nascent tourism industry could hang in the balance.

\* \* \*

That evening, I stood on the lawn at the Grand View and watched two guys knock breadfruit out of a tree with a stick. On my walk, I bumped into a young reporter from West Virginia, who was covering the story for his hometown sheet. He was friendly with Jim Fletcher's father, Bob, and Bob's wife, Kae—they, too, were in Kingstown and waiting for the trial—and offered to share some background on the family, so we repaired to the Surf Side Bar. It was an open-air place right on the water, where Vincies mingled with both tourists and expats and consumed countless bottles of Hairoun, a fine local brew. We ordered conch roti—a sort of whole-wheat burrito stuffed with curried onions, potatoes, and conch—and the reporter launched into his tale.

Bob Fletcher had made his fortune in mining equipment, he said. J. H. Fletcher & Co. dated back to 1937 and currently had about 200 employees based in Huntington. Bob was known as a decent, stand-up guy with a passion for sailing, but his son had led a pampered life. Educated at Choate and DePauw University, where he majored in Spanish literature, Jim went to work for the Fletcher company right after graduation, starting in sales and winding up as its CEO. He was active in Republican politics and once served as the party's chair in Cabell County, running for the West Virginia House of Delegates in 1984 and 1986. He lost both times.

Jim would marry and divorce twice. In 1988, he was named (but never charged) in a drug sweep that netted a Fletcher & Co. accountant and also Penny Rhea Carter, his future third wife. Born Penelia Carter in Olive Hill, Kentucky, she ran with a fast crowd and acquired a nasty cocaine habit that was reportedly costing her between $500 and $800 a week during the late eighties. (After quitting coke, she switched to prescription pills, got strung out again, and wound up in rehab.) To beat the cocaine rap, she turned state's evidence. Penny liked to brag that she carried a gun, and at least one Huntington tavern banned her for flashing it on the premises.

By the early 1990s, Jim Fletcher had become a problem drinker. Friends described him as adrift, in need of challenge, which Penny seemed to provide. He had known her for years, but when the two began dating and frequenting bars together, their affair caught fire. In the autumn of 1993, out of the blue, Jim surprised his parents by phoning them from Bermuda and inviting them to a spur-of-the-moment wedding, where one of his daughters sang his favorite song, the Eagles' "Desperado."

Apparently, Fletcher had second thoughts about the marriage, because he allegedly filed for divorce the following spring. There was a reconciliation, though, and shortly afterward Jim Fletcher retired at the age of 47 (Penny was 33); he and Penny intended to sail the *Carefree*, a Wellington cutter Jim had purchased from his father. The couple spent four months preparing it for an open-ended voyage. They had five children between them, including three school-age kids, but they planned to leave the youngest behind with relatives. The Fletchers set sail from Key Largo in April 1995 with an ample larder of food and booze, plus a Smith & Wesson .22 and 200 rounds of ammunition. The pistol was still in their possession and duly registered at customs when, on August 21, 1996, they entered St. Vincent and the Grenadines.

From the hotel terrace on Sunday morning, I could see a preacher baptizing members of his flock by dipping them into the Caribbean. The downtown area was deserted, with not a single soul in the market, so I walked over to look at the courthouse, an old gray sandstone building that dates from the colonial era. It had a palm-fringed yard and high arched windows dappled with copious pigeon droppings. I peeked through some green shutters at the courtroom inside. It was all polished mahogany, with a gallery for spectators with rows of benches, like church pews. There were ceiling fans to circulate the humid air. Faded photographs of Queen Elizabeth and her consort decorated one wall.

I found the men's prison right behind the courthouse. It looked daunting and medieval, with "A.D. 1872" chiseled into a stone over the front door. The exercise yard was tiny and claustrophobic. Shards of broken glass were sunk into the high concrete walls to discourage the merest notion of escape. The sea was only 500 feet away, but Jim Fletcher never got a glimpse of it, nor could he hear the comforting roll of the surf; for his listening pleasure, he had the rattle of traffic and the braying of goats.

So little was going on in the city I decided to have a look at Bequia, just an hour away by boat. While hymns roared skyward from a congregation on the second floor of a department store, I strolled down to the dock and boarded a ferry, stepping around bicycles and cargo crates and over bunches of green bananas. I headed for the passenger cabin, where an elderly Vincie woman in a Yankees cap sat by herself and watched a Bible scholar from Alabama on SVG-TV, the only island channel, which broadcasts a daily half-hour news program during the week and fills out its air time with shows donated by American evangelists, along with old movies, television dramas, and sitcoms.

When I saw how intently the woman was involved with the TV set, I understood why the *Nightline* episode about SVG might have caused such a furor. It had focused on the Fletchers, and John McWethy, an ABC correspondent with close ties to the State Department—and another college classmate of Jim Fletcher's—declared in no uncertain terms that he doubted the accused could get a fair trial in Kingstown. He interviewed Alan Heath and Arturo Diaz, and they reiterated their charges of bribery and corruption. McWethy located someone to allege that Jolly Joseph had sold drugs—Rudy Hanson, a deckhand from the *Carefree* and hardly an unbiased source. And to end the show, Ted Koppel raised the question why, if SVG was so dangerous, the U.S. government didn't issue a travel advisory.

The Bible program vanished in a few minutes, replaced by a psychedelic test pattern and some hot calypso music, and the ferry chugged away from the dock. There weren't many passengers on board; Vincies look upon the Grenadines as too fancy and expensive, and they don't feel all that comfortable on Bequia or its more exclusive neighbor, Mustique, where Princess Margaret, David Bowie, and Mick Jagger have estates. Some Vincies refer to the Grenadines as "The Land of the Rich and Famous" and regard the island chain as a place whose sole purpose is to cater to the whims of affluent visitors from elsewhere—a decadent and seductive place.

In the Carib language, "Bequia" (pronounced BECK-way) means "island of the clouds." It's the largest of the Grenadines, at about seven square miles, and famous for its aura of romance. When Port Elizabeth, the only real town, appeared on the horizon, the meaning of the name grew clear. It looked idyllic, strung along the great sweep of Admiralty Bay, on a beach of pure white sand. (St. Vincent's beaches, by contrast, are mostly black sand.) The timbered hillsides were a vibrant green and draped with cottony clouds. Though summer is the off-season, some grand cutters and sloops were anchored in the bay. I noticed, too, the fleet of motorboats called water taxis, each ready and eager to do the yachties' bidding.

For a few hours, I explored the beaches and back streets of Bequia. I came upon a fine little bookstore, some good dive shops, and a pharmacy that featured a gigantic display of condoms by the front counter. You could probably get anything you wanted on Bequia, as long as you were quiet about it and didn't disturb the peace. The doors of houses were open or unlocked, and the police didn't carry any guns. In the many bars and rum shops of the port, people were drinking through the early after-noon—island men alone and in groups, island couples, and a few island men with white women. Music played in the background while boys splashed in the sea and fished from a small dock.

Port Elizabeth had an overriding sense of calm about it, as well as an attitude of live and let live. I shuddered to imagine the Fletchers sailing into Admiralty Bay on their tide of noisy disruption.

They had arrived in Port Elizabeth in August 1996. With them aboard the *Carefree* was a Benedict Redhead, a Grenadian deckhand they'd hired in St. Lucia. When they anchored, the island's water-taxi operators circled them, yelling and competing for their business. These locals made their living from tourists and would do almost anything for a price—fetch ice, haul garbage, pick up liquor, or provide transportation. They were hustlers engaged in an aggressive game, and one of Bequia's most accomplished players was Jerome "Jolly" Joseph, a 30-year-old Bequian who lived with his parents on a ridge above the bay. Jolly was well liked, reliable, honest, and good-looking, and he had a solid reputation as a ladies' man.

The Fletchers soon came to depend on Jolly's services. According to reports, Jim had begun drinking heavily, going ashore to buy a fifth of liquor almost every day. Often he passed out early, forcing Penny to cast about for company. Sometimes she toured the bars and rum shops with Jolly and called him her protector. They'd sit close to each other and chat intimately, and it was probably inescapable, given Jolly's history, that some people assumed that they were having an affair. (Penny would deny this to the police.) When Jim was awake, he and Penny brawled in public, and they had an especially loud and ugly fight at the Gingerbread, a restaurant owned by the prime minister's ex-wife. In fact, James Mitchell's family owned the Hotel Frangipani nearby—he'd been born in room one—where Garfield Joseph, Jolly's brother, had tended bar for years. The bonds among Bequia families were tight.

In late August the Fletchers flew back to Huntington to visit their families. They returned to Admiralty Bay at the end of September and resumed their routine. One afternoon, Penny drifted into a narrow Bequia saloon called Buddy's Bar with Rudy Hanson, a new deckhand who'd replaced Benedict Redhead. She allegedly began arguing with three customers, insisting that she was a better navigator than any of them, and warning one fellow that he might lose his job just for the way he was looking at her. She boasted about her pistol and spoke of her desire to shoot a "nigger." ("She was really out of control that evening," Hanson said on *Nightline*.) The argument turned physical, and there was a scuffle that caused enough damage for Jim to have to pay for repairs.

A few days later, on October 6, around 9:35 p.m., Penny and Jim radioed Jolly Joseph at the Frangipani, where he was visiting with his brother, and asked him to take them to the Gingerbread for a late dinner. The restaurant was closed when they got there, however, so Jolly returned them to the boat. And that, they subsequently told police, was the last they ever saw of him. A single shot was heard on Bequia at about 2 a.m., and at dawn Jolly's empty water taxi was found washed ashore directly downwind from the *Carefree*. Its fuel line was disconnected, and two live .22 bullets were rattling around on the floor.

The news traveled the island quickly, and an angry crowd had collected on the beach by that afternoon. "Murderers!" they reportedly shouted at the Fletchers. "You killed him!" Jim and Penny were frightened enough to weigh anchor and head for the open sea, but the St. Vincent coast guard intercepted them. (They claimed that they were only going to visit the other side of the island.) Two days later, a sea captain on his way to the southern Grenadines spotted Jolly's ravaged body adrift near an area called Moon Hole. Although the Fletchers weren't formally charged, the police brought them to Kingstown and questioned them in two separate sessions—for 51 and 54 hours straight—without the benefit of an attorney and without allowing them any food or sleep. They were steadfast in maintaining their innocence.

Four times the police searched the *Carefree*. They discovered a fiberglass storage chest with some reddish stains on it and a bullet-torn rubber dinghy, but the Smith & Wesson .22 was missing, along with 80 rounds of ammunition. (The live bullets in the water taxi matched the one in Jolly's chest, but not the rounds still on the yacht.) Pressed for an explanation, Jim claimed that a disgruntled Benedict Redhead had stolen both the pistol and the ammo back in August. Redhead, working in St. Lucia again, denied it. When Jim was asked why he failed to report the theft, he said that he had reported it, although no such record was ever found.

\* \* \*

On Monday, in the early morning, I joined a big crowd of islanders gathered outside the Kingstown courthouse. A light drizzle was falling, but some people were still dressed in their Sunday best in hopes of landing a seat in the gallery for the Fletchers' trial. A U.S. consul from Barbados was also in attendance, dispatched by the Clinton administration to ensure that Jim and Penny would be accorded "full due process." The Fletcher clan was present in numbers, too—Jim's grown children, his sister, and a few other relatives. Bob Fletcher, who is 82, wore an old blue sport coat and a bolo tie and scarcely resembled the public's idea of a multimillionaire. This was his third visit to Kingstown since his son's arrest.

The accused were already in the courtroom and confined to a tight little dock. Jim was rail-thin, sallow, and blank around the eyes, but Penny acted animated and glanced nervously around at her in-laws and friends. They looked slack and harmless, a couple of suburbanites on holiday, he in a bland business suit that hung on his bony frame, she in the plainest of dresses. It was difficult to picture them as the scourge of the eastern Caribbean, and yet they'd had bad scrapes in almost every port. On St. Lucia, for instance, Penny had yanked out their .22 and terrorized some locals, and the police confiscated the weapon. On Antigua, she allegedly had made loud claims that a black man had raped her. And on Bequia, she and Jim had fought those bitter public battles.

The hum of anticipation in the gallery stopped with the appearance of High Court Judge Dunbar Cenac. He had close-cropped hair, owlish glasses, and an open expression that radiated intelligence and easy authority. He had been up since six o'clock, he said, and would tolerate no nonsense. Jury selection, the first order of business, went without a hitch. A clerk plucked numbered pieces of paper from a cylinder, consulted a list, and shouted out names. In less than 30 minutes, including preemptories, a jury of eight men and four women occupied the jury box.

Cenac then asked the jurors to leave, so that an important issue could be debated. I sat forward, wondering what was up, and studied the barristers grouped around some tables in front of the judge. They were the premier legal hands in the islands, and had tangled with one another many times before. To head the prosecution team—and perhaps to avoid any suspicion of bias—St. Vincent and the Grenadines had imported from Trinidad and Tobago the highly regarded Queen's Counsel Karl Hudson-Phillips and his partner, Gerald Stewart. Judge Cenac had preemptively denied Hudson-Phillips's motion for postponement, as well as a gag order on the media, so the counsel seemed frustrated as he strutted about in his flowing black robe and white bib.

The island's papers, all weeklies, had criticized Hudson-Phillips for his gambits and branded him a carpetbagger, but they showed no ill will toward Richard "Johnny" Cheltenham of Barbados, who was defending Penny Fletcher. Cheltenham was a veteran of 96 murder trials, and his interrogatory style was spare and effective, like a boxer who relies on his jab. But the real star in the room was Ralph Gonsalves, Jim's attorney, a Vincentian of Portuguese descent. Known by some as Comrade

Ralph for his support of Cuba, he led his country's labor party, battled corruption, and hoped to be the next prime minister.

Judge Cenac presented the issue of the moment. He had to rule whether or not Penny's statement about wanting to shoot a "nigger" should be part of the evidence that the jury would hear. At a preliminary inquiry, the three men from Buddy's Bar had described Penny's behavior. "She said she wanted to shoot a nigger because she'd been raped in Antigua," went their testimony.

Richard Cheltenham, the first attorney to speak, proceeded from logic. Penny had not threatened a particular black man, he pointed out—that is, Jolly Joseph. Rather, she had tossed out an idle barroom threat against a class or category of people. Such a general threat couldn't be construed as evidence of murder, Cheltenham continued. It was a non sequitur and simply didn't follow! In rebuttal, Hudson-Phillips adopted a folksy idiom: If you find an egg missing from your henhouse and your dog, a known egg sucker, has been in the vicinity, isn't it fair to assume that the dog may be guilty?

"When you marry it [Penny's statement] to the circumstance of a nigger shot," Hudson-Phillips concluded, wiping his brow with a hankie, "it is a highly relevant bit of information." The barristers in their formal attire turned in a marvelous performance. There was something very stylized and old-fashioned about the way they conducted themselves that had the effect of shoving the victim, Jolly Joseph, far into the background; it was as if the players were more interested in upholding the dignity of St. Vincent than they were in determining the Fletchers' guilt or innocence.

But perhaps all trials revolve around fine points of language in the end. As for Judge Cenac, he was busy taking down the arguments by hand, in pen and ink, instead of relying on a court stenographer. He deliberated briefly before making his decision. There were gasps in the courtroom when Cenac announced that the prejudice of Penny's statement would outweigh its probative value. He would refuse to admit it as evidence.

Then the trial began in earnest. A string of witnesses paraded before the jury to relate discrete bits of information that combined to form a narrative. Their story was thin in places, but it was never wholly unbelievable, even though the evidence, as advertised, was circumstantial. They were, in essence, the prosecution's case, and they laid out the grim tale of the murder and the Fletchers' damning behavior in the days preceding it.

The defense team did its best to nullify the potentially damaging testimony, casting doubts and poking holes. Couldn't Jolly's water taxi have drifted to the same location from elsewhere, rather than from the site of the *Carefree*? Possibly. Didn't other residents of Bequia have .22s? Probably. More than 30 of them? Yes.

It was impossible for a spectator to distinguish the truths from the half-truths and the lies, but I felt the prosecution's case had some credibility. Who else on Bequia had been so recklessly courting disaster? If the Fletchers' gun had indeed been stolen, how had Penny, as reported, shot up the *Carefree*'s dinghy in a birthday revelry just days before the murder? Was Rudy Hanson around on the night of the murder, as he had been at Buddy's Bar? There were plenty of suggestive and unanswered questions, but that didn't mean a jury would or should vote to convict the Fletchers in the absence of any hard evidence.

As the hours passed in the courtroom, I began to understand where Hudson-Phillips and his partners were directing the narrative—toward Benedict Redhead, their key witness. Although Redhead had been fired by Jim and Penny during a dispute and couldn't be considered objective, he was, Hudson-Phillips intimated, the only person who might provide a reasonable motive for the killing: Redhead told the police he had proof that Penny Fletcher and Jolly Joseph were romantically involved. But he wasn't scheduled to recount this proof until Friday, so I took a break from the trial and visited Bequia again myself to see what, if anything, I could find out.

* * *

On Wednesday morning, Slim came to fetch me at the Grand View and drove me to the Kingstown dock, where I again caught the ferry to Bequia. I'd made an appointment to meet with Tom Hopman, one of the publishers of the *Caribbean Compass*, a monthly yachting paper, and an old Bequia hand; he knew as much about the island as almost anybody, and might help describe the often awkward interaction between tourists and locals.

An American from Indiana, Hopman had sailed into Admiralty Bay 23 years ago and could never bring himself to leave for good. With his partner and companion, Sally Erdle,

Hopman still lives on a boat, in fact—a 41-foot Phillip Rhodes "plastic classic" anchored in the bay. He'd known Jolly Joseph well, but he wasn't particularly eager to talk about him.

"Jolly was reliable and honest," he said, repeating what I'd heard from others. "He had the longest-established operation here. He never cut any corners. He wasn't a perfect angel, but who is?"

I asked Hopman about rumors that Joseph had dealt drugs to tourists. He was reported to have died with a substantial savings account in an island bank. Could the murder be the result of a drug deal gone wrong?

Hopman shrugged. He doubted it. "That's an easy enough equation to make," he said. "But Jolly worked really hard. In winter high season, there'll be about 150 boats in Admiralty Bay, and a guy who hustles can earn $1,000 in a single day."

We left Hopman's office after a while and headed to a neighborhood cafe for lunch. Hopman went barefoot and greeted friends along the way. As a waitress took our orders, the sky grew dark and broke open, with the rain falling so fast and in such thick sheets that both the ceiling and walls of the cafe began to leak. An inch of water, a little flash flood, spread across the floor and washed into my sneakers and socks, and I realized that Hopman's feet were bare for a reason.

We moved to a table in a drier part of the cafe. Again Hopman seemed reluctant to speak, and I had a sense that most people in St. Vincent and Bequia (and probably in the U.S. State Department) wished that the whole affair would disappear and allow things to go back to normal.

"They were total loonies," Hopman finally said, shaking his head at their curious actions. They had professed their love for Bequia and hoped to start a charter business with their yacht and also to donate $25,000 to buy books for the impoverished island schools, yet at the same time Jim was capable of offending Rotary Club members by showing up for a meeting so drunk that, according to some Bequians, they had to ask him to leave.

"We've never had any violence here," he went on. "It's the Americans who bring the guns. We had a boat show last May, and the Bequians wouldn't let their children go aboard any of the yachts because they were scared the kids might get shot."

"Bequia's changed in 25 years," I said.

"Yeah, we've got an airport now, and more tour boats are stopping in the port. Bequia used to be for travelers, not tourists."

I asked him if he knew the Joseph family, if they might be willing to talk with me.

"Not now," Hopman said, with some regret. "Everybody here was friendly to the media at first. But they got hurt by all that television stuff. Nobody trusts an outsider now."

I checked into the Hotel Frangipani and looked up the Josephs in the phone book, but they weren't listed. I tried strolling up into the hills, where the roads are rutted and the houses are simple and often in need of repair, thinking I might get lucky and locate them. Families run big on Bequia, sometimes with as many as ten children, so there were lots of boys and girls playing in the streets. They kicked around a soccer ball and dashed after one another, but when I asked about the Josephs, they turned shy and looked away.

That night, I hung around the hotel bar and also hit the Gingerbread and Buddy's Bar, but I soon tired of making inquiries. I felt bad about intruding on people's privacy. They had a right to silence in their time of sorrow, so I finished a last Hairoun, watched the stars blinking above the indigo sea, and admitted that Tom Hopman had been right. On Bequia, for whatever reason, nobody wanted to talk about the murder of Jolly Joseph, at least not yet.

\* \* \*

The evening before Benedict Redhead's court appearance, I visited with Bob Fletcher at The Camelot, the most luxurious hotel in Kingstown, and the most oddly situated, in that it overlooks the slums of the city rather than the Caribbean. Fletcher and his family were sitting on a patio and giving interviews to three reporters, all from West Virginia. Bob still wore his bolo tie, and his thick white hair made him look younger than his years. He knew how to assess a messy situation and tackle it head-on. I had a feeling that he'd cleaned up after his son before, maybe more than once.

There was no arrogance in Fletcher, despite his fortune. That $100,000 payoff looked cheap to him now, he told me with a smile, as we sat down at a table. He must have spent close to half a million dollars on attorneys, hotel bills, and plane fares so far.

Bob Fletcher said he'd always loved sailing, even back when he was navigating a humble sailing canoe around Lake

Michigan. He bought his first real yacht from a boatbuilder on Long Island in 1965. It was a 35-foot sloop constructed entirely of fiberglass, and he called it *Manana* and sailed it happily for 23 years until he traded up to the *Carefree*, which had cost him $250,000. He was very fond of the eastern Caribbean and had passed 11 winters touring the same islands that had brought Jim to grief. He praised the beam wind and the lines of sight, the fine anchorages and the excellent snorkeling.

Bob was at a cancer clinic in Mexico, where his wife was being treated, when he first got word of Jim and Penny's arrest. He jumped into the fray and soon learned what the State Department could and couldn't do on his behalf. The prison conditions were truly awful. His son told him that there were inmates inside who weren't even aware of the charges against them. He wished he could do more for Jim, but he couldn't—his hands were tied. Jim would need the courage to make it through on his own. Meanwhile, SVG was going to have to change its ways if it wanted to join the twenty-first century, he felt.

I wondered if Bob had any thoughts about why Jim and Penny had run afoul of the law. He took a minute. "Well, I think Jim was unfortunate," he said, in a measured voice. "He didn't get on the right side of certain people down here, for reasons beyond his control. I'm real proud of how he's conducted himself. Once you get involved in this kind of thing—and it could happen to anybody—there's no way out."

"Do you think they'll be convicted?" I asked.

"I don't see how," he said. "They've got no gun, no blood evidence, and no motive. Mind you, we're not out to hurt the people of St. Vincent. We think a lot of the country and the location." There was a pause. "I'm just afraid the trial might go to the jury box."

\* \* \*

All the Fletchers were in the courtroom, of course, when Benedict Redhead took the stand in the morning. He looked sheepish about his status as the key witness, hauled reluctantly back to St. Vincent. In a new pair of khakis and a clean polo shirt, with a gold chain around his neck, he appeared tense but forthright as he recounted how Jim Fletcher had hired him "to run small errands for alcohol and cigarettes." He had sailed with them from St. Lucia to Antigua and on to Bequia, and he explained how there, in Port Elizabeth, he had come back from town very late one night and seen Jolly Joseph in the cockpit of the *Carefree* with his arm around Penny "in a lovemakin' position."

Lovemakin' position! The gallery exploded. Hands flew up to cover mouths and muffle all the laughter, while a broadbeamed, stern-faced police matron pounded the floor with a staff and cried, "Order in the court! Order in the court!" until a relative calm was restored.

Redhead, looking downcast, went on with his story, which the prosecution hoped would speak to motive. That evening he'd waited until Joseph had left, then warned Penny that she'd "have to stop doing these things because your husband will eventually start blamin' me." Enraged, Penny screamed at him and accused him of trying to rape her. Jim was drunk and asleep, Redhead told his rapt audience, but she woke him and reported the supposed rape. Jim called her a liar, Redhead said, adding that he never mentioned the embrace again, "'cause I was scared I might be shot by any of 'em." He'd seen Penny flash her pistol many times, so he leaped into the dinghy and slept under an almond tree on shore for safety's sake. When he returned the next day, Jim fired him.

Then came the defense attorneys' chance to question the deckhand. The scenario, the defense suggested, was at odds with his account and cast Redhead himself as the villain. Ralph Gonsalves, his grand voice savoring every syllable, implied that Redhead had actually been pub-crawling in town all evening and was drunk when he got back to the yacht—or "sweet," as Vincies say.

"You were sweet, weren't you?" Gonsalves asked.

"I was not sweet," Redhead said hotly.

In Richard Cheltenham's version, Redhead stripped down to his underwear on his return from Port Elizabeth and drunkenly accosted Penny, who was sitting up reading after Jim had passed out. She resisted his advances, and they grappled around and made such a racket that Jim woke up and came to the rescue. Jolly Joseph was nowhere around, according to Cheltenham.

"James Fletcher slapped you in your face!" the barrister bellowed. "He sent you back to your room and told you he would deal with the matter in the morning."

"No, your honor!" Redhead snapped. He denied every charge thrown at him, clearly offended, before he stepped down. Had he been believable? I thought so. But I thought as well that the real truth lay somewhere between the two different stories.

The prosecution produced one final witness, Inspector Ernest James, a top-ranking police official on Bequia. He had supervised the murder investigation and stated for the record that the Fletchers had been cooperative and had asserted their innocence throughout. He had only one new item to contribute. The stains on the *Carefree*'s fiberglass storage chest had proved to be blood—type O, identical to the victim's. When questioned, Jim Fletcher had claimed that the blood was his. He'd smacked his nose on the lid of the chest while removing a quart of oil from it, he'd claimed. Inspector James had noticed a bruise on Fletcher's nose, but when he'd requested a blood sample for the sake of comparison, Jim had refused to provide it.

And with that, the prosecution's parade of witnesses ended. Opinions in the gallery were evenly divided as to the ultimate worth of their narrative. The defense team responded to it as they might to a merry little fairy tale. Gonsalves argued that the case was too weak to go to the jury, and that the judge should exercise his right to dismiss it. Richard Cheltenham joined his colleague in the push for a "no-case" submission.

"What we have are fragments or scraps of evidence posing—posing, milord!—as circumstantial evidence," he said. Hudson-Phillips, the lone (and predictable) dissenter, reminded the court that circumstantial evidence is by definition composed of fragments and scraps, and he offered a professorial discourse in support of its validity.

Judge Cenac—pen in hand, writing away—listened to the arguments from both sides and advised the court that he would sleep on the matter and render a decision in the morning.

It was a long night in Kingstown for all the principals in the Fletcher case. When morning came at last, the courtyard was mobbed with Vincies awaiting Judge Cenac's verdict. As Bob Fletcher made his gentle way through the crowd, a few locals approached him to offer their support or merely shake his hand—he had become an island celebrity, like it or not—while others kept their distance and grumbled about the special way Americans were treated. Army troops in camouflage uniforms were posted around the courthouse in case of a riot.

Inside the building, Cenac gave a long legal explanation for his decision, going over it point-by-point. It was so quiet during those 45 minutes of discourse that you could hear the blades of the ceiling fans turning.

"The question remains, 'Who shot Jolly Joseph?'" Cenac asked. "There is no evidence before me, direct or indirect, that the accused committed this act." And with that, he instructed the bailiff to release the Fletchers from the dock. They were free.

The courtroom fell to bedlam. Penny Fletcher burst into tears and let her head rest on her husband's chest, while their equally tearful family members rushed forward to embrace them both. Mary Joseph, Jolly's mother, was visibly upset, and there were shouts and hoots of derision everywhere. Jim and Penny Fletcher were soon to board a flight to San Juan, but before they left they paused to make a brief statement. "Justice has been served," Jim said from the courthouse steps. "We bear no ill will toward the people of St. Vincent."

So the affair was over, at least for some of the parties involved. Prime Minister Mitchell rode the ferry back to Bequia with the Josephs and afforded them what comfort he could. Arguably, his situation was somewhat improved—it had been shown that American tourists could get justice in SVG, if that is how you chose to look at it—but the fact remained that Mitchell still had two unsolved murders on his hands and the cries of injustice continued, this time from some of his citizens.

In Key Largo, Jim and Penny gave their only extended print interview, to Mark Truby of the *Huntington Herald-Dispatch*. They described the horror of being in prison and confessed that they'd planned to commit suicide if they were convicted. They blamed Prime Minister James Mitchell for all their trouble. Mitchell was the mastermind out to get them, they believed, because they had embarrassed him by intending to buy books for the children of Bequia. As for the true murderer of Jolly Joseph, Jim hinted that it might have been someone in the courtroom. His love for sailing was undiminished, he stated, and he and Penny might well board the *Carefree* again and continue their interrupted trip.

In late August, when the dust settled, I called Bob Fletcher and asked him if his son might be willing to talk with me. I wanted to offer Jim and Penny a chance to correct the unflattering portrait of them that had been painted in Kingstown. But Bob doubted that they'd consent to a talk—they wished that the business would simply disappear. He agreed to pass my number along to them, at least, but they never called. I spoke with Sally Erdle of the *Caribbean Compass* right after that, hoping to reach the Josephs, but she informed me that the family members were still grieving and in seclusion.

Erdle did have a bit of news, however. In trying to track down Rudy Hanson for a story for her paper, she had discovered that he'd put the Fletchers' yacht in dry dock at a boatyard in Trinidad and had done some repair work while he lived aboard it. Now Hanson had the yacht back in the water and had set sail—possibly for Venezuela, though the boatyard owner wasn't certain—perhaps to meet Jim and Penny at some agreed-upon anchorage in the Caribbean. And one other thing, Erdle said: Rumor had it that the boat's name, *Carefree*, had been rubbed off. I found it difficult to imagine the boat in operation again, its larder stocked and its destination unknown.

*Outside*, 1997

# Ulster Spring: Belfast

In Belfast last spring, I stayed at the Wellington Park Hotel, near Queen's University. It isn't a fancy place by American standards, but the staff is friendly and polite, and if you take advantage of the free breakfasts, you can go straight through until evening on the eggs, streaky bacon, and doughy pancakes that make up an Ulster Fry. My windows looked out on a back parking lot, where empty beer kegs were stored; a front parking lot was protected by a guard, closed-circuit cameras, and a ten-foot-high fence. All the security measures put me off at first, but I soon learned that they had to do less with terrorist attacks than with keeping rowdies out of the lobby bar on weekend nights. Like so many things in the city, they were deceptive, double-edged, not at all what they seemed to be.

In my room at the Wellington Park, I always watched the evening news. Almost everyone in Northern Ireland is addicted to the news, and events of importance are constantly reinterpreted, so that sometimes it's impossible to be sure what really happened. Although the newspapers are expensive—about seventy-five cents on the average—you have to read at least three of them daily, each offering a different viewpoint, to get any sense of the actual. I started clipping stories when I arrived in May, and before long I had such a pile of print that the maids were afraid to disturb it, as if it had a totemic significance.

Quite early in my stay, I saw that it would be impertinent to take a judgmental, overly sympathetic, tongue-clucking attitude toward the Troubles. Local people become agitated when outsiders carry on about the sadness of Ulster, and they are doubly offended when an American does it, since our own history is so violent, racist, and imperialist. It's fair to say that journalists, even some of those in town, are regarded as a lower form of life. The easiest way to start a pub fight is to mention Beirut in reference to Northern Ireland. The reporting in English papers is roundly despised, because it often treats the Irish as if they were unwashed children in need of moral instruction.

Only foreign TV crews are heaped with more abuse—they disseminate the sensational images that give Belfast its bad reputation. There is a much-talked-about tragedy involving a French crew that, facing a deadline and unable to find anything dramatic to film, hired a few punks to drink too much, knock each other about, and toss a petrol bomb over a wall. The bomb supposedly killed a milkman and his teen-age son.

The hotel where most journalists bunk is the Europa. It's an ugly concrete slab near the city center, bombed so often it has a spot in the *Guinness Book of World Records*. When I first walked by, I wondered how it had ever passed architectural muster; nobody had told me yet that you can put up anything in Belfast as long as you pay off the Ulster Defence Association or the Irish Republican Army. These paramilitary organizations, especially the I.R.A., like to be thought of as pure in heart, but both thrive on graft and corruption, and they control the building trades in most of Northern Ireland. Sometimes they work hand in hand to shake down developers and contractors, plowing their profits into Swiss bank accounts, dummy corporations, and arms shipments from Libya.

The best aspect of the Europa is its location, right across from two of Belfast's oldest and finest pubs, the Crown Liquor Saloon and Robinson's Bar. The National Trust owns the Crown, and it has a Victorian atmosphere, with stained-glass windows, elaborate woodwork, and a series of cozy booths called snugs, which have curtains for privacy. If you sit in a snug with some oysters and a glass of stout, it's easy to imagine liaisons between men with handlebar mustaches and women in rose-colored garters. Robinson's, where the barmen wear blue-and-white striped shirts and long aprons, has a Gay Nineties feel. The clientele in both pubs is a mixture of Protestants and Catholics, and religion, as a topic of conversation, gets about as much play as trigonometry, baseball, or the breeding habits of newts.

In Belfast, the nineteenth century isn't a distant memory. The city is still a monument to the Industrial Revolution, all brick and iron and grit, and its style remains resolutely working class, long on muscle and short on frills. Around 1900, it had a population of about four hundred and fifty thousand, the largest in Ireland, and almost everybody was employed by the shipyards or the linen mills. (Today, the population is about three hundred and fifty thousand, and is rising again after two decades of decline.) Its industries didn't collapse until the nineteen-fifties, so you meet lots of middle-aged people who were sent off in their youth to work in factories.

Often they had harsh childhoods, sleeping two or three to a bed, using a backyard privy, and doing their homework by candlelight because electricity was too dear. Alcohol ruined many fathers, and mothers made some extra cash by taking in laundry and boarders, or scrubbing floors. Families were big (bigger on the Catholic side), and they occupied the sooty row houses you see in most districts even now. The houses fan out in every direction before giving way to farms, hills, and open fields.

The phone book for Northern Ireland lists twenty-six pages of farmers. They still drive into town on Saturdays to visit their relatives, do some shopping, and have a few pints of beer. The ones I met were not unsophisticated, but they all wanted to know how Belfast, so physically compact, had become so prominent in the eyes of the world—as if geographical size were a measure of notoriety. They would insist that the city is just "a wee small place," and it's true that you can walk from one end of town to the other in a couple of hours. If you take a central route, you notice hardly any signs of a conflict, only some broken windows or a vacant lot gone to rubble.

The full weight of the Troubles can be felt only in the Catholic ghettos, where the British presence is most evident. When you consider that the I.R.A. has fewer than two hundred activists in Greater Belfast, it's astonishing how much money is being spent to keep an uneasy peace. About sixteen thousand troops are scattered from Antrim to Armagh, and the Royal Ulster

Constabulary has an armed force of about thirteen thousand police.

Coming out of Robinson's one afternoon, I nearly bumped into four British soldiers on foot patrol. They held rifles against their chests, crept forward in a semi-crouch, and craned their necks to check the roofs of surrounding buildings, probably in response to a rumor of a sniper. They wore regimental berets and jungle camouflage, and all four had pimples and wispy mustaches. I was struck by how jittery and inexperienced they looked. Their assignment was difficult and a bit embarrassing, since they had to track an invisible enemy through an obstacle course of cyclists, elderly matrons, schoolchildren, and women pushing prams.

I could tell that they wanted to appear noble and brave but it wasn't going well for them—and yet at every moment their lives were in danger. The Army is composed of just such young men thrust into just such hopeless, confusing predicaments. The soldiers are often recruited from England's depressed industrial areas, and it must shock them to travel north on their military adventure only to arrive in a city that looks, smells, and tastes exactly like home.

\* \* \*

If there was one thing I didn't expect in Belfast, it was lovely weather, but the spring storms that blow in from the Irish Sea stayed away, allowing the chestnut and elder trees to blossom. The temperature rose into the seventies, and the Botanic

Gardens, adjacent to the university, were filled with picnickers, lovers, and sunbathers. They stretched out on blankets or on the grass and listened to radios—U2, Van Morrison, Hank Williams singing "Jambalaya." Everywhere, men strutted around bare-chested to show off their tattoos, which ran the gamut from snarling tigers to hearts melting in rings of fire. A few amateur jobs were also on display—inscriptions such as "MUM," "UDA," and "PIRA" which had been done with safety pins and ink on nights when the beer got mixed with strong cider and then with whiskey.

Along the Lagan River, which flows down from the hills, a handful of men sat on campstools holding long poles and offering a bait of maggots to fish that seemed to have no interest in biting. The Lagan is a murky, slow-moving stream in a state of decay, polluted with chemicals and other waste. When children go for a swim, they head for one of many leisure centers around town, where for about a quarter they can splash and paddle in a big indoor pool. The centers are part of a government plan to combat violence by promoting exercise—the theory being that adolescents who have exhausted themselves in athletics will be less likely to join in the ritual rock and bottle throwing that occurs on every Peace Line, especially in summer.

Peace Lines crisscross working-class Belfast, separating Protestant and Catholic turf and creating a sectarian map that bears little relation to the city as it appears in official atlases. The map gets drummed into every child as soon as he or she can walk, and it colors the way everyone thinks about space and property. For boys and girls who live in Ballymurphy, a tough

Catholic slum where poverty is endemic, Belfast is no larger than a few square blocks. This causes a mental as well as a physical diminishment: children are deprived of the right to dream of a future that might be any different from the past. The pressure to conform, to abide by the myths and traditions of an inbred group, is enormous, and it comes at them from all sides—from parents, siblings, and priests.

It is often said that the Troubles have left a scar on entire generations in Northern Ireland, and to some extent this seems to be so. Children who have been exposed to the horrors of terrorism do sometimes suffer from nightmares and other problems associated with post-traumatic stress, but most of them survive intact and begin to develop a resilient personality that may be peculiar to Ulster. It's a personality built upon rock—quiet but defiant, with an inner strength that anchors one in reality. The inducements to paranoia are so constant that people become ultra-sane; they turn into no-nonsense types who seldom indulge in flights of fancy.

Words are mistrusted in Belfast, because they can be fickle, twisted around, put to a variety of purposes. The best poets in the North still write formal verse, with much of the tension buried under a surface of restraint. If you scratch the surface, you're likely to touch a frustrated naturalist, somebody who longs for the exactness of taxonomy. It's considered bad manners to put on airs. At a literary gathering one night, I heard a fine poet in excellent health announce that he would read a poem about his funeral—it was really a loving catalogue of what he'd miss when he *did* die—and, before he could begin, a dishevelled man in a mud-spattered shirt rebelled against the conceit, shouting, "Is the funeral to be soon then, Michael?" The entire program lasted just fifteen minutes, and copious wine and beer were served throughout, free of charge.

In Belfast, both men and women tend to be soft-spoken, direct, honest, bawdy, and intimate. Surprisingly, you encounter very little bitterness or self-pity. Instead, a manic good cheer often holds sway, particularly during the evening hours. Everybody seems to have a heightened awareness of the passing seconds, and a determination to squeeze all the juice from them. But at the same time no one is romantic about living on the edge; rather, people worry about becoming inured to the misery around them, about losing the ability to feel. In every neighborhood, regardless of its religious bias, I found a powerful craving for the ordinary, for normal life—for peace.

Still, the city can be so pleasant that an illusion of normalcy sets in. On those warm spring mornings, I'd leave the Wellington Park and walk down University Road and Great Victoria Street toward the center, going by Queen's, where students were hustling to classes, and then passing through Shaftesbury Square, where workmen in overalls were hammering away on a Kentucky Fried Chicken outlet, piece by franchised piece. Usually, the sight of creeping Americanism is appalling, but Belfast is so insular that the presence of Colonel Sanders can be viewed as a healthy sign. As an old plumber said to me once at the Crown, "Maybe we've been blowin' up the place to let a little light in."

Of all the spots where the hopeful light shines, the city center is the brightest by far. It's a pedestrian shopping district about a mile square, bounded on every side by a spiked iron fence. To enter it at any point, you must go through a gate, where civilian search officers stand guard. Ten years ago, everyone was stopped and frisked; packages were unwrapped, the contents of purses dumped out, and men had to empty their pockets. A Catholic from the Falls Road, in the heart of the ghetto, might be strip-searched, merely because of an incriminating address on a driver's license. People darted in and out on business, rarely lingering for fear of being the victim of a paramilitary operation. The area was deserted by five o'clock in the afternoon, and at dusk the gates were locked, allowing the Army to begin its ceaseless patrols.

But now, because Belfast is much more stable, the center is animated and upbeat, with shoppers eating pizza and ice-cream cones, resting on benches, or gazing into windows. Land Rovers circle, soldiers march, police in flak jackets gather intelligence, but they lose their intensity in the sea of human energy swirling about them. In most department stores, the security is less intrusive than at Bloomingdale's in Manhattan. On corners, newsboys hawk the Belfast *Telegraph,* crying "Te1-*ly!* Tel-*ly!*" in the nasal voices of Dead End Kids, while disgruntled gamblers emerge from betting shops, blinking, cursing, and casting scraps into the gutter. The scene looks so calm and unthreatening that you get lulled into thinking that the Troubles must be easing; but then, inevitably, something happens to remind you where you are.

\* \* \*

The first person to be murdered while I was in Belfast was Terry McDaid, an unemployed Catholic bricklayer. He lived uncomfortably close to a Peace Line in Tiger's Bay, a Loyalist stronghold, and while he was watching TV with his wife and his parents, sipping a cup of tea before bed, two gunmen broke into his house and shot him at point-blank range. The killers, who were rumored to belong to an outlawed paramilitary group, fled in a stolen Cortina and ditched it off the Shankill Road, in hard-core Protestant territory.

According to the Royal Ulster Constabulary investigators, the murder appeared to be sectarian in intent, committed solely to produce a wave of fear and bad blood. McDaid had no ties to the I.R.A. or the Republican cause, and was known as a quiet, unassuming fellow who tinkered with cars and machines and liked to take his children swimming.

In the morning, I expected the city to be paralyzed, but everyone was carrying on in the usual way, riding buses to work or to school, and I began to understand how ritualized terrorism has become in Northern Ireland, and how few people are directly endangered by it. The impression you get abroad is that anybody in town is fair game, and though that may have had some validity in the past, it doesn't anymore. If you avoid certain tense areas, such as the Falls and the Shankill, your chances of being harmed are minimal. The number of civilian deaths has dropped steadily in recent years, and in 1987 only sixty-six civilians died. Even this figure is misleading. When a psychopath runs amok, he often does so within the handy framework of the Troubles (as Michael

Stone did in Belfast, throwing grenades into the crowd at an I.R.A. funeral), and this can skew the statistics.

In a barbershop that afternoon, a fiftyish barber put scissors to my hair and shyly explained why he had no desire to visit San Francisco, where I live. "I'd be skeered of the earthquakes," he said, in thick Ulsterese, proving again that the idea of risk is relative. There are virtually no homicides in Belfast, no muggings or drive-by shootings, and none of the bizarre mass murders that make America so distressing. Furthermore, the violence has a recognizable rhythm, much like a poker game, rising or falling as the stakes change, and you can almost predict when an incident will occur—although you never know for certain who or what has been targeted. If an uneventful week passes, you can feel a growing tension in the streets, and everybody starts to be more cautious. There are more troops around, more R.U.C. vans and coppers on the beat, and they keep multiplying until something explodes.

For an outsider, it was fascinating to watch the press deal with McDaid's murder, transforming the poor victim into a martyr. His picture was featured on every front page, sometimes next to a photograph of his wife in her wedding gown. He looked curly-headed and inoffensive, a typical enough lad of twenty-nine. The actual killing was described in gruesome detail: we learned that the children slept through the shots, that McDaid's mother was nicked in a leg, and that his widow tried to battle the intruders by swinging around a vacuum cleaner. The locals seem unable to get enough gossip about the private lives of the lately departed. All the papers cater to this taste, adopting a confidential tone.

The murder was reported to be especially irritating to the R. U .C. because it didn't follow the established pattern—McDaid had been chosen at random. Such random killings used to be standard, but they've almost vanished from the terrorists' repertoire, partly because of the efforts of the British to make the city safer, and partly because of the way the leading paramilitary groups are currently conducting their business.

For instance, a subgroup of the Ulster Defence Association, the Shankill Butchers, once made a career of slaughtering Catholics by slitting their throats, but since 1979, when eleven Butchers were sentenced to life imprisonment, attacks on innocents have been few and far between. Instead of wreaking havoc, the U.D.A. now squirrels away the money it skims from its drinking clubs and its protection rackets, while simultaneously burying caches of arms in sympathetic rural villages against the possibility of an Armageddon. The U.D.A. isn't revolutionary or idealistic; it most resembles a Chicago mob of the nineteen-twenties, dispatching thugs to sell "insurance policies" to publicans and shopkeepers.

The Irish Republican Army also profits from illegal schemes, but its devotion to its long-standing campaign to drive out the British cannot be questioned. At its core are a handful of canny veterans, who identify themselves with liberation movements worldwide and offer a philosophy that is a poorly digested bit of Marxism. Divided into cells, the I.R.A. is highly disciplined, and controls every downtrodden Catholic neighborhood, punishing petty crooks and unruly juveniles by kneecapping them, some-times with bullets or a Black & Decker power drill. The degree of crippling one receives is supposed to reflect the gravity of one's crime. Anybody who fails to heed such a warning may wind up floating in the black waters of Belfast Lough.

The I.R.A. has a revolutionary manual, the Green Book, and its members look to it for advice on everything from muni-tions to resisting police interrogation. Such interrogations can be brutally sadistic, for the R.U.C. uses beatings, threats, humili-ation, and other kinds of torture to extract confessions. I heard stories about prisoners forced to stand naked for hours in a win-ter chill, about bashings with cords and truncheons, and about men having to subsist for months on a diet of cold oatmeal and warm water.

In the face of such treatment, the Green Book urges a volunteer to remain "COOL, COLLECTED, CALM, and SAY NOTHING." The bulk of the I.R.A.'s money still comes from partisans in the United States, who are often bilked into think-ing that they're giving to widows and orphans, not to terror-ists. Each member of the organization receives a small weekly stipend of about thirty-five dollars, and from supporters in the community he may get free groceries and amenities, and plenty of free drinks.

The military arm of the I.R.A. is known as the Provisional I.R.A., or Provos for short. The Provos can do crackerjack work, but they also botch their missions. After I left Belfast, a Provo bomb meant for a British patrol on the Falls Road accidentally blew up at a leisure center, killing or maiming several children and adults; a bomb meant for a High Court judge killed a Protestant family of three instead; and a bomb meant to destroy a military vehicle in County Tyrone failed to detonate because cows chewed through its green detonator wire. In each case, the I.R.A. made its excuses, but it remains dedicated to violence and explains its errors by saying that accidental casualties happen in any war.

In some quarters, there is a naïve belief that the I.R.A. is invincible, but that isn't so. The group was almost defunct in 1969, when the Troubles began; its arsenal consisted of just ten rifles. The British deserve credit for reviving the Republican dream, since England's indirect rule in Northern Ireland had so abused the civil rights of the Catholic minority—denying it jobs, education, and decent housing—that the I.R.A. hardly needed to recruit.

The first British soldiers to invade Ulster were a walking advertisement for the opposition. It's not difficult to imagine how out of context they must have looked, marching down alleys and cobbled lanes, past horse carts, peat-roofed cottages, and gangs of awestruck kids. The soldiers rousted old married couples from their homes. They pushed around priests and women, and tanks began to roll through districts where nobody owned an automobile. All the prejudices of the realm were made manifest, and law-abiding citizens, people who had always paid their taxes and saluted the Queen, picked up rocks, bottles, and bricks and started hurling them in outrage and self-defense.

The ranks of the I.R.A. soon swelled to bursting, but it had no single leader and didn't yet see itself as a guerrilla band.

Factions fought for control of the organization—and for control of the cash pouring in from overseas. In the early seventies, the Provos, responding to Loyalist atrocities, embarked on a disastrous campaign of car bombings and blowing up places of public assembly, like hotels and restaurants, many of them in the city center.

The campaign is supposed to have been devised by John Stephenson, who was born in England, of an Irish mother, and who turned Republican while doing time with some I.R.A. boys in Wormwood Scrubs prison, changing his name to Sean Mac-Stiofain. (A Belfast joke has it that the worst Irish are always Englishmen in disguise.) Many civilians died in the bombings, and sympathy for the I.R.A.—and contributions to it—took a serious dip. A paramilitary group, too, must respect the bottom line, so the I.R.A. refined its methods, eliminating a source of bad publicity, and these days it tries to hit only representatives of the Crown while they're unarmed, off duty, or asleep.

\* \* \*

In Catholic West Belfast, I became friendly with Laura McIlhennon, an American who is married to a native of the city and has a house off the Falls Road. Before I visited her, I was advised to be careful. In the Falls, there's a casual air of menace that a stranger recognizes immediately. You feel that a single false step might lead you down the wrong path. The look of the area is also disconcerting. Some blocks are ravaged, strewn with trash, marked by half-demolished buildings, boarded-up windows, piles of broken glass, and walls covered with pro-Republican graffiti. Wherever you go, people keep an eye on you, trying to figure out your purpose, wondering if you're with the security forces. Sinn Fein, the political arm of the I.R.A., has its headquarters in Andersonstown, a neighborhood in the Falls, so surveillance throughout the area is heavy and incessant.

Laura lives in a part of the Falls called Clonard, or sometimes Little India, because the streets have names like Bombay and Kashmir. Her house is similar to those around it, built of brick the color of ashes, and fronting on a ribbon of concrete sidewalk. Her street is narrow and seldom carries any traffic, so on nice afternoons women sit outside on kitchen chairs, taking a break from the dusting or the cooking to smoke a cigarette. There is an ease to such moments, a familiar intimacy reminding you what a tightly knit community the Falls is, with mothers living three doors down from daughters, and almost everybody having at least one relative within shouting distance. The nearness of kin is a great comfort, and even when people earn enough money to move to a better part of town, they do so reluctantly.

Rain or shine, children are always running around on Laura's block, both boys and girls, dozens of them, playing tag, kick the can, and other games. For the most part, they come from families struggling to get by, and they look their best in school uniforms, all polished and rosy-cheeked, but at other times you can read the poverty and neglect in their soiled T-shirts, ragged trousers, and dirty faces. There's a lot of rough wrestling, pushing, and shoving among them, and they swear vigorously, too. Once, I saw a bunch of tough little boys pretending to be soldiers, chasing a lame old dog and taunting it with sticks. When the dog howled, they just laughed and kept after it, driving it down an alley.

Laura's house dates from the turn of the century. She paid about sixteen thousand dollars for it in 1986, using the proceeds of an inheritance. It's three stories high and shares common walls with its neighbors. The rooms are compact and have low ceilings. You walk directly into a parlor furnished with a couch, two armchairs, a stereo, and a TV. On some shelves are books pertaining to the Troubles, including three histories of the I.R.A. and two biographies of Ian Paisley. There's a small fireplace, and Laura burns coal and peat in it every winter—peat is cheap and sweetly aromatic.

A plate-glass window looks out onto the street, and when somebody goes by on the sidewalk, which is flush against the house, he seems to be striding right through the parlor. A kitchen, tidy and functional, is behind the parlor. It has a door that opens onto a cement backyard, maybe five feet by ten feet, but the door hasn't worked properly since a soldier kicked it in during a raid. The view from the kitchen is of Mackie's, a foundry the I.R.A. keeps bombing, because it hires many more Protestants than Catholics.

On the second floor, up a treacherous staircase, are two small bedrooms and a bath. More stairs lead to an attic, which is slowly being remodelled and turned into a study. In all, the house is pretty and adequate, if a bit cramped—probably an average accommodation for a family in the Falls, although many people are renters, not owners. The poorest Catholics, those who depend on welfare, would be delighted to have it, since at the moment they must live in government-owned blocks of flats around town.

Those flats are overcrowded and run-down, as hideous as our worst urban-housing projects. Pipes leak, rats and mice scurry about, toilets overflow and are never fixed. An apartment suitable for two might be home to six. It might have a broken stove, and no electricity or central heating. The roof of the building might well be full of holes. Every complex of flats is packed with alcoholics and teen-age hooligans, and the R.U.C. is constantly on patrol, often provoking the violence it ostensibly seeks to contain.

Laura is in her early thirties, bright, independent, and articulate. She met her husband, Barry, six years ago, when she came to Belfast as a graduate student to do some research toward a master's degree in Irish history. Barry used to be a butcher, but then was unemployed for more than two years, having got tired of cutting meat. He worked at a shop in a Loyalist district, and it took him an hour and a half to get there by bus, and just as long to get home. One evening while he was waiting at the bus stop somebody took a shot at him for no reason, further reducing his interest in the commute. For several months he was on the dole, making almost as much as he did on the job. He played a lot of golf—it's a passion in Ulster—and talked of going into the catering business, but in July he got a job as an on-site technician for a construction firm.

In 1978, when Barry was twenty-two, he was arrested for throwing a petrol bomb during a riot, and was imprisoned at Long Kesh, which is known as the Maze, on account of its H-block shape. (A petrol bomb is gasoline mixed with soap shavings in a glass bottle; a saturated rag serves as a wick.) He spent almost four years there and briefly shared a cell with Bobby Sands. For about half his term, he was "on the blanket," joining more than three hundred other Catholic prisoners in a protest against being denied Special Category Status—a status that allowed men to wear their own clothes, move about freely, and, in general, be treated like political prisoners, not ordinary convicts. Refusing to put on a uniform, Barry went around naked under an Army blanket, rarely washing his hair or bathing. Even with the protest, his sentence should have been much shorter, but there is nothing logical, or even very fair, about the British treatment of protesters.

At Long Kesh, the guards were mostly Loyalists, and that added to the tension. They assumed that anyone from the Falls must be a Republican and quite possibly in the I.R.A.— an assumption that's as wrong today as it was then. There are people in Clonard who despise the I.R.A. and wish it would disappear, but they don't speak out in public, for fear of reprisal. A large percentage of the youngest prisoners had no political beliefs at all when they were jailed. They had tackled a soldier or run a barricade in the heat of a moment, and they were shocked at being dealt with so severely. (Protestants, too, have been arrested for rioting, but in much smaller numbers.) Once the men were inside, living in miserable conditions and being pushed round by their keepers, they were easy prey for Republican propagandists and quickly became radicalized, learning under the tutelage of seasoned professionals to hate the British.

Sometimes Laura feels that Barry hasn't completely recovered from his time inside, and I was told similar things by other women who'd married former prisoners. It is routine for the men to be depressed and to lack direction. They went into Long Kesh as innocents, but they returned in a hardened state, with a long list of unaddressed grievances. Like prisoners of war, they had been through an experience that is nearly impossible to put into words. A man released from the Maze is an odd combination of hero and victim, and in the Falls he acquires a badge and stripe for having survived. He enters a caste of abused, powerfully emblematic individuals whose value to the I.R.A. cannot be overestimated.

\* \* \*

One afternoon, Laura gave me a tour of the Falls. We started near her house, on Cupar Street, at the most depressing Peace Line in Belfast. It is a brick wall about twelve feet high, chipped by bullets and scribbled upon, which separates Clonard from the Shankill Road. Built in 1972, it's supposedly a barrier to keep the warring factions apart, but many Catholics believe that the real intent of the British in putting it up was to define the limits of the ghetto and simplify matters for the Army and the R.U.C. The wall makes such a dull, primitive statement that you can't look at it for long without getting angry.

Years ago, before the Troubles, Catholics used to cross over to the Shankill to do their shopping. They assumed, with good reason, that Protestants got better bargains than they did. You can still do this, and I crossed over by myself one afternoon and was surprised to discover how much the two neighborhoods resemble each other. They are about the same size, and have about the same scale and population density. The same amount of free demolition work appears to have been done to them. Although the murals and the graffiti in the Shankill all praise the U.D.A., not the I.R.A., a visitor unfamiliar with the local political signs and symbols might be hardpressed to differentiate it from the Falls on a dark night.

From Cupar Street, Laura led me past Clonard Monastery to the Falls Road, a busy thoroughfare, that links one Catholic district to the next. As we strolled along, she stopped now and then to greet her friends, most of whom were young married couples. "How you keepin', Eamon?" she asked one man, reaching down to pat his small daughter on her sunbonnet. Laura doesn't have any children of her own, which makes her an anomaly in the Fails, where broods still run to six or eight. Every pub we went by was smoky and crowded, including the infamous Felons' Club, where Republicans hoist glasses in honor of their dead and imprisoned comrades, whose pictures decorate the walls.

The sad truth is that the Falls has little except drinking to offer as entertainment. There are no movie theatres, no theatre companies or amusement parks, no discos, hotels, or ice-cream parlors. A video store did open recently, and among its most popular tapes are such Provo favorites as *The Deer Hunter*, *Apocalypse Now*, and anything else having to do with Vietnam. Whenever new businesses try to come in, the I.R.A. does its best to discourage them, leaving people no choice but to patronize its various clubs, where the beer is always a third cheaper than it is in regular bars, and where you can hear a bit of approved, traditional music on weekends. Young men and women may not like the clubs, but they'll go anyway to save some money, and also because they know they'll be safe.

The Falls is a ghetto, but it isn't necessarily a slum. At its center, there's a big, lush park with rolling lawns, finely tended athletic fields, and sparkling flower beds, and Laura and I walked through it. Farther on, we came to a side street where the houses were rather elegant, with yards and gardens, and roses climbing on trellises. We never went more than a couple of blocks without passing a church. A few of them were humble and impoverished, but more often they were the nicest buildings in the vicinity. One convent had grounds as lovely as a French château, its trees, fountains, and benches secure behind a wrought-iron fence. To be anywhere close to it was to feel the nearly organic power of Roman Catholicism in Belfast, and to realize how deeply its roots extend, binding family to family over generations.

After a while, I became aware of how many men were gathered on corners, idly talking or just staring into space. A majority of them were in their late teens or early twenties, and they had the rough, bored, intransigent air of those who are eager for something—anything—to happen. The unemployment rate in the city is officially twenty percent, but in parts of the Falls it's more than forty per cent. In Ballymurphy, about half the heads of households are unemployed. There are some cunning ways to stay afloat; one is "doing the double"—going on the dole, while earning additional cash by part-time work and getting paid off the books, and another is committing petty thefts.

Any delivery truck parked on the Falls Road with its back doors open may be liberated of some merchandise, which will then be sold in alleys, where the black-market trade is brisk, or through an ad in the classifieds, under the heading of "Unwanted Gift." You'd be amazed by what people don't want—TV sets, tape decks, couches, washers, dryers. A man without a job can also make some spare change by running errands for the I.R.A., acting as a go-between or as eyes and ears in a section of town where a Provo's presence might be noticed by the R. U .C.

On these street corners, you can see the conflict of Ulster in embryo. For every soldier on patrol in the city center, there are six patrolling in the Falls, along with police convoys and inspectors performing surveillance duties, driving around in unmarked vans that have small antennas on their roofs. The area is often crawling with men in uniform, so that you can't go out to buy a quart of milk without encountering a roadblock.

Laura told me that the troops are better trained than they used to be, but she still resents the constant infringement of her civil rights. A copper may have wonderful manners, but you still don't like him knocking on your door at three in the morning and asking if you'd please let him have a quick look around your attic. The I.R.A. comes calling at odd hours, too, taking over houses as bases for its missions, and this constant pressure, the quality of living in suspension, never knowing when you'll be violated next, rubs everybody's nerves raw.

There is a humorous side to the pressure, of course, as there is to almost everything in Belfast. In Little India once, right after a bombing, Laura peeked through her lace curtains and saw two slack-jawed, pasty-faced men in dark suits standing outside, about to ring her bell, and she flew into a panic. Former prisoners are picked up over and over again for questioning, so she hustled Barry out the back door and waited a few moments before letting the men in. They turned out to be Mormons promising salvation and handing out brochures about Salt Lake City. Meanwhile, Barry, who's a military buff, had wandered off to watch a bomb squad run its robots through the debris on the next block.

But there's nothing funny about the attitude of the young men hanging around on corners. If a soldier comes within yards of them, they bristle. It's a reflex action, pure and simple—a knee-jerk response created over the last two decades. They're hostile because they've been taught to be; antagonism toward the Army is part of the code of living in the Falls. And, regardless of how hard a soldier tries to counteract the hostility, he's destined to fail, for what has been bred in *his* bones is a sense of moral superiority—the colonial impulse in a nutshell—along with a desire to serve a high ethical standard he's been subconsciously instructed to believe that the Northern Irish can never grasp.

These confrontations occur daily. A soldier passes by on his rounds; he may nod or look stern, or make a small attempt to be cordial, but whatever he does will be met with derision.

The young men (and sometimes young women) will turn away. They may swear, spit, or mumble insults. If children are close by, they may throw stones and then run and hide. And if the soldier makes the slightest move to retaliate, perhaps only by asking to see someone's I.D., he pushes the situation nearer to the boiling point. He's supposed to be above provocation, keeping a stiff upper lip, like the guardsmen at Buckingham Palace, but it is a supremely difficult task—the same task Great Britain has set itself in trying to defuse the I.R.A.

An army caught in such a bind suffers morale problems, and when soldiers return to England from the North they're often confused. Some of them claim to have been bothered less by the fear of death than the frequent humiliation. They talk about how it feels to have a gob of spit land on your cheek, or to be castigated by children, or to stand silently at attention while a woman old enough to be your grandmother calls you vulgar names. The R.U.C. is even more susceptible to this subtle, peasant warfare. Its members are paid well for accepting hazardous duty in Ulster. But alienation from the community seems to get to them after a while, and they have soaring rates of alcoholism and divorce. Suicide is rare in Northern Ireland, but since 1978 thirty-three R. U. C. men have killed themselves. All but two of them used their own service revolvers.

\* \* \*

The last place Laura took me was Milltown Cemetery, in the upper reaches of the Falls Road, where the I.R.A. buries its dead.

Though the cemetery occupies a large plot of land, it wasn't the first thing I noticed as we approached. Instead, my eye fell on Andersonstown Barracks. It stands on a low hillside just beyond the massed gravestones, and its buildings are a blackish gray and seem to be made of a durable, hard-edged metal. Every foot of fencing around the complex is topped with coils of concertina wire. From the fence to the barracks runs a net of steel mesh, to intercept grenades and other missiles. A soldier stationed at the barracks must feel that he is living in a cage, always looking out at a society from which he's excluded, and this has to contribute to the Army's sense of isolation and, ultimately, to its despair.

The rows of graves that stretch toward the horizon must also play on the soldiers' minds. For the wealthy, there are monuments of granite and marble, but nearly everyone else lies beneath a simple concrete slab inscribed with his or her name, a comforting or sentimental message, and the dates of birth and death. Some graves are marked only by homemade crosses, two sticks of the plainest wood nailed together. Grass grows in clumps throughout the cemetery, and paths worn into it connect one relative to another, an aunt to a distant cousin, illustrating again the bonds of family. At Milltown, you can see how an innocent victim of the Troubles, a boy accidentally shot or a girl burned in a fire, reaches out to touch, however lightly, every person in the Falls.

On an elevated patch of ground, in the shadow of the barracks, the I.R.A. has its graves, more than fifty of them. A green picket fence sets the area apart, and as you wander from headstone to headstone you feel the grip that the dead hold over the living in Catholic Ulster, their undeniable power. There is a collective historical weight in the loss of so many sons and daughters, and it is a weight not easily shed. For a Republican, giving up the cause is the same as delivering an insult to fallen comrades. Yet in Northern Ireland there are ironies even in cemeteries, and when I came to the grave of Bobby Sands, a man with a Protestant name, I thought how curious it was that the I.R.A.'s greatest saint should have moved the world through passive resistance, not violence.

\* \* \*

One means of getting away from the intensity of Belfast is to ride a train into the countryside, where the troops and insurgents are few. I did this on a pleasant Sunday, going to the Botanic station and boarding a local to Bangor, a pretty seaside town northeast of the city. Across the aisle, a boy was tapping his sister on the knees with a badminton racquet while their dog howled, and this bit of domestic comedy, too, had a calming effect.

The train chugged over the Lagan and wound around the lough, and down in the marshy channels we could see children probing the muck for tadpoles and frogs, and dropping them into buckets. Soon a mild smell of salt blew in through the open windows, and we passed by suburbs with houses that were new and often quite impressive. They belong to Protestants of the upper class—judges, barristers, doctors—with some Catholics sprinkled in. As a friend put it, money tends to soften prejudices.

Bangor has a prosperous, conservative, tight-lipped air. Once, it was just a resort village with a small fishing fleet, but now commuters searching for peace occupy its hills, its flatlands, and its budding tracts. A three-bedroom house in Bangor isn't cheap; in a depressed real-estate market, it costs at least a hundred and twenty-five thousand dollars at the current rate of exchange. But there is still a village quaintness to the streets, and little hotels and guesthouses overlook a rocky strand dotted with kelp. The Troubles don't hit you in the face as they do elsewhere; instead they're translated into the overzealous scrutiny you get in moneyed enclaves—a scrutiny that has less to do with religion than with the fact that the residents have something of material value to lose.

It was lunchtime, so I stopped at a place called the Sands and had to ring a buzzer to be admitted. This crude and mostly useless sort of security causes embarrassment, and a woman who must have owned the restaurant joked about it and led me to a table in a hushed dining room. For three dollars I ate a price-fixed meal of roast lamb. As a waitress spooned turnips and potatoes onto my plate, she remarked on my accent and mentioned, blushing, that a Canadian had been in last week. Such information is always offered tentatively, with a quiet expectancy, as if the speaker were waiting to be reassured that other foreigners would be arriving shortly.

The sun was lower in the sky when I came out, and the afternoon warmer. It's hard to describe how appreciative everyone is for the small gift of decent weather. The chance to play a round of miniature golf on a lawn by the sea, to sit on a stone jetty and bask, to stroll on a beach with a lover and not have to think about bombs or rifles, it is no accident that the travel agencies in Belfast advertise vacation trips to Majorca, the Canary Islands, and the Costa del Sol, or that cabbies save up for junkets to Fort Lauderdale. Imbedded deep in the struggles of Ulster is an unspoken dream of being healed.

On the train ride back, toward evening, a man sitting next to me held his pink-skinned baby girl on his lap and cooed to her sweetly, talking in nonsense syllables. In the presence of a moment of tenderness, I found myself understanding as never before that the ultimate goal of terrorists, whether conscious or not, is to destroy such human impulses, and to create an illusion that those of us on the outside have nothing in common with those who are suffering. We are meant to turn our backs, to be disgusted and sickened, to stay away. The darker and more bitter the landscape appears, the larger the profits to the paramilitaries.

It was dusk when we reached the city. Instead of heading for the Wellington Park, I walked toward the center. An Elvis impersonator was doing a show later at the Limelight Club, and a few trendy students were already hanging around in front, their hair upswept and moussed into pompadours in homage to the King. The pubs near Shaftesbury Square were filling up, too, and out of them poured loud jukebox music. You hear it said that the electric night life in the city is a byproduct of its atmosphere of risk, but I always felt that it came from the breaking down of barriers, the smashing of taboos which occurs when young Catholics and young Protestants rub elbows. Old Orangemen may be set in their ways, just as aged Republicans are, but among the young, even some of those trapped in ghettos, there is a tremendous desire to be free of the burden of the past.

* * *

The Avenue Bar isn't a place any stranger to Belfast would wander into on a whim. It's a drab corner joint downtown, not far from the absurdly named Unity Flats, where poor Catholics and a few poor Protestants live, and it has nothing to commend it other than the ordinary tavern attractions, like beer, gossip, and a plate of hot food. The interior is plain, and the floor is pocked with black marks from stubbed-out cigarettes. In spite of its anonymity, the pub was bombed twice in the seventies, and to get in now you have to press a buzzer, as two men did on a Sunday afternoon in mid-May before committing a spray job.

In paramilitary parlance, a spray job is a mass murder, and the usual instrument is a submachine gun. At the Avenue, one of the murderers, a member of the Ulster Volunteer Force, took such a gun from beneath his coat, aimed it at the twenty or so regulars drinking and talking, and opened fire. As the bullets sailed around, customers dived to the floor and tried to hide behind upturned tables. Some threw bottles and pint glasses, shouting for help. The attack did not last much more than a minute, and when it was finished the murderers left as calmly as they had entered, climbed into a stolen taxi, and drove off.

A passerby walking his dog later described the scene inside the pub. What he saw was two men stretched out in pools of blood, and a third man near them, a bone sticking out of his leg, who was crying, "I've been shot! I've been shot!" All three of them died before they reached a hospital; ten other patrons were wounded and required stitches and surgery.

The spray job followed a pattern set by the McDaid murder, though on a grander, more vicious scale, and the ritual responses to the crime were familiar. First, the full newspaper treatment, with pictures of grieving widows, the victims' bodies, and children trying to peek into the pub as workmen washed the blood from the sidewalk. Then the statements of outrage and condemnation from bishops, ministers, and politicians. A call for peace by relatives of the dead, and then the moment of apotheosis, when the dead themselves took center stage in the pomp and pageantry of funeral corteges that moved to cemeteries through streets lined with mourners. There were flowers, prayers, and many tears.

At the same time that these rituals were going on, various parties were engaging in a war of disinformation, hoping to shade the event in a way that would benefit them. Sinn Fein, the political arm of the I.R.A., claimed that the police had been slow to arrive, even though a barman had pushed a "panic button" connected to the North Queen Street R.U.C. station, and that this dragging of heels always occurred when Catholics were under attack. The Ulster Volunteer Force issued a widely ridiculed rewrite of the murders, maintaining that its "soldiers" had been after a pair of I.R.A. men and had inadvertently killed and wounded civilians through human error. The R.U.C. rejected the U.V.F.'s account out of hand, and released documents to show that its emergency squad had reached the Avenue within minutes of the alert.

When news of the Avenue Bar massacre came over the television, I was in the Wellington Park, and I went into the lobby pub to watch the reports. The physical sensation in the aftermath of such violence is always the same—a queasiness in the pit of the stomach, as if you were in a plane that had taken a sudden drop in altitude. I stood next to a middle-aged man in a cardigan who was muttering about the stupidity of terrorists, and we struck up a conversation. When I told him I was a writer, he grew wary, but in time he turned friendly, and introduced himself as Stan Wright. He was a Protestant, his father had been in the military, and he'd recently returned to Belfast to take over a large company that supplies educational materials to schools. His wife and children, he said, were still in Dublin.

Wright was the first person I met who talked about the guilt many Protestants feel over the indignities that Catholics have suffered in Northern Ireland. A Catholic discussing the Troubles tends to be high-minded and proud, fiercely confrontational, and in no doubt about the ethics of the matter, while a liberal Protestant will lower his eyes or look away, or remark on how disgraceful the situation is, just as liberals from the American South used to do during the civil-rights movement.

The comparison is apt, for there's a Belfast version of a redneck who, instead of promoting peace and understanding, tries to join a paramilitary group, or a right-wing lodge, like the Orange Order, where men old and prematurely old drink to the ascendancy of William of Orange. Catholics, for their part, are fascinated by the experience of American blacks and by the rise from slavery, and books like *Roots* are often assigned to secondary-school classes.

When I mentioned to Wright that I had found a positive, even a hopeful, side to daily life in Belfast, he nodded vigorously and invited me to visit his company, where both Protestants and Catholics were employed, in about a sixty-forty ratio. The company operates from a warehouse in Newtownabbey, some five miles from the city center. There's a field behind it, and during summer teen-agers gather to indulge in the usual skull-bashing and hurling of epithets, although, as Wright noted dryly, they'll take a break if a good soccer game is on TV.

Wright once had a job with Xerox, in London, and he's brought an enlightened style of management to the company. His workers find it exhilarating. Even with the boss out of earshot, they told me how pleased they were to be able to play a radio while they were loading trucks, or to wear jeans to the office every now and then. Some old-line Belfast firms are downright Victorian, enforcing strict dress codes and docking laborers for each lost minute on a time sheet, so the slightest acknowledgment that employees have rights causes a stir.

What I saw in the warehouse was another example of how Protestants and Catholics are willing to cooperate if they're given a chance. One young Catholic woman, a clerk, offered me an account of her journey to visit a Protestant co-worker at home, on the Shankill Road. "My mother warned me never to go there," she said, with a laugh, "but it wasn't bad at all. I thought the men might be carryin' pitchforks, you know?" It isn't that people expect the past to be erased, much less forgotten, but that they don't want their future to be limited by its follies and its excesses. In Ulster, there's a middle-ground constituency waiting for a politician brave enough to articulate its concerns.

For Wright, doing business in Belfast has some peculiarities—not being able to deliver orders because of a roadblock, for instance. There are problems with phones going dead, and with graffiti. Hooligans hit the warehouse at night, scrawling UDA or PIRA in crimson, and you can't just paint over the letters, because the neighbors might construe that to mean you were in league with the other side. So Wright has to call in the municipal authorities with buckets of whitewash. Other small problems plague him, too, but he has decided to stay on. As I was leaving, he shook my hand and gave me a pen-and-pencil set—an ideal gift for a writer, he joked.

\* \* \*

In the days before I left Belfast, there was a big explosion at the Royal Ulster Agricultural Show, at Dalmoral Showgrounds, on the outskirts of town. No one was hurt. The R.U.C. said a gas main had blown, while the I.R.A. claimed it had set off a bomb to kill some R.U.C. security men. The I.R.A. did not accept credit for the bomb that went off near a military base in the Falls, slightly injuring three civilians and two soldiers, and destroying a Chinese takeout joint. Patrons of the Laurel Leaf bar next door heard a "deafening blast," then found the ceiling collapsing, its pieces splashing into their pints.

Obituaries still ran on the second page of every paper, and the nostalgia column in the *Irish News,* a Catholic sheet, told how in 1921 a citizen, John Smyth—incidentally, of the Catholic faith—had been shot dead by Protestant gunmen as he was proceeding to his home.

Though I had been in the city for less than a month, I knew that when I met people for drinks or dinner these incidents would not be mentioned, or would be mentioned only in passing, with disgust—tossed aside dismissively, considered too boring for further comment. It was inevitable that somebody at a pub would make a joke about a fire sale of eggrolls, just a little charred, going on at the Laurel Leaf. There were many jokes about two new portable toilets that had been installed downtown—coin-operated models from France, which the Deputy Lord Mayor blessed by being the first customer. For additional comic relief, everyone turned to the plan of an architectural consultant, who was bandying about a scheme to build a new hotel in the Falls, near where another hotel had closed after a bombing attack, in 1983. This palace would have eighteen rooms and a twenty-lane bowling alley.

In Belfast, things are almost never so bad that a laugh can't help. A "craic," the locals call it, as in "It cracks me up," and whenever I heard the expression I'd think of a fissure through which all kinds of pressure and negativity could be released. A line from a poem by Louis MacNeice also kept rumbling around in my head: "Belfast devout and profane and hard." This appraisal of the place still seemed accurate to me—as accurate as it must have been when MacNeice, who grew up in a brick row house, wrote it. The toughness of the city both shields and hides its heart, and serves, too, as a mask for slow, steady signs of change.

The taxi-driver who took me to the airport was a woman. She and her husband had recently bought a nice house in the country, at a bargain price, from a police officer who was departing in a hurry, under death threats from the I.R.A. As we wound through the Falls, she pointed to the spot where an angry mob at a funeral had beaten and shot to death two British soldiers last winter. Here was my final taste of sightseeing, Ulster style.

Down the street, we came to a roadblock. All around it troops were swarming, taking a bead on pedestrians with their rifles while simultaneously pinning three men against a car, and for the first time I felt the sort of worry every person in Belfast must know intimately—a worry that one's luck has run out. As the saying goes, "He was in the wrong place at the wrong time." But a soldier merely waved us through, not even bothering to ask a question, and I made it to my plane in plenty of time.

*The New Yorker*, 1988

# The Crazy Life:
# Youth Gangs in L.A.

The first time I met Manuel Velazquez, he greeted me awkwardly, unable to shake hands. He had cut himself on a broken bottle while crawling around in a tunnel to read a new graffito, and a doctor at a local clinic had sewed him up with seventeen stitches and wrapped the wound in cotton, gauze, and tape. Manuel was stoical about his injury, seeing it as an unfortunate but perhaps necessary consequence of his job, which is to keep teenage gang members in the San Fernando Valley from killing one another in wars.

In Los Angeles County, there are an estimated fifty thousand youth-gang members, and about a hundred of them are expected to be murdered this year. In the old days of youth-gang warfare, the days of *Blackboard Jungle* and *West Side Story*, a boy might arm himself with a knife or a homemade zip gun, but now in times of trouble he has access to .357 magnum pistols, hunting rifles with pinpoint scopes, and Uzi semi-automatics from Israel.

Manuel works for Community Youth Gang Services Project, a private, nonprofit organization. Under the auspices of the city and the county, Youth Gang Services operates a twenty-four-hour hot line and has teams patrolling fourteen sectors of Greater Los Angeles where gang activity is heavy. There are four people on each team, and they pair off as partners and work nine-hour shifts. Five days a week, from Tuesday through Saturday, they hit the streets at eight o'clock in the morning and do not quit until the bars and discos close, at two.

They drive Dodge Colts and carry two-way radios and identification badges, but they do not have any weapons or powers of enforcement. On their rounds, they inspect graffiti, listen for rumors of impending battles, and spend a lot of time chatting with gang members. With the lightest touch imaginable, they try to save lives. There are moments in the field when they seem to be doing open-air therapy, taking in all the wild, eccentric griefs of the young.

Rahsaan Cummings works in the Hawthorne area, south of Los Angeles. Rahsaan is in his early thirties and wears shades, black Levi 501s, and a gold chain. When he frowns or scowls, he gives an impression of ultimate toughness. Like most of his peers at the agency, he is intelligent and street-smart, as well as hyperconscious of how the image of youth gangs is manipulated in the media.

One afternoon, at Hawthorne High School, I heard him discuss this with a few members of the Rebels, who were on their lunch break, standing around and combing their hair. The

Rebels are a white gang, and Rahsaan did not know them well, so he broke the ice by saying,

"You Rebels? Yeah, you are. I've been seeing you dudes over by the 7-Eleven. You'll be buying your beer, smoking shit, having that shit in you."

The Rebels thought this was funny and cool, and they opened up, and soon the talk turned to a TV documentary that had aired recently. Nobody had liked it, because it was too sensational and falsified issues.

"You know how it is," Rahsaan explained. "People come down here, they have a concept in mind. Then they just find what they need to fill it."

The landmark work in the sociology of gangs is Frederic M. Thrasher's *The Gang*, published in 1927. Thrasher was a founder of the Chicago school, a methodology that stressed the importance of interviews and direct observation. In pursuing his study, he observed more than a thousand Illinois gangs before arriving at his well-known theory that gangs are largely a phenomenon of immigrant communities.

According to Thrasher, they represent an ethnic group in transition, waiting out its adolescence until it can be assimilated into the mainstream. The underlying assumption is that the attractions of a so-called "normal" life—a job, a family, a house in the suburbs—far outweigh the attractions of a life of crime. Over the years, Thrasher's ideas would be repeated, with variations, in many other studies, monographs, and books, and they still echo in current sociological theory, coloring the way youth-gang members are perceived, making them seem distant, opposite, always somewhat less than human.

In Los Angeles County, there are Hispanic youth gangs whose histories go back almost a century, involving three and sometimes four generations of men. There are black gangs of such size, sophistication, and economic well-being that they put many small corporations to shame. There are gangs of Chinese teen-agers who run gambling emporiums as skillfully as old Vegas hands. When immigrants come to Southern California, their children form gangs—Korean, Vietnamese, Filipino, Honduran, Salvadoran, Nicaraguan, Guatemalan. There are Samoan gangs and gangs from Tonga, and they feud with each other just as their ancestors did on the islands. Increasingly, in affluent suburban towns, there are gangs of white teen-agers, kids from decent homes, who—the saying goes—"have everything," and still take to the streets.

\* \* \*

In many ways, the San Fernando Valley is the quintessential suburb of Los Angeles. It lies roughly northwest of the city center and has more tract homes and shopping malls than the entire state of Maine. The valley does not make you think of surfboards and blue skies but of hot rods, toreador pants, and men with crew cuts—all the icons of the nineteen-fifties. Its twenty or so linked towns have a generic look, enhanced by thousands of franchises, and the differences among towns are registered in terms of money, not style or philosophy. A wealthy neighborhood is merely a poor one transfigured, with greener lawns, bigger swimming pools, and better-quality ranch houses. There is a tendency to see the valley as either a beautiful fulfillment of the American postwar dream or a nightmarish wasteland, but it is an actual place, with actual problems, and those concerning wayward teen-agers often wind up in the lap of Manuel Velazquez.

The house that Manuel rents from his wife's family is in Sylmar, a quiet town at the northern tip of the valley, where you still find horses and corrals on the borders of subdivisions. When I made my first trip to visit him, he was sitting in his living room nursing his battered hand.

Manuel is twenty-seven years old, of medium height, and put together solidly, with the broad chest and muscular shoulders of a college wrestler. He has a few extra pounds above his belt, but they don't make him look soft—they just add to his mass and density. His hair, wavy and black, falls over the collar of his shirt, and his round, rather Indian face shows little emotion unless he knows himself to be among friends. His manner toward strangers is polite but wary. If he is distrusts somebody, he may run that person around. He has run certain observers of the youth-gang scene up hillsides and down dismal alleys in search of scoops. The scoops fail to materialize, being no more substantial than snipe. There is an air of calm about Manuel, a gentleness. In his three years on the job, he has been punched, kicked, scratched, bitten, and almost shot in the line of duty.

The area Manuel patrols covers about twenty square miles. He once took me to El Cariso Park on the outskirts of Sylmar, so that we could see the town from above. On the way, he kept pointing things out. He stopped by an open meadow where hang gliders were sailing to earth from an outlying mountain, and pointed to an extravagant ranch in the distance. "That used to be Clark Gable's," he said, in his melodious voice. "Some nuns have it now." As we drove toward higher ground, he showed me some cracks in the road and told me that an earthquake had caused them. He has lived in the valley almost all his life and prides himself on knowing everything about it.

In time, I learned which franchise has the best hamburgers (Bob's Big Boy), where to watch Valley Girls in action (Sherman Oaks Galleria), and what the trendy kids at San Fernando High School were driving (Nissan and Toyota trucks, and VW bugs with nose bras).

On that first morning in Sylmar, Manuel informed me in a casual way that a friend of his, Joe Mendez, was going to drop by to talk about youth gangs and music. As if on cue, Joe pulled into the driveway, made a sharp right, and parked on the lawn. He is short, slender, lithe, and energetic. He has hair that reaches almost to his waist, prominent tattoos on both forearms, and a heart-shaped earring in his right ear.

Although Joe plays in a heavy-metal band, Mad Whip Thunder, he disapproves of some heavy metal music, and he had brought with him a few albums by the groups that were hottest in the valley—Slayer, Venom, and Wasp. He gave me the album covers to look at, and I saw gore and half-naked women in bondage. An axe severed a head. Here were whips, chains, and cartoony slaves in iron masks. "Welcome to Hell," it said on a Venom album.

The primary audience for heavy-metal music is teen-age boys. In the San Fernando Valley, they form gangs, either as stoners or punks. Manuel began to notice their emergence five or six years ago, and he remains fascinated by them. These gangs, almost exclusively white, have no inner-city roots, no history, and their members do not come from poor families. Hispanic gangs are known as traditional, because they follow well-developed patterns of behavior, and also because it is traditional for a boy to join one to prove his manhood. In their actions, they are predictable, while the new white gangs keep flying off in odd directions.

All gangs are territorial by nature, but the territory that many punks and stoners wish to claim is more imaginary than real, a sort of psychological free space to which parents and teachers won't have access. At the start, they were innocent of crime and fought only in self-defense, but they are slowly becoming more aggressive—selling dope, running schoolyard extortion rings, and buying weapons on the black market.

In the living room, Manuel has a big stereo, and Joe played a Venom album on it. The music had the typical blazing electric sound of heavy metal, though maybe a bit faster, louder, and more diffuse. I couldn't understand the lyrics, but Joe said that they were evil, satanic, and harmful. In his opinion, heavy-metal bands had gone too far in trying to upstage one another. Both Manuel and Joe believed that their influence was profound. In the streets, they said, arguments often began over the relative merits of bands.

Gang members adopted the clothes, mannerisms, vices, and ideas of rock stars. If a heavy-metal star got busted for drunk driving and manslaughter and did only thirty days in the county jail—that had happened to Vince Neil, the lead singer in Mötley Crüe—they saw it as proof that the system was corrupt. It was cool to drink, cool to flout the law. An intelligent kid might be able to react to heavy metal as theatre, Manuel believed, but a dull or confused kid took its messages seriously. If a kid had no parental guidance, no filter between him and the music, its anthems, however bizarre, burned into his brain with all the power of gospel.

\* \* \*

The Colt that Manuel drives is gold and has a Youth Gang Services sticker on a window. I rode with him that afternoon, and so did Joe. On a night shift, Manuel tries to make three loops through the valley, but he seldom completes them, because there are seventy-one gangs around, and a certain percentage of them are always doing something wrong. Day shifts are much easier: Manuel works schools and parks, record stores, malls, and burger joints.

Whenever he has a chance, he stops to read graffiti. He has an honest passion for them. He sees the walls of the valley as a huge bulletin board on which gang members scribble their encoded secrets, and he unravels their writing as raptly as a cryptologist. He is fond of the tunnels, or pedestrian walkways, that cut beneath freeways. The tunnels are about forty feet long and ten feet high, and have inviting walls of white stucco. If necessary, Manuel will get down on his hands and knees to look closely at a mark; he doesn't always watch for broken glass. I soon grew accustomed to trailing behind him as he led us on tours, using the antenna of his radio as a pointer.

"This here, it's the 'A' for 'Anarchy,'" he said in one tunnel, touching a black "A" in a circle. "You find a lot of these. Punks write them. Half the punks, they don't know what anarchy means. They just try to shock you. Same with swastikas. You tell them what a swastika means, they wish they didn't write it. Here's 'FFF'—'Fight for Freedom.' That's a white gang. Some of them are into white-supremacist stuff. Adolf Hitler, Charlie Manson. Lot of stoners been in here, man. Look how many band names are in here. Iron Maiden. Metallica. Ozzy. Look, Joe, here's a Mad Whip Thunder."

"All right!" Joe said.

"Most of this is just kids showing off, you know?" Manuel said as we continued through the tunnel. "They get a thrill out of it. But this one here, it's bad. See this?" I saw a name in red spray paint. Through it ran two parallel strokes in icy blue. "The blue, he belongs to a Crip gang. The red, he's a Blood. All the black gangs in L.A., you're either a Crip or a Blood. Bloods wear red. Crips wear blue or black. You remember how Richard Pryor used to do that cripple-legged walk in his night-club act? Crips walk that way sometimes. This Crip, he snuck over into the Blood's territory to make that mark. It's bold, man. It cancels him out. He's challenging the Blood, saying he's not afraid. If he'd got caught over here, he would have been in trouble."

Trouble can mean a beating. It can also mean death. Gangs like to get rid of an enemy with a drive-by shooting. Bystanders are often hit, too. A gang member under the age of eighteen usually pulls the trigger, because he has special status under the law and is less likely to be tried in an adult court.

In prison, he joins a prison gang to protect himself. The most important ones in California are Nuestra Familia, Mexican Mafia, Black Guerrilla Family, and Aryan Brotherhood. Like most street gangs, they are formed along racial lines. They offer expert instruction in mayhem. Only about eight per cent of all California inmates are gang-affiliated, but they account for ninety per cent of prison crime. When a killer is released at the age of twenty-five, having served the maximum term allowable by law, he returns to his neighborhood as a hero. In Hispanic gangs, this is part of a cycle known as *la vida loca*—the crazy life.

"It didn't use to be that way," Manuel said. "When we were coming up, if you killed somebody or got caught at anything you were stupid."

"Now they get a tattoo to advertise it," Joe said. "If a kid dies, he's really famous. His name goes up on walls."

"Lot of 'hope-to-die's around, man." In addition, there are "wanna-be"s —kids eager to be in a gang, eager to make a reputation by being bold, bad, or insane. This is not always easy to accomplish. In traditional gangs, where the power structure is rigid, only a handful of members are hardcore criminals, and they are likely to be specialists. A gang might have a knife expert, an expert driver, and perhaps ten or twelve others with specific jobs to do. The rest of the gang is composed of between seventy-five and a hundred members. Their function is mostly social.

They go to parties, hang out, and dress in a prescribed style, but they keep a distance from the inner circle. All this changes during a gang war, when everybody becomes bold, bad, insane, and probably stoned.

Every month, Manuel files a report on what he has learned in the field. He charts trends, and ranks gangs according to their potential for violence. His report is combined with reports from other teams, fed into a computer at Youth Gang Services headquarters, in East Los Angeles, and stored in a permanent file.

From Sylmar we drove toward Pacoima. It is a blue-collar town, where the tract homes are sometimes in need of paint and the lawns in need of cutting. Its poorest sections have a faded, gray look, as if they had been ineptly copied from an original. Although it was about two o'clock and most schools were still in session, there were teenagers and children wandering on nearly every block. I would glance out and notice a drugged boy or girl ambling along in herky-jerky steps. Manuel knew many of them by name. When he waved, they would make their determined way over to us and carry on a brief, disjointed conversation. They had the abstracted quality of astronauts touching base with earth.

In a housing project covered with graffiti, we came upon a teen-ager, Hispanic, a member of a traditional gang, who wore the classic outfit of a *cholo*—a flannel shirt buttoned up to the neck, a pair of baggy black khakis with a split cuff, and a hairnet over slicked-back hair. (The baggy pants are good for concealing a weapon strapped to a leg.) His teeth were rotting, and his eyes were glazed. He was standing in the middle of a street with two friends and told us happily that his court-appointed lawyer had just helped him to beat a rap for possession of PCP. As he spoke, cops on horseback, looking grandly out of proportion, cantered through the project, shaking their nightsticks and searching for drugs.

"They took me in, man!" the teenager said excitedly. "They confused me with somebody else. They got me in there, and then they had to set me free!"

"So how's it been?" Manuel asked.

"Real quiet. Nobody's looking for any trouble."

On a block outside the project, a girl flagged us down and asked for a ride. She had a user's pale, indoor skin, splotchy and dull. Joe knew her. She had recently tried to sell him some recording equipment, brand-new, at a cut-rate price, insisting that her boyfriend didn't need it anymore. Now she gave Manuel directions as he drove, being very explicit about which streets to avoid. When we dropped her off, in a residential area, she drifted foggily toward two young men who stood yards apart in frozen postures.

"Now she owes us," Manuel said. He would keep tabs on her, seek her out as an informer.

Around the corner, we pulled up to another teen-ager. Manuel was quite fond of him. He said the boy was honest and smart, a good kid. "So what's happening, man?" Manuel asked as he shifted into neutral. "I thought you were supposed to be in school."

"No, man," the boy said. He had a goofy smile on his face. "I couldn't take it anymore."

"So what are you going to do now?"

"Get a job, maybe. Do some kind of work."

"Maybe we can help you." Youth Gang Services had contacts, a few job training programs.

The boy was acting jumpy. "Yeah, well, O.K.," he said, and he dashed off.

"You know why he didn't want to talk, don't you?" Joe asked.

"Too stoned," Manuel said. "PCP."

PCP is phencyclidine. Originally synthesized by Parke-Davis in 1956, it was intended to be a new, nonvolatile analgesic and anesthetic. It worked fairly well, but it caused some severe side effects, including hallucinations of the schizophrenic variety. People complained of feeling dead, or as though they were dying. PCP first surfaced as a street drug in the nineteen-sixties, when it was sometimes sold as LSD, mescaline, or THC, the active ingredient in marijuana.

From the beginning, dosage control has been a problem, and users routinely flip out. PCP is usually smoked in small quantities, added to marijuana or ordinary cigarettes. Some users say it produces a mild, drunken euphoria. They feel giddy, a little numb in the extremities, and don't know what their bodies will do next. They lose their inhibitions. In gang-related homicides, the killers are often under the influence of the drug.

Because a PCP high can be mild, many teen-agers think of it as a harmless substance. In fact, the drug is insidious. It collects in brain cells and body fat, and users may suffer terrible flashbacks, physical disabilities, and severe depression. Overdoses are still common. A user can go into PCP psychosis and develop a "light or flight" reaction—ready to run from or tackle anything spooky. Such users become truculent and superhumanly strong. Cops tell stories about kids doing pushups on a freeway, drowning in a shower stall, and gouging out their eyes.

Once at his house, Manuel gave me a clear-glass vial that had formerly contained liquid PCP and asked me to sniff it. It had a strong chemical odor. Young dealers dip Sherman cigarettes in the liquid and sell them as "Sherms." A vial costs between a hundred and a hundred and fifty dollars, and translates into a profit of about five hundred dollars. In the valley, a teen-ager can also buy marijuana, prima (a joint sprinkled with cocaine), LSD, methamphetamines, cocaine, crack, and heroin. The only category of drugs not currently in favor is downers.

\* \* \*

As you ride through the streets, there's a bad moment that comes when you understand that what you've been witnessing is not an isolated phenomenon but a pattern, even a way of life. For me, the moment came in a run-down neighborhood of a valley town when Manuel stopped outside a tract house where two teen-agers were standing in a littered front yard smoking cigarettes and holding hands. I'll call them Bud and Lydia.

Bud was Hispanic. Lydia was white. Manuel wanted me to meet them, because they belong to a new type of stoner gang, in which races and sexes mix freely. Bud had a sparse mustache. He wore a black heavy-metal T-shirt and a ballcap. He looked like a kid who knows how to fix things and ought to be working in a shop or a garage. Lydia wore a sweater and tight jeans, and when she spoke she said everything at least twice and kept picking invisible bugs off her arms. Her parents didn't know she was in a gang—that's often the case with white kids.

While Bud talked music with Joe and a couple of other gang members, Lydia leaned against the car and asked Manuel about a summer softball league. She had played in it the year before, and her team, all gang girls, won a pennant. She was excited about the softball league, because it had been a significant achievement for her to get to the games, all thirty-six of them, and stay straight enough to show off her athletic ability. During the games, nobody was allowed to drink or do dope—not even homeboys from the neighborhood, who were rarely in a sober condition. Almost the entire season had passed without a fight, and then some gang guy from Van Nuys turned up at a game with a shotgun and spoiled a perfect record.

"So, Manuel," Lydia said, flicking her hair from her face. "Are we going to get our trophies, or what? We were supposed to get some trophies."

"That guy ate cheese on us," Manuel said.

"He ate cheese on us?"

Manuel nodded. A cheese-eater is a rat. This cheese-eater had promised to donate two hundred dollars for trophies, but he had not come through. The softball program itself cost only a few hundred, but Manuel had no funding for the coming summer. He couldn't bring himself to tell Lydia. Kids in gangs are hard to motivate, and they lose faith quickly. In softball games, Manuel sometimes has to change the rules to let them have an extra strike or two at bat. They hate to lose, because losing is all they know.

The gang rented this tract house and used it for parties and hanging out. A thin woman, slightly older than Lydia, stood in the open doorway, balancing a baby on a hipbone while she smoked. She had the casual grace of somebody relaxing on a beach. Lydia thought she might be pregnant herself, but Bud was denying that he could be the father. While she was complaining, a late-model sedan pulled up at the curb opposite us and the air began to crackle.

The young man who got out of the driver's side was about twenty years old. His hard little eyes took in everything at once and simultaneously rejected it. You could tell that he was never going to be pleased or satisfied—not by drugs, sex, or money. Some combination of forces had turned him sour, and he was in the business of spreading that sourness, using it to taint, to misrepresent, and to control. He didn't make a move toward our car or do anything to acknowledge our presence, but he informed us wordlessly that he was on to us.

The other gang members were drawn toward him. I felt a knot of fear in my stomach. It came not from any imminent danger but from the possibility that something nasty could easily occur. I found myself considering escape routes, looking around for objects to duck behind. The young man was a time bomb. As we pulled away, Manuel told me that he had already been arrested twice for attempted murder. He had beaten both raps.

* * *

San Fernando High School, home of the Mighty Tigers, is Manuel Velazquez's alma mater. It is famous in Los Angeles for producing first-rate athletes and being tough. In Manuel's senior year, the football team played its games at night, and all the Mighty Tiger fans were searched, so they'd be discouraged from attacking their opponents.

"We used to say, 'We lost the game but not the fight,'" Manuel said as we fell into line behind some VW bugs and imported trucks that were creeping, low-rider style, around the school building. Classes had just let out. About five per cent of the students at San Fernando High are gang members, Manuel thought, and their extracurricular activities require the attention of two armed security guards. There is also a narcotics agent from the Los Angeles Police Department, and I saw him peering, oblivious of parody, over a row of hedges.

By inclination, Manuel is an artist, and he has fond and slightly rueful memories of a former art teacher at the school. "Her name is Melanie Taylor Kent," he explained once. "You ever heard of her? She does silk screens. Mayor Bradley has some. So do some Hollywood stars. She's really well known, man. I can't believe how bad we treated her sometimes. We were always being rude. One time, she kicked me out of class, and I didn't think I'd ever come back. But I came back. She was a good teacher. Her way of teaching was the classical way. You got to dominate the basics—same as with yourself. I used to think I'd be a regular kind of painter, but now all I care about is murals. Other people can paint clowns. I don't want to be painting any trees or flowers."

For inspiration, Manuel looks to Los Tres Grandes—Orozco, Rivera, and Siqueiros. When he was a student at nearby California State University, Northridge, he dropped out, travelled to Mexico City, and lived there for eight months, studying their work. This was a fine time for him, a time of growth and change, during which he began to understand more deeply his connection to Hispanic culture. He came away from it with a feeling that he owed a debt to his family and neighborhood.

In the valley, he has painted murals on the sides of church annexes and schools. His subject matter is always optimistic, and, even in the drabbest circumstances, his colors are bright and radiant. When the summer Olympics were held in Los Angeles, in 1984, Manuel got a commission to do a mural on a parking garage, and he enlisted several gang members to help him. He called the mural "Wall of Dreams." It showed children going through transitions, getting older, dreaming. They turned into teachers, lawyers, doctors. He remembers the stifling heat, and also a French cyclist who—against the warnings of Manuel's apprentices—left his bike unattended for a minute to tie his shoe. Somebody made off with it, and the police brought in helicopters and rousted every house in the vicinity.

Manuel stopped every now and then to chat with students. In dealing with teenagers, he follows a single rule: he must never be ahead of them or behind them but always with them, refusing to patronize, granting their world an absolute integrity. He will discuss a pimple, an insult, or a bad lunch. Without comment, he listens to the most baseless complaints, the most absurd bragging, and the grossest expressions of self-pity. He is not always approving, but he shows his disapproval so lightly that it turns into compassion. In his view, every teen-ager in the valley is a potential victim, easily swayed, easily hooked on drugs, messing around with a number of things whose power he or she cannot fathom.

It happens on occasion that Manuel becomes especially involved with someone. He introduced me to a beautiful girl who was sitting on the front steps of the school and strumming a guitar. Around her were many admirers, each in hot pursuit. Manuel was trying to keep her from falling into the trap of a teen-age marriage. She was interested in music, so he sometimes arranged for her to go to Mad Whip Thunder concerts, and he went by her house and talked with her mother and sisters, hoping to forge a link that would let her see that her life was open, not closed.

Another kid was on Manuel's mind in those days—a big, rebellious kid from a white punk gang in another section of the valley. The kid had been missing from his usual hangouts for about a week, disappearing into a maze of shopping malls and video arcades. Manuel wanted me to meet him, because the kid was flirting with the border that separates mischief from trouble, but he didn't know when he would make contact again. He thought we should go look for him in about a week.

* * *

Around Los Angeles County, when you are bored or lonely or have time to kill you take to the freeways, joining seven million other licensed drivers on loops, cloverleafs, and figure eights, and wishing you were many miles closer to the ocean. One morning, I drove from Burbank, where I was staying, to Reseda, in the western part of the valley, and visited Metal Blade Records to pick up a catalogue. Metal Blade has been in business for three and a half years, producing albums by local bands and licensing imported records from Europe. Metal Blade has an impressive list. It handles Slayer, Bitch, Malice, Satan, Tyrant, Destruction, Hellhammer, Sodom, Nasty Savage, and Future Tense.

Turner's Sporting Goods, in Reseda, has a gun counter that stretches along one wall of the store. In glass display cases, there are Walthers, Smith & Wessons, and Berettas. At Turner's, a 9-mm. Uzi semi-automatic costs $599.99. It weighs about eight pounds, has a collapsible stock, and—with the right parts—can be converted in a few minutes into a fully automatic weapon, firing countless rounds. I found a brochure on the counter advertising Firing-Line indoor shooting ranges, which are open to the public seven days a week.

At the range in Northridge, I inquired of a clerk what sort of pistol I should buy to defend myself. Without hesitation, he recommended a German Ruger. "Reliable," he said. I held a Ruger in my hand, feeling the heft of it, that stunning sensation of being armed.

In my motel room, I was reading lots of papers. That morning, in the *News Daily,* which is published in the valley, there was a story about a Northridge woman who had been mistaken for a burglar and shot with a .30-30 rifle while she was delivering papers. A jury had awarded her four hundred and seventy-five thousand dollars in damages. Another story told of a Los Angeles narcotics officer accidentally shooting a fellow officer in the thigh while trying to hit an angry Rottweiler. Another story told of an argument in the Chimneysweep Bar, in Sherman Oaks, that had spilled out into the streets, where one customer shot another with a handgun.

Yet another story told how three youth-gang members, ages sixteen to eighteen, had been seriously wounded in a sidewalk shooting on West Venice Boulevard, in downtown Los Angeles. The shooting took place only hours after Assistant Chief of Police Robert Vernon announced a tough new approach to enforcement that would rid the city of gangs. He gave few details.

\* \* \*

In Hawthorne, a suburb south of the valley, crack was making its usual inroads. Because the processed cocaine came in chunks for easy smoking, it was often referred to as rock. For about twenty-five dollars, you could buy three or four tiny rocks— enough to keep you high for maybe an hour. In part, the drug's popularity was due to a scarcity of good-quality marijuana on the streets. Various state and federal efforts had helped to dry up the weed supply, pushing dedicated users in a much more serious direction.

A crack high is a fast trip up and a fast trip down, with none of the mellowness of marijuana, and people often experience an intense desire to repeat it. Even those who'd never tried cocaine before were investing in it, because it was so neat and clean—no sniffing, no sinus problems or bloody noses, no dirty needles. Crack was cheap, available, and formidably addictive. The demand for it had brought out dealers by the score and pitched several gangs into a heated competition for turf.

"On some corners you'll see five or six dealers," Joe Alarcon told me when he picked me up at a 7-Eleven store in Hawthorne on a quiet Tuesday night. Joe, a square-jawed military type, plans to go into police work when he finishes a college course in business economics. His partner, Jeffrey Harper, grew up in a dreary housing project and made his way out of it with the help of a dedicated mother and a talent for putting a basketball through a hoop. He has been with Youth Gang Services for four years—a year longer than Joe—and he can spot a deal going down from a distance of better than two hundred yards. In the course of our rounds, he and Joe would show me parks, bars, restaurants, and even taco carts where dope was being openly sold.

Almost as soon as we left the 7-Eleven, we were in an apartment complex near Inglewood, where a drug bust was going down. The police had sealed off both ends of the block with cars and motorcycles. About fifteen men and women in handcuffs were sitting on the pavement. Street lamps cast an eerie yellow glow over the scene, while residents gathered in doorways, holding coffee cups or cans of beer. They had the dazed expressions of those who gather at a fire or an auto wreck, wanting to know what has happened and yet somehow unable to process the information. The apartment complex was a nice one, with bougainvillea and jacaranda creeping over trellises, and palm trees swaying in a light Pacific breeze.

Such arrests are common in Los Angeles County and have the effect of briefly interrupting the flow of commerce. A dealer makes so much money on crack or heroin that he or she can hire an attorney and be back at work in a day or two. Some gangs keep an attorney on retainer, and they are sophisticated in other ways, as well.

For instance, a teen-age runner may wear a pager on his belt, get his instructions over a radio, and make his deliveries on a motor scooter. In certain areas, drugs are transported from point to point on school buses. In serious cases, where large quantities of cocaine are involved, an arrest creates a vacuum and leads to a battle between gangs for the relinquished turf—"gang-banging," it's called. One weekend while I was in the county, nine youth-gang members, all Crips and Bloods, died in fighting over turf in south-central Los Angeles.

We left the apartment complex, made a few turns, and passed a shoddy liquor store. In its parking lot were two Mercedeses, a new Trans Am, and a stretch limo. It is impossible to estimate the size of the drug trade in Los Angeles County, or how many millions of dollars it generates.

"We used to have a Chevy Malibu," Jeffrey said. "Everybody thought we were narcs."

"Guys pretend to be narcs," said Joe. "They put on a cheap suit, drive around, flash an open wallet, and rip off dealers," he said. "It's not hard to do."

In another neighborhood, we passed through an alley behind some sleepy little bungalows. A concrete wall nearby had recently been painted over, so no graffiti were visible. The county has several projects to discourage kids from applying their tags. Workers from Project Heavy paint over writing as quickly as possible, but they can't keep pace with the many young authors at play. For the owner of a broad canvas, such as a warehouse, graffiti removal can be a significant expense. National Paint has developed Anti-Graffiti Clear Coat, which forms a sort of varnish on a building and allows writing to be cleaned off with solvent. At National, business is brisk.

Youth Gang Services teams sometimes intervene on behalf of property owners and bargain with gangs about graffiti. Joe and Jeffrey had just negotiated a truce with Tepa, a Hispanic gang, and they were congratulating themselves on its success—no marks on the wall—but then they found "Tepa" scrawled on the trunks of two palm trees.

Around ten o'clock, we drove into a housing project and saw a boy on a bicycle, alone, riding around in circles. He had two or three sweaters on, and also a hooded sweatshirt, and he had pulled the drawstring of the hood tight, so that only his face from eyebrows to chin was showing. He was ten years old, and both his older brothers had been in a youth gang. One was in prison; the other was dead.

The boy lit up when he saw Jeffrey. "Hey, Harps!" he cried happily. "When you going to play us in basketball, man? We are going to whip you, Harps. You know it's true. Me and my homeboys, we are going to do in Youth Gang Services the way

Louisville did in Duke in the N.C.A.A.s. My vertical leap is very strong, man. I am getting very far up into the air."

"His vertical leap's very strong," Jeffrey mused to Joe.

"Hey, Harps, it is! So listen, when you going to bring around a team to play us?"

"May be on Saturday. Can you be here on Saturday?"

"On Saturday?" the boy said. "We *can* be here."

The history of the streets is often a history of failure compounded over generations. The boy was in school now, Jeffrey said, and was doing reasonably well, but it would be difficult to keep him there. His parents were hardworking, they were trying with him, as they had tried with their other sons, but they had few resources. Every day, the boy met gang members around the project, and they were slowly sucking him in. Did he have the courage, the machismo, of his brothers?

Every day, the boy rode his bicycle home from school, rode it through the parking lot where his brother had been shot. He knew all the details of the murder. His brother was walking home from the movies with his pregnant girlfriend when somebody from an enemy gang rolled out from under a car, pulled the trigger of a rifle, and killed him.

\* \* \*

Marianne Diaz-Parton, the leader of Youth Gang Services Team 14, in Hawthorne, comes from an affluent suburban family. When she was growing up, she had spending money and all the clothes she wanted, and she made straight A's in school. She was contented enough as a child, but once she reached adolescence she started to rebel, and joined a tough youth gang—pulled toward it by the usual mix of drugs, sex, and power.

Hawthorne was newly integrated at the time, and there was racial tension in the schools. Marianne was thrilled to be able to stroll into class and know that she did not have to take any insults from white girls. She had backing, and it meant so much to her that she vowed to do anything for her gang. Her bond to its members was almost mystical, a primary source of her identity, and when somebody in the gang's chain of command, a higher-up, asked her to drive to Santa Monica and shoot some rivals Marianne did it.

She was fortunate in that she failed to kill the two teenagers she shot. The Lennox police investigated, and they arrested her within days of the incident. Marianne was surprised by the gentle treatment she received. Nobody beat her or shook her down. She did not suffer any hassling until she went to prison. She got a fairly mild sentence, and ended up serving three years.

During that time, she learned a lesson about misplaced loyalties. A deputy sheriff from the Lennox gang squad, Ken Bell, used to visit her, urging her to make something of herself, to use her intelligence, but not one member of the gang she was willing to die for ever came to call. Gang members did not send her money for cigarettes, they did not mail her magazines or books, they did not write her a single letter or postcard. She could have rotted in the joint for all they cared, so she turned against them and decided to change her life.

I said, "Suppose they had visited you—what then?"

"I don't know what would have happened," Marianne replied.

We had this conversation at the Youth Gang Services office in Hawthorne, a utility shed in a large municipal park. Marianne and her partner, Rahsaan Cummings, had finagled it from the county, and though they'd cleaned it and swept away the cobwebs and bugs, it was now thickly layered with dust and furnished with chairs off the scrap heap.

Marianne is twenty-seven years old, with long auburn hair feathered away from her face. On her right hand she has a chola cross in blue ink—a souvenir tattoo from her gang days—and when I asked her where she got it, she laughed, and said, "Any homeboy with a sewing needle can give you one of these." Marianne was sniffing. She had a cold, and she was going to be wed on the weekend, and complained that her energy level was low. "I usually move faster than this," she told me. I thought she was moving plenty fast; in motion, she looks inexorable, full of purpose. "It's not only poor kids who get into trouble," she said. "It's rich kids, too."

When Marianne and Rahsaan work a shift together, Rahsaan usually drives. He drives with flair and agility, and makes the wearing of a seat belt automatic. From approximately eleven-thirty in the morning until one o'clock in the afternoon, they shuttle back and forth among three or four schools, so there isn't much waste in the operation.

One of the places they visit is Lloyd, a "continuation" high school, which caters to kids who have been bounced out of every other school and are on a last-chance mission to get an education. Lloyd is not as big as San Fernando High, but it also has two security guards, armed with nightsticks, and they were on the front lawn enjoying the sunshine when we arrived. Marianne knew one guard well, having traded information with him in the past, and she shook his hand through an open car window. "So how you doing, man?" she said.

"It's been real quiet," the guard said. He was a cheerful black man in his late twenties, who did not show any particular attachment to his uniform. He seemed to regard it as a strange and slightly humorous circumstance of his life. "Real, real quiet."

"I heard that problem kid, he dropped out again."

"Yeah, he did."

"Well, if you see him around, you tell him to cool it," Marianne said. "Little Watts"—a hard-core youth gang in the neighborhood—"is looking for him."

"Little Watts are packing heavy," said Rahsaan. "I heard they bought some Uzis."

"Uzis?" the guard said. "Is that right?"

I asked Rahsaan where a bunch of teen-agers get weapons like that. "From the same people that give them rock cocaine," he said.

"That rock is bad stuff," said Marianne. "Girls in the projects, they'll do anything for a twenty-five-dollar piece. They lose all self-respect."

Information continued to make the rounds. The Compadres had just shot a guy. Lennox 13 was also preparing for more action, having lost some members to prison. "They courted in twenty new guys in Fullerton," said Rahsaan.

"A Crip got shot over on a Hundred and Fifteenth and Simms, man," Marianne said. "For two hundred dollars. Can you imagine that? Two hundred lousy dollars! They shot him bad, man. He's never going to have any babies."

The other security guard came over to the car. He was black, too, and new on the job, but he was already thinking about advancing himself. He wanted to know how much workers at Youth Gang Services got paid.

"They start you at eleven hundred a month," Marianne told him. The guard began to back off. "I make fifteen, but I've been there for a while. You get medical and dental. You're working for the agency, you know? It's a good job, but it's no picnic."

I had been collecting statistics, and I added this one to my list. For trying to save the lives of teen-agers, you earned eleven hundred dollars a month. For trying to teach teen-agers, helping them to better themselves, you earned about seventeen hundred dollars a month—slightly more than a mail carrier. For graduating from law school and dealing with the legal problems of teenagers, you earned about forty-five hundred dollars a month. For working at a TV station and making a documentary about teen-agers in gangs, you earned about eight thousand a month. For being a movie star and killing teen-age actors with a prop Uzi, you earned an incalculable sum.

\* \* \*

The Insanity Boys have always been a good-time group—no big trouble, nothing terrible going down. They party on weekends, do a little writing, maybe drink some beer and do some smoking. About forty of them were gathered in the parking lot at Hawthorne High School, milling around a white Nissan truck at recess. They were teen-agers in all their abundant variety–stubby, gargantuan, brilliant, stupid, shy, aggressive, utterly normal.

The Insanity Boys come in many colors. They dress in a myriad of styles. The truck's owner was a short, curly-haired kid in a Harry Belafonte calypso shirt and blue clam digger trousers. He told me that the truck had once been stolen and stripped, but the cops had found it for him in Huntington Beach. "I had to go down there to get it," he said.

"You expected them to deliver it to you?" asked a friend.

The Insanity Boys were listening to Power 106 on a radio. Power 106 is popular with youth gangs, playing a dance mix of up-tempo songs which covers a spectrum of eternal teen verities. Almost all the vocalists are female, and they sing in high, quavery voices, as if they were heading for a date to the prom. When men sing, they use unthreatening falsettos, a la Michael Jackson. The big hit that spring was Miami Sound Machine's "Bad Boy":

> Bad, bad, bad, bad boy
> You make me feel so good

Marianne was not in the mood to let the Insanity Boys lounge around and sunbathe. She felt that they were slipping and sliding, losing their focus. For one thing, they had written up the walls of a new shopping mall. "You know you're not sup-posed to be writing in there," she lectured them. "I don't want to see your names when I do my shopping." But she was much angrier about some other writing they had done. A dude from Little Watts had crossed out an Insanity Boys graffito, and they had retaliated by making marks that linked them to Lennox 13. "You think you know about Lennox 13, but you don't," she told them. "If you get involved with them, you'll be gang-banging pretty soon."

"If trouble comes to us, we'll be ready," one kid said.

Rahsaan corrected him. "You think you're ready."

"I'm not saying we're looking for trouble. But if trouble comes, we're ready."

"You're not ready," Rahsaan said.

"Little Watts is packing, man," said Marianne.

"Then we'll pack, too," said an Insanity Boy. He had braces on his teeth and weighed about a hundred pounds.

"Don't you be talking like that," said Marianne, glaring at him. "You think it's a game. It's no game, man. You don't need to be involved with that stuff. You got all kinds of opportunities around you."

A tall, pudgy teen-ager who did not belong to the gang appeared on its fringes, lifted a foot, and extended a sneaker for us to examine. The sneaker was slashed in three or four places, cut to ribbons. "That crazy dude, he just came up to me out of nowhere," he said, laughing. "He came up and used his knife."

Across the parking lot, a few Rebels were chatting among themselves. They were white kids, stoners, fifteen and sixteen years old, and they wore the obligatory heavy-metal t-shirts. But, more than anything else, their hair set them apart, flowing from their heads in such lush cascades that I was reminded of a Breck-shampoo ad. Every ounce of protein in their bodies appeared to be concentrated in those follicles. After Rahsaan introduced himself, he jived for a while, warming them up. "So you been going to classes, man?" he asked a Rebel who bore an uncanny resemblance to Jimmy Page, of Led Zeppelin.

"Somewhat," the Rebel said, rather nervously.

"So you into music, man?"

"Yeah."

"What do you play?"

"I'm a singer."

"That's cool," said Rahsaan, not missing a beat. "What's this I hear about Satanism. You Rebels, you into that?"

"Aw, no," the Rebel said. "We just mainly party."

The Rebels wanted Rahsaan to arrange a football game with another gang. Like many youth-gang members, they enjoyed sports but hated coaches, uniformity, and rules about hair length.

I talked to a Rebel who was carrying a big ghetto-blaster. He came from a good family and kept a decent average in school. He owned a stereo, a TV, and a VCR. He had an electric guitar. Still, he spent much of his free time in the streets. He said that the Rebels had recently put together a party pad in a vacant lot near a freeway. They had carted in a couch and some old chairs, and in the evenings they'd gather with their musical instruments, their amps, speakers, and girlfriends. They would build a fire and mess around, not making a lot of noise, but an old lady in a house by the pad had complained, and the cops had come around and busted them.

The bust was nothing, really, just a minor harassment, and the Rebels were already back in business, planning a kegger at a local park that weekend. "Drop by and check us out," he said.

Rahsaan shook his head. "It's too cold out there, man."

The Rebels said that was O.K. It made the girls cling to them.

In summer, the action around Hawthorne shifts to the coast—to Hermosa Beach, Manhattan Beach, Redondo Beach. The Rebels would drift with that tide, and so would the Insanity Boys, driving to the ocean in caravans and raving for adventure. They would brush up against Compadres, Little Watts, and Lennox 13. If they went north, to Venice, they'd run into hard-core Crips and Bloods, as well as motorcycle gangs. They'd meet beach rats, surfer punks, and skateboard stoners eager for a fight. In time, one of them would mistakenly respond to a challenge. According to Marianne, he would do it fearlessly, as if in a dream. "When you're a kid, you're not afraid of anything," she said. "You don't think you're ever going to die."

\* \* \*

The kid Manuel Velazquez was looking for—I'll call him Jody—is fifteen, white, and big for his age. Manuel gave me his case history as we set out from Sylmar one morning. Jody lives in a middle-class valley town, in a quiet neighborhood of apartments and single-family houses.

He has one brother. His room is large, private, and plastered with posters of punk-rock bands. "You'd have to use a scraper to get them off the walls," Manuel said. Jody wears the same clothes for days on end and often needs a bath. He smokes, drinks, and does almost anything on a dare. His father is dead, or simply missing—Manuel wasn't sure, because he had heard different stories. His mother has an administrative job, but she works long hours, and Jody spends much of his time alone. Since his last birthday, he has done poorly in school, and his behavior has become much more radical. "Fifteen," Manuel said. "That's when they start pushing everybody's buttons."

A frustrated kid learns how to manipulate his elders, provoking them, forcing them to drop their masks. In class, Jody ragged his teachers and gave them little respect. At home, he was disobedient. When a riot broke out at his high school, with punks and stoners battling each other, he was fingered as a ringleader and expelled. He transferred to another school, but his gang activities had increased. He was arrested once for a petty offense. He kept pushing his friends, wanting them to be more outrageous. When the other gang members backed down from a fight with some rivals, Jody accused them of being cowards and "talking smack." So they got rid of him—"jumped him out"—turning him into a free agent, a wanderer.

From the moment Manuel met Jody, shortly after the riot, he had tried to make the boy aware that he was heading for serious trouble. When Jody got arrested, Manuel said to him, "You think it's cool to be busted, don't you? Well, it isn't. The next time, they'll drag your mother into court. They'll insult her, maybe tell her she's unfit. Are you going to allow that to happen?"

But he doubted whether Jody was paying much attention. The kid was headstrong, and Manuel was amazed to see him following the same course that had led so many Hispanic teen-agers to disaster. This course could be mapped out, step by step. After failure in school and a few casual brushes with the law, a kid begins to view himself as an outsider, beyond redemption. He will reject everyone who has rejected him. His loyalty to a gang grows, and he is drawn more deeply into crime. He may confirm his status as a lost one by buying a weapon. In the streets, a handgun costs about twenty-five dollars.

Sometimes Manuel compares a kid like Jody to an apple that has fallen from a tree. "People can see it lying on the ground, but they don't pick it up," he told me. "They wait for a while. They ignore it, go do something else. Then, when they finally reach down and touch it, they find out it's rotten."

We started looking for Jody in Van Nuys. Manuel parked on a broad boulevard and led me through a vacant lot where beer cans were strewn among knee-high weeds. Punks hung around there, he said. A night club called Hot Trax was nearby, and a murder had occurred outside it a few months ago—a Viet-namese teen-ager had shot a white kid in an argument over a girl. To the best of Manuel's knowledge, the victim was the first white gang member in the valley to die in a shooting. But the police refused to classify it as a gang-related homicide, because the Vietnamese youth did not belong to a gang.

That bothered Manuel. He believed that the killer would not have used a gun if he hadn't been outnumbered—white kids had been taunting him, waving sticks and baseball bats. While the victim was stretched on the pavement, a friend dipped a finger in his blood and wrote "FFF" near his body. That fact vanished from newspaper reports in a matter of days, and Manuel felt that the white community was protecting itself, denying that its gangs existed.

In grade school, Manuel had first begun to distrust whites. He was a good student, but the only prize he ever won was for jumping rope. Academic awards went almost exclusively to white children. As a boy, he came to expect such subtle forms of discrimination, and when he was thirteen, predictably, he joined a neighborhood gang. He remained a member until he was stabbed during a fight at San Fernando High. He remembers being caught in a pack of kids, wrestling, shoving, and punching, when, out of nowhere, a blade flicked into sight and thrust itself from the tangle of bodies into his upper chest. It left a small puncture below his right collarbone. All the classrooms were locked, most of the teachers were in hiding, and police sirens wailed in the distance.

Manuel ran away with the rest of his gang. They urged him to go to a hospital, but he was afraid. He was also afraid to go home, because then his father would have to be interrupted at work, and that would mean even more punishment. At last, he stopped at an emergency room and let a doctor apply butterfly bandages. His wound seemed miraculous to him, an initiation into another phase of the gang process, and it convinced him that he was on a path that would lead him to prison or an early grave. So he quit and underwent counseling at school to help him with his anger. "We did role-playing," he told me with a smile. "I even got to play a mean white person, man."

In Van Nuys, there's a General Motors plant, where his father has worked on the line for more than twenty-five years. "One thing I'll always remember about my father is the back of his hand," he said. "But I understand it, you know? He had a hard life. He kept having to go back and forth across the border, bringing in family. My great-grandmother, she was in the Mexican Revolution. She dressed up as a man to smuggle troops around. My grandfather was a bracero for a while, working in the fields. He had thirteen children. He got arrested once and did a year in jail. He died of alcoholism.

"My mother and father used to take us to Mexico City, so we'd know where we came from. They wanted us to know our culture. Diego Rivera is still my hero. The way he combined art and politics. His feeling for people. Once, my father told me if I ever went to work in a plant he'd really be angry with me. He even got mad at me when I took this job. I think he wanted me to finish college, but for me college just obstructed learning. In my neighborhood, I grew up with about twenty boys. Eight of them are dead now. Some committed suicide. You could consider them almost like brothers to me. People say, 'Why did it happen?' But it's really 'Why did we let it happen?' Who are you going to blame it on, really?"

All afternoon, we looked for Jody. I had a feeling that Manuel was tracking a ghost from his past, seeing himself in the boy, trying to break a cycle before it completed itself in destruction. We cruised through parks, checked shopping malls and pizza parlors. Again, I saw the drugged kids walking the streets. Sometimes, on the periphery of schools, they stood by playground fences with their fingers threaded through the mesh and stared at the buildings in a posture of intense longing. In the United States, only about seventy per cent of all teen-agers graduate from high school. The percentage is lower in the San Fernando Valley.

In the late afternoon, Manuel admitted defeat. He thought about phoning Jody at home, but Jody's mother had forbidden him to do it. Manuel had visited her once to express his concern, and she had become so upset with his talk of guns and violence that she called him names and threw him out.

\* \* \*

Detective Randall Pastor, of the Burbank Police Department, was among the first in the San Fernando Valley to identify groups of white teen-agers as gangs. He is a big, bulky, physically intimidating man in his late thirties, and he serves as secretary to the California Gang Investigators' Association, which has affiliates in nine other states. When I went to talk with him, he was waiting at the end of along corridor, looming outside his office with his hands buried in his pockets and his tie loose at the collar. In many police departments, the juvenile division is a joke, staffed by malcontents and officers heading for an early retirement, but there is nothing funny about Pastor. "They call us kiddie cops or diaper detectives," he said, engulfing my hand in his.

In the past, a cop in juvenile had little to do except roust truants, chase runaways, and lecture shoplifters, but in the eighteen years Pastor has been on the force juvenile crime has taken an exponential leap, even in small towns. In fact, Burbank is really just a small town, having grown up around Lockheed Aircraft during the Second World War. Its streets are clean and orderly, its municipal buildings fly the flag, and yet an increasing number of its teen-agers are threatening to run wild.

At one point in our conversation, Pastor showed me a snapshot of some spiky metal rods that were used in a homicide last December. Three members of Burbank's only significant Hispanic gang, high on PCP, had beaten up and then shot a Mexican teen-ager from Cypress Park, who had recently moved to the valley. The case had been turned over to the county's hardcore prosecution unit, but other counties did not have such support systems. "Suppose a Crip gets paroled to Arizona," Pastor said. "He takes with him everything he knows about crime and introduces it in a new area."

In Pastor's jurisdiction, Burbank Punk Organization, or B.P.O., is the most active white youth gang, with between twenty and twenty-five members. In spite of its moderate size, the gang generates a tremendous amount of graffiti. Its crimes usually fall into the legal category of malicious mischief or vandalism, but for Pastor either category is too broad. In Burbank, white teen-agers have ripped the plumbing from a restroom at a drive-in. They have poured phosphorus on cars, blown up trashcans, and thrown the blade of a lawn edger through the window of a house. Pastor does not accept such acts as "innocent fun." To discourage them, he likes to "shake, rattle, and roll," making lots of very minor arrests, in the hope of creating a climate in which a kid has to think twice before he misbehaves.

Not everybody agrees with Pastor that rowdy suburban kids ought to be classified as a gang. The argument goes, There's a difference between making a youthful mistake—say, getting drunk and slashing someone's tires—and conspiring to sell cocaine. When I asked Pastor about this, he produced a state-task-force report on youth-gang violence and read me its definition of a youth gang: "A gang is a group of people who interact at a high rate among themselves to the exclusion of other groups, have a group name, claim a neighborhood or other territory and engage in criminal and other anti-social behavior on a regular basis."

The task force considered the problems facing law-enforcement agencies, and it made a number of recommendations. In effect, the force suggested a major revision of the existing criminal code, stripping away many of the protections that are now afforded to minors. It asked for increased penalties for drive-by shootings and other gang-related homicides, and for the possession and sale of controlled substances. The courts should be allowed to detain juvenile probation violators for up to a year. There were provisions to ease the laws of search-and-seizure, and to amend the death penalty so that it could be applied to anybody who killed a witness in a trial.

As a working cop, Pastor felt that such changes were necessary. The current laws did little to deter juvenile crime, and they sometimes hampered him in doing his duty. But he was also willing to address some of the cultural issues surrounding youth gangs, and he spoke about them in leisurely fashion for half an hour or so.

"Kids today are out of control," he said. "I don't care if a kid is seventeen years old or three years old, he has to have rules. Parents are afraid of their kids. I can't always blame them. Some of these kids in gangs are bigger than me. It's hard for a single parent—especially for a woman. Around our house, my wife doesn't let our children get away with anything. One time, my twelve-year-old daughter wouldn't finish her milk at breakfast, and my wife marched down to the bus stop with a glass and made her drink it.

"If you don't have responsible parents, you won't have responsible kids. Yesterday, we picked up a girl for joy-riding. Her dad won't take her back, so she has to go through the probation systems, which is a real pain in the butt. I get between two and five calls a week from parents who want me to take their children into custody. Everybody looks to cops or courts or social workers for relief. You'd be surprised how many kids in gangs tell me they want to be cops. They don't have any role models. Sometimes there isn't a person in the world who cares whether they live or die."

\* \* \*

One more time, Manuel and I went looking for Jody. He had heard from his co-workers on the night shift that the boy was hanging around Sylmar, where he had been transferred to yet another school. They didn't know whether he was really attending classes, or even whether he still lived at home, but at least he was behaving himself.

For a while after his punk gang dumped him, he had talked of joining a traditional Hispanic gang, which would offer him the boldness he'd been seeking. In exchange, he would be able to do favors for the gang, passing into neighborhoods where Hispanics couldn't go. For Jody, this would have been a ticket to prison, so Manuel was glad to hear that he'd decided to cool it instead, apparently happy enough to be on his own.

We left Manuel's house on a warm morning in June. He wore his standard work outfit of jeans, high tops, and a shirt with the tails hanging out. He'd been on vacation for a month, and he was suffering the re-entry blues. In relaxing, he had let his defenses down, and he needed some time in the streets to develop the crust—like a surgeon's—that enables him to deal with little doses of horror on a daily basis.

We got into the Dodge Colt. It had a fresh dent in a fender where a woman had backed into it. As we drove, Manuel explained that his primary worry was that Jody would now fall into the juvenile-justice system. When a kid has to go before a judge, he works on his excuses. The excuses often have some validity, but for a kid in court they become a kind of passport, establishing his credentials as a "troubled youth." The system is set up to cope with troubled youths.

In Manuel's eyes, it endorses failure. It makes a kid believe that failure has always been his destiny, that he has fulfilled, however perversely, his obligation to society. "Around here, every kid has problems," he said. "Every kid has excuses. There are a million reasons to fail and only a few to succeed. That's the truth of it. You shouldn't lie about it. If you come up through the streets, it's hard to get an education. It's hard to get a job. But you can't feel sorry for yourself. Because then you're finished."

We were cruising through towns that were familiar to me now—through Pacoima, Arleta, Panorama City. The day was balmy, and as we stopped at corners to talk to kids, I could smell a trace of chlorine in the air, the vapors off a swimming pool. I found myself recalling summers from my own teens, hanging around a suburban schoolyard to play baseball or meet girls, and I marveled at the remarkable innocence of that time.

In the thirty years or so since Elvis Presley sang "Heartbreak Hotel" on TV, the music of young people had become more raw and aggressive, and often more despairing. The drugs they used were stronger, more addictive, and more widely available, and the traps that had been set for them were far more insidious. In a crucial sense, they were being denied the luxury of making a simple mistake—a few wrong turns, and they were strung out or in prison. That so many teen-agers had accepted all this as the given of their lives was an ongoing tragedy.

Jody eluded us again that afternoon. For the moment, he was missing in action, maybe lost for good. At Manuel's house, we parked the Colt and stood outside for a bit and chatted. I asked him if there was really any way to deal with gangs.

"Just to deal with gangs, no," he said. "You make new laws, criminals always find a way to get around them. If you want to deal with gangs, you have to deal with parents and families.

You have to deal with schools. You have to deal with the whole environment."

Since gang activity was continuing to increase, spreading to new segments of the community, I wondered if Manuel had any hope that his work would make a difference.

"You can't get depressed about it," he said. "You know, with the people on my team, I tell them they have to make their job fun—even though it's a crummy job. It's got lots of negatives, but lots of positives, too. Once you start an input into somebody's life, you begin to influence them, you break the monotony. Some kids, they don't know any other kind of life. What we do, it's like throwing a wrench inside an engine. It screws up the structure. Suddenly, you're a part of their lives. That's good to feel. Sometimes it's like I can almost control what's going on. It's like having a sixth sense. Like seeing into the future and controlling it. That's when you know you're doing your job."

*The New Yorker*, 1986

# Two: Diversions

# Still Truckin':
# Jerry Garcia and
# the Grateful Dead

Here is Jerry Garcia, the rock star in middle age. He has always been our most improbable pop-culture idol, somebody to whom the playing matters more than the posing. At fifty-one, a halo of gray hair fringing his head and his gray-white beard indifferently trimmed, he resembles the proverbial unmade bed. The merest of filaments divides the man from the performer. His clothing onstage is his clothing offstage—a T-shirt, baggy sweatpants, and a pair of sneakers. The absence of style is a style itself and suggests an inability to abide by anybody else's rules. He's the rebellious child grown up, not so much above his youthful audience as insistently a part of it. In refusing to be adored, he inspires a kind of love. Hunched over his guitar and scarcely moving a muscle, he becomes a larger instrument through which the music travels. While the crowd focusses on the notes that drift from his fingers into the air, he does his best to disappear.

In a sense, Garcia is defying gravity. Nobody else in the history of rock and roll has ever watched his popularity advance with each passing year. Until recently, with the repackaging of such geriatric rockers as Aerosmith and Rod Stewart, most performers could be counted on to go down in flames before their fortieth birthday— better to burn out than to rust, as Neil Young once put it. Garcia himself upheld the old tradition by nearly self-destructing a couple of times. When he turned fifty last year, he weighed almost three hundred pounds, smoked three packs a day, survived on junk food, never exercised (he needed a roadie to carry his attaché case), and had a serious drug problem. He appeared to be headed for an early grave, but he had the good luck to collapse instead. Forced to confront his mortality, he changed his ways, adopting a vegetarian diet, cutting down on cigarettes, taking long walks, swallowing vitamins in megadoses, and even hiring a personal trainer to tone a body that had given new meaning to the concept of shapelessness.

I caught up with Garcia shortly after he launched his recovery program. Like most veterans of Haight-Ashbury in its prime, I felt a special kinship with him and wondered how he was weathering his transformation into an American icon. For aeons, his band, the Grateful Dead, have had their headquarters in Marin County, where I live, so I arranged a meeting backstage at the Oakland Coliseum before a concert.

Garcia is a native San Franciscan. He is the second of two sons, and his father, Joe, a musician who had led both a Dixieland band and a forty-piece orchestra, named him in honor of Jerome Kern. Joe Garcia liked to fly-fish, and on a camping trip one spring he was swept to his death by a raging river. Jerry, who was five at the

time, witnessed the drowning. In its aftermath, his maternal grandparents, who lived in the blue-collar Excelsior District, took him in.
He was a sickly, asthmatic child with a rich fantasy life. Although
he was given piano lessons, he did poorly at them and showed no
special aptitude for music. He preferred to read, immersing himself
in E.C. Comics and the sci-fi novels of Ray Bradbury and Edgar
Rice Burroughs, and he also drew and painted in his sketchbooks.

His mother, Ruth, reclaimed him when he was ten. She
owned a sailors' bar and hotel downtown, and Jerry became its
mascot. He had already developed a knack for independence,
roaming the Excelsior while his grandparents were at their jobs,
and he liked to hang around the bar, later describing it as "romantic and totally fun." School bored him. Homework was a dumb
idea, he believed, and he had to repeat the eighth grade, because
he wouldn't do any. In an auspicious conjunction of the planets,
the onset of his adolescence coincided with the birth of rock. He
was particularly fond of Chuck Berry, Gene Vincent, Little Richard, and Buddy Holly. For his fifteenth birthday, in 1957, he asked
his mom for an electric guitar like the ones he'd seen in pawnshop
windows. She must have had a nose for trouble, because she gave
him an accordion instead.

\* \* \*

Notes from Oakland on a mild December evening: The Coliseum, a cavernous, echoing concrete structure, has the architectural distinction of a bunker. About fifteen thousand Deadheads,
a sellout crowd, were waiting behind sawhorse barricades in the

parking lot when I arrived. I had assumed that there would be a rousing party going on backstage, but the Dead are so old and have done so much partying that now they hole up in separate dressing rooms and conserve their energy before a show. Roadies were taking orders for dinners, which the band members would eat between sets, and were moving equipment around.

One roadie had the task of caring for Garcia's custom-built guitar, which is the near-equivalent of a Stradivarius. It's called the Tiger, because the luthier who made it—Doug Irwin, of Santa Rosa—inlaid a tiger of brass and mother-of-pearl in the guitar's ebony face. Wherever the Dead go, the Tiger goes, too. They tour three times a year for three to four weeks at a time, and often bring their families. For the last couple of years, they have been the highest-grossing concert act in the business, with last year's receipts amounting to more than thirty-two million dollars.

Garcia was in his dressing room, sitting on a couch before a picked-over tray of fruit. When I walked in, he rose to greet me. Up close, he was much bigger than I had expected—broad-shouldered, and with an aura of physical power. He looked both fit and alert. Some musicians extend a hand delicately, as if it were a baby bird about to be crushed, but Garcia's grip was firm and strong. It spoke of his unguardedness. The tip of one finger on his right hand was missing, chopped off by his brother in a woodcutting accident when they were boys.

Garcia's eyes were merry behind tinted glasses. He sat down again and leaned forward, eager to start. He's a wonderful talker, in fact, and converses in much the same way that he plays, improvising and letting his thoughts lead where they may. There's an intensity that comes off him in ripples when he's enjoying himself, and it doesn't seem to matter who or what the source of his pleasure is. If he were to formulate a philosophy, it could probably be boiled down to this: If it's not fun, don't do it. He had performed thousands of concerts, and yet he was truly looking forward to another one. In an ideal world, he said, he'd be playing somewhere six nights a week—twice with the Dead, twice with the Jerry Garcia Band, a small group meant for more intimate venues, and twice with an acoustic group on his five-string banjo.

Before Garcia turned to rock full time, he fronted a jug band, Mother McCree's Uptown Jug Champions. In some respects, he finds acoustic music more challenging to play. He had recently made an acoustic album with the mandolinist David Grisman, and he was pleased that it had been nominated for a Grammy. He and Grisman have been collaborators since they met at a bluegrass festival in 1964. A lot of Garcia's friends are old friends, people he's known for twenty or thirty years.

I complimented Garcia on the album, and it seemed to unsettle him a bit; I'd heard that he was his own severest critic.

"That makes me feel good about myself," he said, with a shrug, as if he were not yet convinced of his talent.

Among the tasty things about the album, I went on, was the variety of its selections—Hoagy Carmichael's "Rockin' Chair," Irving Berlin's "Russian Lullaby," B. B. King's "The Thrill Is Gone."

Garcia allowed that he liked music of every kind and delighted in experimenting. He mentioned that he had once sat in with Omette Coleman, the jazz master, at a recording session.

"How was that?" I asked.

He laughed. "Like filling in the spaces in a Jackson Pollock painting! Ornette's such a sweet man, though. He gave me a lot of help."

The curtain was about to go up, and Garcia needed some time to get ready mentally. He still has bouts of stage-fright. To relieve them, he uses a mental trick that he learned in the nineteen-sixties, when any food or drink around was liable to be dosed with psychedelics. Once, at the Avalon Ballroom, he saw an enticing chocolate cake backstage, but he was sure that somebody had doctored it, so he contented himself with a lick of frosting rather than a slice. The cake's baker soon turned up and announced that the frosting had seven hundred doses of STP in it. Sinking, Garcia went on a very bad trip indeed. He imagined that some Mafia hit men were in the crowd, waiting to kill him. The only way he could survive, he thought, was to be humble and play for mercy—for his life. "And it worked!" he exclaimed, laughing again. "I'm still alive!"

I stayed around for the concert. The atmosphere was festive, with the audience batting balloons back and forth. Oddly, I didn't smell any marijuana, a scent that, along with the refractory odor of patchouli oil, had characterized the Dead concerts I used to go to at the Fillmore Auditorium. Some people were obviously stoned, but they'd done their smoking in private. The average Deadhead is often portrayed as a glassy-eyed, long-haired wretch in a tie-dyed T-shirt, but I didn't see many of those types. The fans were mostly middle-class white people in their twenties and thirties. They had the look of young professionals masquerading as hippies for a night, eager to bask in the recollected glow of the sixties.

When the band came out, the Coliseum seemed to levitate for a second or two. The music kicked in, and the Deadheads started dancing. They danced right through both sets, on the floor or by their seats, for three straight hours, as if they'd been drilled. It was pretty strange, really. At the Fillmore, none of us knew what we were doing, and our evenings had often been as amorphous as the pulsating blobs in a light show. The Dead in middle age were a curious sight, too—ordinary guys, graying, and miles removed from any glitter. I could have been watching myself onstage, but that was always part of the band's appeal for my generation: we were them, and they were us. For the young people around me, the show must have had the texture of a fantasy in which their parents actually listened to them and understood their deepest secrets.

The bond between the Dead and the Deadheads was extraordinary. Garcia would tell me on another occasion that the band aimed for such a target. He felt that it happened at about forty percent of their concerts, but they could never will it into being. Hearing his lovely, bell-clear notes again, I was heartened to think that the Dead were still in search of the miraculous, chasing after those moments when your flesh pops with goose bumps and the hair stands up on your head. What the band created for their fans was a benign environment where a person could be loose, liberated, free from inhibitions, and without any fear—fifteen thousand happy dancers, and no violence anywhere. The band took all the risks.

* * *

How the Dead, once nearly buried, have ascended: Early in their career, Garcia and company endured the usual music-industry scams and rip-offs, and they decided to take control of their destiny. Their first four albums had not sold well, leaving them in debt to their label, Warner Brothers, but they recouped with two straight hits in 1970, "Workingman's Dead" and "American Beauty," both primarily acoustic and distinguished by the richness of the songs and the band's clean, crisp playing. That same year, they acquired a small shingled house on a suburban block in Marin to serve as their offices and began handling their own business affairs. In 1972, they tipped off their fans to their new free-form operation by inserting an apparently harmless message in the liner notes of a live album recorded on tour in Europe. "DEAD FREAKS UNITE!" the message read. "Who are you? Where are you? How are you? Send us your name and address and we'll keep you informed."

With one gesture, the Dead eliminated the barriers between themselves and their audience, and established a direct flow of communication. Although the Dead Freaks turned into numberless Deadheads and came to require elaborate attentions (there are ninety thousand Deadheads on the American mailing list and twenty thousand on the European list), the band's offices have remained in the same little house. It's as if the Dead were superstitious about tampering with the magic, so booking agents, publicity people, and accountants are all crammed in like family. The Dead still meet about once a month in a boardroom to discuss their projects. Initially, the meetings were free-for-alls, Garcia says, but somebody dug up a copy of "Robert's Rules of Order," and they riffed on it until they had devised their own warped version of parliamentary procedure.

I stopped by the house shortly after the Coliseum show, walking in through the back door, as I'd been instructed, because anyone who uses the front door is presumed to be an unwanted visitor.

The universe that the Dead have evolved, a parallel reality that permits them to function, is built on such fine points. In the old days, it was virtually impossible to apply for a job, but if you were to wander in and start doing something valuable they might hire you. Many staffers have been with them for ages, and they are very well paid. The band even floats them loans to buy homes and cars. The prevailing staff attitude seems to be a hybrid strain of hippie good vibes and nontoxic American capitalism. As Garcia once said to me, the Dead are a rock band that disguises itself as a California corporation.

Garcia arrived at noon, by way of the back door. Fresh from a session with his trainer, he claimed, only half-jokingly, that the unfamiliar oxygen racing through his system had granted him a weird new aerobic high. "Weird" is a favorable adjective with him. He uses it often to describe experiences he has enjoyed. If an experience is really weird, it gets elevated to the status of "fat trip." A fat trip is anything that pleasantly rearranges the brain cells—say, bumping into Charlie Mingus drinking Martinis from a thermos in a Manhattan park, or landing in the same Amsterdam hotel as William Burroughs, or going up the Nile on a boat after a gig at the Great Pyramid.

We settled into a funky room off the kitchen that could not technically be described as decorated, and I asked Garcia about his accordion.

"Oh, it was a beauty!" he said. In the heat of conversation, his voice rises, and he grins with the relish of a man who's sinking his teeth into a steak that he shouldn't be eating. "It was a Neapolitan job. My mother bought it from a sailor at the bar. A little later, I got a Danelectro guitar and a Fender amp. I taught myself to play, and pretty soon I was fluid in a primitive way. I picked up a trick or two from my cousin Danny—he knew some rhythm and blues–but the most important thing I learned was that it was O.K. to improvise. 'Hey, man, you can make it up as you go along!' In high school, I fell in with some other musicians—beatnik types, the pot smokers. My only other option was to join the beer drinkers, but they got into fights. I kept getting into trouble anyway, so my mother finally moved us out of the city to Cazadero."

Cazadero is in the coastal redwoods of Sonoma County. It's a wicked spot for a teen-age exile, a damp, spooky resort town that is deserted for nine months of the year. "I hated it there," Garcia went on. "I had to ride a bus thirty miles to Analy High, in Sebastopol. I played my first gig at Analy. We had a five-piece combo—a piano, two saxes, a bass, and my guitar. We won a contest and got to record a song. We did Bill Doggett's 'Raunchy,' but it didn't turn out very well. Things in Cazadero got so bad that I enlisted in the Army.

"I wound up in a thirty-man company at Fort Winfield Scott, at the Presidio, right back in San Francisco. That company was choice! We did lots of ceremonies, stuff like flag-raising. The guys rotated from the city to Korea and Japan. I started going out at night to see my friends, you know, and I didn't always make it back in time for work. I was piling up the AWOLs, and the commander was worried that I'd queer the deal for the other guys. So he called me in and asked me, 'Garcia, how'd you like to be a civilian again?'

"In all, I did about eight months in the service. After that, I went to the Art Institute in San Francisco for a bit, to study painting. I wasn't playing guitar so much—I'd picked up the five-string banjo in the Army. I listened to records, slowed them down with a finger, and learned the tunings note by note. By then, I was getting pretty serious about music—especially about bluegrass. In the early sixties, a friend of mine and I toured the bluegrass festivals in the Midwest. We had a tape recorder and sometimes got to jam. We met all the greats—Bill Monroe, Reno and Smiley, and the Kentucky Colonels.

"When I got back, we formed our jug band. Bobby Weir was in it, and so was Pigpen"—Ron McKernan. "Pig was our front man. He was a natural, an old soul. The rest of us were loose wigs, but Pig had it together. He knew instinctively how to work a crowd. We did gigs around Palo Alto and Stanford University. I made a little money giving lessons, but we were usually broke. For a while, I lived in my car in a vacant lot in East Palo Alto. That's where I met Hunter." Robert Hunter, the main lyricist for the Dead, is another of Garcia's old friends. "He was living in his car, too. He had these cans of pineapple in his trunk—I don't know where he got them—and I had some boxes of plastic forks, so we'd meet every morning for breakfast and use my forks to eat his pineapple.

"It was an exciting time. I'm a cinephile, and I remember going to see a Richard Lester film one night—'A Hard Day's Night'—and being blown away by the Beatles. 'Hey!' I said to myself 'This is gonna be fun!' The Beatles took rock music into a new realm and raised it to an art form. Dylan, too—he's a genius. It wasn't long before the jug band became an electric band, the Warlocks. We recruited Billy Kreutzman as our drummer. He'd been working at the post office. I didn't think bass guitar was important, but the first guy we had was pretty bad, so we brought in Phil Lesh. Lesh was this wonderful, serious, arrogant youth, a composer of modernist music. He only played the trumpet then, but he had perfect pitch.

"The Warlocks worked the lounge circuit in bars on the Peninsula. We did pop covers, mostly, except for the last set— then we got weird and jammed. Our big break was getting involved with Ken Kesey and his bunch. They invited us out to La Honda. We brought our gear and played for about twenty minutes. Crash! Bang! It was like the war in Grenada, man! We were weirder than can be, and they loved it. When Kesey started putting on the Acid Tests, in 1965, we became their house band, the Grateful Dead. Sometimes we played for hours and were brilliant. Sometimes we had to be dragged onstage and only lasted for three minutes. The really neat thing was that we didn't have to be responsible."

* * *

Deadheads are everywhere at present. For the band, they are a blessing and a curse. Their fealty translates into huge profits, but they also imply an unwanted responsibility. Sometimes they make a prisoner of Garcia. He can't wander about in Marin County or anywhere else the way he once did. When the Deadhead phenomenon began to snowball, five or six years ago, he was concerned about its cultlike implications and tried to sabotage it by being nonresponsive and pretending that it didn't exist, but since then he has seen that it's too directionless to amount to a serious threat. He accepts it as a logical consequence of the Dead's tribal impulse. Besides, Deadheads are quick to be critical, he says, whenever the band is lazy, sloppy, dull, or just plain bad. Still, he isn't entirely comfortable with them, and never speaks a word from the stage, because he's afraid of how it might be interpreted.

Garcia puzzles over the Deadheads. He is trapped inside their obsession and can only probe at it from the inside. He thinks that the band affords its followers "a tear in reality"—a brief vacation from the mundane. The Dead design their shows and their music to be ambiguous and open-ended, he says; they intend an evening to be both reactive and interactive. A Deadhead joins in on an experiment that may or may not be going anywhere in particular, and such an opportunity is rare in American life. The Deadhead world is multireferential and feeds on itself. A fan's capital is measured by his or her involvement with the band over time, by the number of shows attended and the amount of trivia digested.

And there's a lot of trivia. For example, a computer whiz kid in New Hampshire publishes an annual journal called *DeadBase* that attempts to quantify the entire experience of being a Deadhead. According to a survey in *DeadBase '91,* the average Deadhead had attended seventy-five Dead concerts in his or her lifetime and had spent $1,571.40 on band-related activities such as travel, lodging, and blank tapes during the past year. *DeadBase '91* catalogued every song that the band had played on tour, clocking each different version. "Picasso Moon" had lasted for six minutes and seventeen seconds in Orlando, but it had gone on for seven minutes and three seconds in Sacramento.

In a section called "Feedback," the Deadheads rated such items as the security force and the concessions at each concert venue. The worst security was in St. Louis, they maintained, while the best venders were in Essen, Germany. They voted on the most improved song ("Picasso Moon") and on the song they'd heard quite enough of ("Throwing Stones"), and they offered some suggestions for locales for future shows—the Grand Ole Opry, Easter Island, and Intercourse, Pennsylvania.

Nostalgia is built into the Deadhead system. A new convert has always missed the golden age and can only sample its essence by listening to a veteran's tales and tapes. Deadheads also swap war stories. As Garcia puts it, "They sit around and tell how they went to a show once and got stranded in Bumfuck, Idaho." Some Deadheads—a minority—include hallucinogens in the formula, even though the band discourages drug use at concerts. Garcia savored his sixties incarnation as Captain Trips, but he would never suggest that anybody imitate him. (His last transcendental acid trip was in the sixties, at Olompali Ranch, in Novato. He developed three-hundred-and-sixty-degree vision, died a few thousand times, and saw the word "All" float into the sky before he turned into a field of wheat and heard "Bringing In the Sheaves" as a coda. "I think I unravelled every strand of DNA in my body," he says. "I felt both full and empty. I hardly spoke a word for two months, but it was worth it.")

According to a story in USA Today, undercover agents from the Drug Enforcement Administration have lately been infiltrating Deadhead throngs and busting people who are selling LSD, and as many as two thousand Deadheads—most of them young, white, and male—are currently serving severe prison terms of up to forty years. Here lies the unwanted responsibility. It's as if by virtue of having been around when the LSD genie escaped from its bottle, Garcia and the Dead were somehow expected to coax it back in.

\* \* \*

Away from the spotlight, Garcia leads a simple life. If he has any taste for possessions, he keeps it hidden. He has been a creature of the road for so long that he's never had much of a home. After the recent breakup of his second marriage, his house in San Rafael went on the marker—it made the newspapers when a real-estate agent fell into the swimming pool—and he now rents a furnished condo in Tiburon, in Marin. It's an unfancy place, but he likes it for the view of San Francisco Bay, and also because his four daughters live nearby and he hopes to stay in closer touch with them than he used to. The eldest, Heather, is twenty-nine and plays first violin in the Redwood Symphony Orchestra, and the youngest, Keelin—her name is Irish—is just five.

"They've been very generous to me," he told me, with true appreciation. "I've been mostly an absentee parent, after all."

Garcia has had to grow up in public, and he can be troubled by what he regards as his personal failings. The guilt comes from his upbringing as a Roman Catholic, he thinks. He talks readily about his early religious training, and how the Church, with its mysticism and its hierarchical structure, influenced his view of the world. There is a story he tells about how he fudged his First Communion. He had no sins to confess, so he made some up and lied to a priest. Then the lie became a sin, and existence took on complications: he wasn't in a state of grace anymore. Catholicism planted a dissonance in him, he believes, by rubbing against his grain. "Maybe it's good to have something big that's beyond you," he says. "All that magic and mojo power. Sin becomes ever so much more juicy!"

It can take Garcia all day to get out of his apartment. Always the last to bed, he is slow to get going in the morning and can spend hours puttering. He may start by listening to some music, anything from Haydn string quartets to the Butthole Surfers. He has always been an avid reader, and currently champions the books of Terence McKenna, an amateur anthropologist and a psychedelic explorer.

He may decide to fiddle with his Macintosh and generate some computer art, or open a sketch pad and begin to draw.

It's surprising what a good draftsman Garcia is. The best of his drawings are witty, spare, and whimsical. They're very different from his guitar playing—not so rigorous or so practiced. As a guitarist, he labors to make his playing look easy. He never gets caught being showy or calling attention to his technical mastery. What you hear sometimes in a trademark Garcia solo is a plangent kind of longing, a striving after an unattainable perfection.

One evening, I went over to his apartment for dinner. We had some Chinese food cooked without any oil and, to prevent an overdose of health, some good champagne. After eating, we watched *Naked Lunch* on a laser disk. Garcia is a big fan of Burroughs; he considers the writer a paragon of weirdness. Midway through the film, a loud snoring noise interrupted the clacking mandibles on the soundtrack. I looked over, and Garcia was dozing, even though we'd been chatting a few seconds before. He kept sawing logs for about five minutes and then woke abruptly, as bright and as cheery as ever.

Failing asleep like that was a habit of his, he said. He could—and frequently did—take a catnap anywhere, in public or in private. There was something revealing about the sudden sleep. He put out so much energy all the time that he was bound to run low every now and then. It seemed that for him the existential dilemma would always be the same: How could you get to the edge of things without going over the edge?

* * *

The last time I saw Garcia, the Dead were reluctantly in rehearsal—they *hate* to rehearse—for a summer tour. Garcia's mood was still jolly. He was sticking to his fitness program and was eager for more oxygen, not less. He and Robert Hunter had written a couple of new songs that were as good, he said, as anything else they'd composed in a long time. (In *DeadBase '91* the fans had strongly agreed that "the Dead should write more new material.") The future was opening up before him, and he had the optimistic manner of somebody who has started dreaming again in middle age.

In the end, it seemed to me, the Dead's success isn't really so mysterious. They work hard and enjoy what they are doing. They never underestimate their fans, and give them full value for the dollar. People are delighted to go to a concert and return home knowing that they got more than their money's worth. The Dead are responding to the need for joy, celebration, and ritual, and they have struck a nerve.

The next major bit of fun in store for Garcia was a scuba-diving trip. He dashes off to Hawaii whenever he has a few free days in his busy schedule. "Diving takes up a lot of the space that drugs used to," he told me. "It's an active, physical form of meditation. I could never do a sitting meditation, like the Buddhists—I'm way too restless. In the water, you're weightless. It's so silent—you're like a thought. When I begin to relax, the songs start happening in my head." A descent into the ocean, he went on, was similar to a dive through the layers of human consciousness: "You see the obvious stuff first, like the beautifully colored fish. Then maybe you notice a peculiar lichen on some coral, and then you notice something else. You learn reflexively, always taking in information. Once I get going, I might fin around for a couple of miles. It's an ecstatic experience, really. I love it almost as much as I love the music."

*The New Yorker*, 1993

# On Luck and David Milch: A Screenwriter's Education

On December 26, 2008—St. Stephen's Day in Dublin, a celebratory occasion—in the midst of a festive meal, I received the sort of phone call—life enhancing, potentially debt reducing—most writers dream about. On the line was David Milch, the acclaimed creator of *Deadwood,* inviting me to L.A. to collaborate on a series about horse racing he hoped to develop for HBO. The call came as a surprise. Milch had hired me to write the pilot script for such a show three years earlier, but it languished in limbo, and I'd given up on the project.

That was a mistake, I learned. David trusts to instinct and impulse, only acting when the spirit moves him. In an industry that thrives on conformity, he's an original. He has a genuine literary pedigree, having studied with Robert Penn Warren at Yale and taught there for a dozen years, and he also holds an MA from the Iowa Writers' Workshop, where he operated an LSD lab on the side that eventually forced him to swap Iowa City for

Cuernavaca to stay one step ahead of the law. His character, it might be said, is built on such polarities.

I first met Milch in the mid-1990s during *NYPD Blue*'s stellar run. A writer on his staff, knowing David admired *Laughing in the Hills,* my book about the track, arranged an introduction. Maybe the idea for a racing series was already percolating, because he couldn't have been more gracious, eager to include me in his orbit. He asked if I'd like to write an *NYPD Blue* episode, and I jumped at the chance, failing to mention that I'd never read a script, much less written one.

To get up to speed, I hung around the 20th Century Fox lot and soaked up the atmosphere. Often I felt like Tod Hackett in *The Day of the Locust,* marveling at the actors passing by in costume. Milch tried to steal some time for a private chat, but he was far too busy and suggested I stay at his house for a night, where he'd be less distracted. A problem on the set delayed him, though, and his wife, Rita, greeted me instead, then took off for a school play with her kids, leaving me alone with six dogs, a bowl of instant ramen, and a Lakers' game on the tube.

Around ten o'clock, David arrived at last. He apologized for being so late, excused himself to go upstairs, and came down in his pajamas. To my credit, I didn't bat an eye. The talk soon turned to racing. Milch owned a string of quality Thoroughbreds—including Gilded Time, who won the Breeders' Cup Juvenile Sprint in 1992—and showed me some of his trophies. He had a few horses stabled at Golden Gate Fields across the bay from Marin County, my home back then, and wondered if I'd look in on them. If so, he'd gladly pay me. And—by the way—was I doing okay, financially speaking? If I needed any "walking around" money, he'd be happy to provide it.

I'd heard about Milch's legendary generosity toward writers. He'd kept Richard Yates and Terry Southern afloat when their energies and bankrolls flagged in old age, and they were just two of many. Though tempted, I hovered slightly above the flat-broke meridian and thought it would be churlish to accept his offer. But I'd laid out a fair bit of cash for motels, meals, and gas, and asked David if he reimbursed visitors for their travel expenses.

"Sure," he replied. "What'd it cost you? About a grand?"

I did the math. "More like six hundred."

Milch dashed upstairs again and returned with six crisp hundred-dollar bills. "Never ask for less," he advised. That was my first Hollywood lesson.

I went home and cranked out the script in a couple of weeks. What could be easier? Writing for TV was a breeze compared to the infantry slog through knee-deep mud that a long prose work demanded. Fox paid me a princely sum, too, but David never expressed an opinion. Should I give him a call? I decided against it. If he hated the script, he might ask for the money back. Better to carry on with my own work, I figured, only to be shocked when, months later, someone in Milch's office alerted me to the fact that "my episode" was about to air.

"You might not recognize it," he warned. "David does a lot of rewriting."

I admit to a brief burst of pride when my name flashed on the screen, but it was all downhill from there. Only three or four lines of the dialogue I'd written had survived. The rest of the script, 95 percent, belonged to Milch and his staff. He'd turned the story into a darker, richer, and more soulful vehicle than I'd been capable of imagining. The experience was humbling. My effort looked threadbare, and the credit I got, along with the residuals it would bring, seemed undeserved, another instance of David's generosity.

Fortunately, he forgave or forgot my amateurish performance. Or—equally plausible—others before me had fallen short of his exacting standards, so perhaps he'd expected no better. Whatever the case, I was relieved he wanted to see me again when our paths next crossed in 2005. I'd moved to Dublin by then and had flown to California for a writers' conference in Squaw Valley, then headed south to visit friends in Santa Monica, where Redboard, Milch's production company, is located.

David asked me to stop by for lunch. That summer he was shooting *Deadwood,* often hailed as his masterpiece. Never had his gift for language been so lavishly displayed—worthy of Shakespeare, the critics raved. For the first time, too, he was running a show by himself, casting the actors and directing the directors. As a certified Hollywood bad boy, now reformed, he'd always been stuck with a minder in the past—often Steven Bochco—but he'd earned his freedom, and it suited him. He had the look of a contented man.

He collected an entourage around noon, maybe a dozen guests in all—staffers, interns, strays—and escorted us to L.A. Farm, a pricey restaurant down the hall, where he picked up the tab for everyone. It must've cost five hundred bucks or so, yet he did this almost every weekday, taking evident delight in playing the host. The same spirit of largesse led him to charter a plane to fly his friends to Gulfstream Park in Florida for Gilded Time's big race in '92. If the horse hadn't won a two-million-dollar purse, Milch couldn't have afforded to pay for the flight home.

Over coffee, he leaned toward me and whispered, "Have I got a series for you." It involved horse racing, he went on, and a real estate deal with the governor of Kentucky, where we'd film the show at Churchill Downs—*if* the governor, currently under indictment, made good on his promises. "The guy assures me it'll be fine," David said, somewhat halfheartedly. He—Milch—couldn't go anywhere near the set for fear of contracting gambling fever, so I'd be the one in charge—a job for which I was spectacularly unqualified, although I kept my mouth shut once again.

After lunch, we returned to David's office to talk further. The room was large and airy, and it lacked any hint of formality or pretension. The mismatched couches and chairs might have been on loan from a fraternity house. Though Rita's colorful paintings hung on the walls, along with some eye-catching photographs—a Cartier-Bresson, Sugar Ray Robinson at the wheel of a Caddy convertible, the great heavyweight champ Jack Johnson flexing for the camera—Milch seemed oblivious of the decor and had imposed instead a willful disorder.

Pages torn from scripts and notes in the maestro's tiny southpaw scrawl littered the floor, as if to demonstrate his writing took precedence over any concerns about material things. "Here's how I work," he could've been saying, "and if it makes you uncomfortable, too fucking bad." He treated his sleek black Mercedes with the same indifference. Getting into the car could be a challenge, what with the empty CD cases and old *Daily Racing Forms* strewn about. Anything could turn up inside—a shoe maybe, or the Louisville Slugger I once unearthed from the debris.

I sat on a couch, while Milch stretched out on the carpet to ease the pressure on some painful ruptured discs. An aide entered and set a tape recorder on the floor next to him. Tape recorders can be found in every Redboard office, because David does some of his best thinking in the moment, riffing on plot twists and flights of fancy, inventing characters out of whole cloth, and serving up a steady stream of fleeting inspirations that would otherwise be lost. He improvises as freely as a jazz virtuoso, with the same dreamy intensity.

He elaborated on the show for me. In part, the plot referenced the tragic downfall of Calumet Farm, once Kentucky's pride. There'd be a villain based on J. T. Lundy, who ran the farm into the ground. A great stallion would die as Alydar had, possibly a victim of foul play. Milch added some fictional elements to the mix—an old trainer who owns an extraordinarily talented colt, a mobster who covets the colt, and a fiery woman jockey determined to make it in a man's world.

"Sarah Jessica Parker wants to play her," Milch let drop, and I nodded dumbly, learning my second Hollywood lesson. Everybody's susceptible to star power, regardless of how sophisticated or jaded they pretend to be. After the conference, I blurted to my wife, "And guess who'll play the lady jock? Sarah Jessica Parker!" which, of course, never happened.

In an hour or so, David was done. He popped out the cassette and tossed it to me. "Go back to Dublin and write the pilot," he said, and I did, with due diligence and honest effort this time. I spent six weeks on the job and sent the script by email to Santa Monica. Then I waited—and waited. One afternoon, I discovered a check in my mailbox, but Milch remained silent again, choosing to tackle the mystical surfing series *John from Cincinnati* rather than the horses. That left me out in the cold, or so I believed, until his call on St. Stephen's Day.

After our talk, without asking any questions, I bought a one-way ticket to L.A. I had faith in Milch and thought I knew what to expect. I could count on him to treat me well, and to rewrite my copy as he saw fit—a prerogative he deserved, given his mastery of the craft. I knew, too, that he'd be under pressure from the network. *John from Cincinnati* had lasted only a single season and puzzled the same critics who'd loved *Deadwood,* and his next show—*Last of the Ninth*, about New York City cops in the 1970s—never saw the light of day, even though HBO spent a reported ten million dollars on the pilot.

The racing series sounded special, though, close to Milch's heart. He'd been crazy about horses since he was a child. His father, a surgeon from Buffalo, used to take him to Saratoga every summer, where he placed his first bets at the age of six, with the help of some older confederates. Over the years, he'd poured a small fortune through the pari-mutuel windows, once losing a million bucks on a particularly bad afternoon. As an inveterate gambler, he must've understood the show would be a risky venture, but how could it be otherwise, with a title like *Luck*?

\* \* \*

Los Angeles greeted me with 72-degree weather when I landed in early January, a balm after the Irish winter. I dragged my jet-lagged self to Redboard, where Milch, enthused and excited, quickly addressed the question of my weekly salary—five times higher than I'd have dared hope for—and installed me in an apartment by the beach at his own expense. As I walked to the bar at Hotel Casa del Mar to watch the sunset that evening, I found it impossible not to imagine a radiant future for myself.

The next day, we got down to business. The Kentucky governor was history and so was Churchill Downs—we'd set the piece at Santa Anita instead—and so, too, was my script. It no longer reflected what Milch had in mind. His vision for the series had grown broader and more inclusive, focusing on the hothouse universe of the track and the many diehard players—jockeys, trainers, agents, railbirds—who labor under the illusion that a transformative bolt from the blue will someday change their lives for the better.

David scoffed at the notion. "You know what luck is?" he asked. "It's when you wake up in the morning." We should be grateful for every breath we draw, I took him to mean, but our longing gets in the way.

Redboard proved to be an eccentric place to work, designed to accommodate Milch's idiosyncrasies. He refused to carry a cell phone, for example, not knowing how to use one, so a land line was always in easy reach. Computers baffled him completely. He'd never surfed the Internet or sent an email and only read the emails he received as hard copies. At inspired moments, he liked to indulge in the liberty of gathering the troops and reading aloud an instructive passage from *Billy Budd* or Kierkegaard while occupying a battered leather armchair that seemed, by its very nature, to encourage his professorial leanings.

He kept most outsiders at bay, but dogs were welcome to roam freely. Sometimes two or three padded around, most memorably a giant Newfoundland with a gas problem, and David would lower himself to their level for an ear-scratching session. There were no cocksuckers in the canine kingdom, only gentle souls to be petted and praised. He also had a soft spot for children, and if he spied a tot in the lobby, you could count on him to wander over for a bit of small talk.

Adjacent to his office was the "writing room," where a typist sat before an Apple Mac, perennially at the ready, should Milch choose to start dictating. He wrote that way, consulting notes at times but more often winging it, lying on his side or assuming a modified lotus position in deference to his bad back. He enjoyed performing for an audience, so the dictation had a theatrical flair. His words appeared in script form on three computer screens deployed around the room, allowing any observers on the floor or a sectional couch to follow along.

The script was slow to gather steam. Milch confronted the blank computer screens with palpable fear and trembling. ("Before I write," he liked to say, "I pray.") I assumed he'd have the pilot blocked out by now, but he came at it from scratch just as I did. I'd never been able to outline a book in advance. It was too inhibiting, plus it foreclosed on the happy accidents that keep one alive to the flow, so I felt sympathetic toward the maestro. He'd crawled out on a limb. In a medium devoted to the formulaic, he paid a price for his literary aspirations.

After much hesitation, he dived into a scene about a Chilean horse arriving at Santa Anita by van, where a crooked bloodstock agent is waiting. Milch combed over the dialogue with infinite care, deleting a word or turning a sentence on its head until a previously lifeless exchange sounded right, true to the reality he aimed to serve. He'd close his eyes, rock back and forth, and massage his scalp so vigorously his hair stood up in ragged cowlicks. He looked electrified, as if wired to the very dynamo of creation. All writers recognize the sensation of breaking through a barrier to discover what they've been struggling to say, but it was high drama indeed to watch the breakthrough enacted.

Along with his quest for the right word, Milch was a stickler for authenticity. He spent hours talking about vans and transport with Darrell Vienna, a trainer friend, only to scrap the scene with the Chilean horse in the end. The scenes I wrote met with a similar fate, consigned to a file labeled "other stuff." I was disheartened until I realized we were amassing the bedrock material of the series, a loose-limbed first draft. Our lack of progress still bugged David, though. If he fell into a funk, everyone at Redboard walked on eggshells. Even on a productive day, he was loath to celebrate. "That's not bad," he'd say, giving himself the tiniest conceivable pat on the back.

At lunch, he tried to lighten up. As a newcomer, I aroused his curiosity, so he peppered me with questions. Was I of the faith, he asked, meaning, "Are you Jewish?" (No, I told him, though there are Jews with a surname that's spelled differently but sounds the same.) Had the wart under my left eye been properly examined by a specialist? (As a doctor's son, with a doctor brother, Milch often manifests as a doctor manqué.) And the apartment—did I find it comfortable? It's terrific, I said, with a little galley kitchen where I cook my meals. He regarded me suspiciously, as if cooking were akin to sorcery.

One morning, under the guise of research, he invited a few of us to Santa Anita. His real mission was to check out a colt for sale, although he supposedly didn't own horses anymore—at least not for the record—because his wife took a dim view of his costly hobby. But the Pamplemousse was no ordinary nag. A big three-year-old roan, he had Kentucky Derby potential. His trainer, Julio Canani, later became the model for *Luck*'s Turo Escalante, described in the pilot script as "a Peruvian trainer of acknowledged accomplishment and sordid repute."

At Canani's barn, a groom paraded around the Pample-mousse for our inspection. The colt was as impressive as adver-tised, a one-hundred-and-fifty-thousand-dollar purchase as a yearling, but Milch was put off by how he moved, favoring a back leg. (The Pamplemousse later suffered a tendon injury that kept him out of the Derby.) While David dickered with Julio, I toured the barn on my own, glad to be on the backside again. I watched a bowlegged goat with huge testicles hobble past, fol-lowed by a rooster pecking at the dust, and talked with the Mex-icans filling feed tubs and mucking out stalls.

To no one's astonishment, David decided to hang around for the races. His table at the FrontRunner Restaurant was the best in the grandstand, smack on the finish line. He held court there for a motley crew of pals with nicknames like Jimmy the Hat. A tabletop TV showed simulcasts from four or five other tracks, and he bet every race, marching poker-faced to the high rollers' window—minimum wager five hundred dollars—at five-minute intervals. Only when he hit a big exacta did he drop the sober mask and insist on spreading around the wealth. We all pocketed four hundred dollars.

Gradually, the script began to take shape. If I was no match for Milch in terms of dialogue, structure, or psychological acuity, I felt confident enough to handle the narrative sections, those blocks of prose that establish a scene. "The racetrack's backstretch world is waking to its business," I wrote, inspired by our visit to Canani's barn. "The Big Horse hears riders' voices, snorts and nickers from other stalls, some mariachi music on a tinny radio, a groom chattering in Spanish as he wraps a stable pony's bum leg." The bowlegged goat earned a walk-on, too.

With the atmospherics in place, David set the story in motion. The Big Horse's trainer, known only as the Old Man, arrives at the track with his dog, Bruiser. He carries a bag containing a frosted doughnut and absentmindedly gives it to his night watchman, who informs him that his colt has slept well. They gossip about the Pick Six jackpot on offer, and the Old Man wonders if he ought to let his horse strut his stuff. Nothing much "happened," but the scene was still very moving. The handful of lines spoken, deliberately prosaic, acquired an emotional depth by virtue of being so true to the situation—and by what Milch had left unstated.

By early March, he'd gained some real traction and had fallen into a productive routine. He read the script at home every night, then incorporated his fixes in the morning. With ten or twelve tolerable pages written, he felt on top of things, and my contribution—largely moral support and some minor editing—wasn't essential anymore. Probably, too, he'd awakened to the fact—or been made aware of it by his accountant—that what he'd agreed to pay me, in a moment of excess, would be too much even for an Emmy winner, which I most certainly was not.

I stuck around for one more week. David bought me a farewell lunch at the Buffalo Club—originally owned by Buffalo natives toiling in Hollywood, including Milch—and expressed how much my help had meant to him. I took this with a grain of salt but thought better of it later. He wasn't the type to bullshit. Moreover, he harbored a belief that we—human beings—are all connected in ways we sense but can't articulate. If I concentrated hard in the writing room, not even speaking, did that forward the progress of *Luck*? Maybe so. The maestro seemed to think so, anyway.

\* \* \*

After I'd departed, Milch polished the script for another six months, and an assistant emailed a revised version to me and some others five or six times a week. He wasn't seeking any feedback, just keeping the loop intact. I read the most recent dispatch over breakfast in Dublin every morning, watching the piece grow sharper and leaner as he trimmed the fat and knitted the various threads together more tightly. It was an oddly compelling spectator sport. I cheered when the writing went well and felt dismayed when it floundered, but all the while I was learning.

The Old Man acquired a name—Walter Smith—ideal for his taciturn, plainspoken manner. David saddled Joey Rathburn, a jockeys' agent, with a stutter that reflected his anxiety-ridden state. Chester "Ace" Bernstein was the most complex character and the toughest to illuminate. Loosely modeled on the fabled mob fixer Sidney Korshak, Ace was in transition, caught up in the act of becoming. Often confused and unsure of his motives, he vowed not to repeat his past mistakes. As he coped with the challenges of aging, he saw in the nobility of the racehorse a chance at redemption.

When Milch turned in the final draft of *Luck,* HBO gave him an immediate green light, although not the carte blanche of the *Deadwood* era—not after two straight disappointments. Instead the network coupled him with Michael Mann, the A-list movie director, who'd supervise the casting and direct the pilot, as Martin Scorsese did on *Boardwalk Empire.* By all accounts, Mann loved the script. David respected Mann's eye and couldn't argue with his record at the box office, but how well they'd get along, considering their sizable egos, was a matter for conjecture.

In January 2010 I returned to L.A., settled into a furnished studio—I was paying my own rent this trip—above Planet Raw, a vegan restaurant far from the beach, and reported to Redboard, where there'd been some changes in my absence. The office was crawling with interns now. Some were troubled—a drug problem, say—and in need of Milch's counsel and support, but most were aspiring screenwriters basking in the maestro's aura and hanging on his every word. He paid them a "living wage" of fifty grand or so for their six-month stint, and fed them a daily takeout lunch on which they visited a ferocious appetite, leaving a trail of burrito wrappers and half-eaten burgers in their wake.

David had also hired John Perrotta, a racetrack insider, who'd run breeding and training farms in Kentucky, Florida, and New Jersey. (Jay Hovdey, the *Racing Form*'s witty columnist, later became the third member of the writing team.) As Milch put it, "John knows where the bodies are buried." Like the boss, Perrotta was a gambler, be it on poker or the ponies. He and I were charged with writing scenes for future episodes, in case HBO picked up the series. Additionally, John would serve as a technical advisor during the shooting of the pilot, relying on his expertise to enhance Michael Mann's grasp of the track's fine points.

Perrotta also had the unenviable job of talking down the officials at Santa Anita. They were thrilled about *Luck* at first, eager for the publicity it would bring to a dying game, but they developed cold feet after reading the script. In particular, they objected to a scene in which a horse breaks down, fracturing a leg. But for David that scene was integral. It drew a line in the sand. He was full of disdain for sugarcoated movies like *Seabiscuit* that played fast and loose with the facts, and wanted the viewers to know up front they were in for a truthful, if occasionally rough, ride.

In due time, the officials swallowed their reservations. How could they not? *Luck* had generated a buzz in town, and actors were supposedly begging for roles. Sam Shepard as the Old Man? That rumor made the rounds. Even Sarah Jessica Parker merited a mention again, but the big fish was Dustin Hoffman, and Milch was angling for him. Hoffman would be the perfect Ace Bernstein, David thought. He was the right age, intelligent and supremely talented, although demanding—"higher maintenance than God," as somebody once said.

We lived on a steady diet of whispers until the afternoon Milch strolled into my office unannounced. He looked tired but happy. "We got Dustin," he said, flopping onto the floor to pet Oscar, Perrotta's Welsh corgi. With Hoffman on board, Nick Nolte was the next star to sign on—he, not Shepard, would play Walter Smith. As part of the package, David took on Dustin's two sons as interns and then Brawley Nolte, who supplied us with avocados from his dad's back forty in Malibu.

In early March, on the first day of principal photography, I set my alarm for 4:00 a.m. and reached Santa Anita in Arcadia just as the sun crested the San Gabriels. A crowd had already gathered on the apron of the track. Almost everyone associated with *Luck* put in an appearance, whether or not they were scheduled to work. Hoffman and Nolte chatted over coffee at Clocker's Corner, while the crew prepared to shoot the first scene of the day—a confrontation between two degenerate gamblers arguing about the Pick Six ticket they proposed to buy.

Then the head-butting began. As the cameras rolled, Mann's assistants made certain Milch and his staff steered clear of the action, confining us to the periphery of the set—too far from the actors to hear their lines—and barring us from the "video village" where Mann could review each take. In one fell swoop, we were reduced to the lowly status of second-class citizens. Nobody bothered to explain. The assistants were only following orders. Perrotta and I were stunned, but David must've known in advance his presence wouldn't be required or possibly even tolerated.

Still, he chomped at the bit. *Luck* was his baby, after all, and he felt protective and inclined to ignore the agreed-upon division of labor. But Mann was no pushover and enforced the terms of the deal as he understood them, unwilling to grant David any leeway to coach the actors or fiddle with the script at the last minute. Fair enough, one might say, but it grated when Mann altered a line or two of dialogue himself. Worse, he failed to heed Perrotta's advice, and that led to the kinds of mistakes that the hardcore racing fans were sure to notice.

Under such constraints, Milch grew sulky. He'd put in a day at Redboard, then go back to the set to mingle with the players at lunch or hang out in his trailer. Maybe he indulged in a magical belief that Mann's resolve would weaken, but that was the longest of long shots. Power in all its manifest glory was on display, so David eventually gave up and surrendered to the gravitational pull of his table at the FrontRunner.

Sometimes I joined him there, and that was almost always a mistake. Around high rollers, one throws caution to the wind. It's like catching a virus. Instead of my usual miserly five- or ten-spot bets, I invested twenties and fifties, trusting the tips so agreeably offered. Three came at me in rapid succession one afternoon. Perrotta alerted me to a "live" horse at Gulfstream Park, who lost; Milch touted a mare Darrell Vienna trained, who lost; and both experts assured me that a recently gelded colt in the fourth race at Santa Anita couldn't miss. The colt lost.

With alarming speed, I dropped two hundred bucks and beat a hasty exit from the grandstand, only to miss Milch's astonishing reversal of form. His losing streak ended, and he won a hundred grand or so over the next few hours. "You left too early," he chided me in the morning, giving me a five-hundred-dollar voucher to compensate for the cash I'd tossed away. He'd papered the track with money to celebrate his victory, in fact, laying Ben Franklins on anybody who had the wit to approach him with a hand extended, palm up.

More often I stayed away from the FrontRunner and killed the time by roaming. "*Luck* Credential" read the laminate around my neck, so I was set upon by track employees who fancied themselves actors—a much higher percentage than I'd have predicted. They mooched around, hoping for a bit part or a screen test. Milch was an even bigger target, but he had a strategy for dealing with the wannabes. He sent them to an acting coach he knew from *Deadwood* and paid for the lessons to prepare them for the roles they'd never get. For David, that was easier and less messy than saying no.

I ate constantly as I roamed. Between the gargantuan breakfasts and lunches that union rules required, I nibbled at the snacks on the food carts that circulated—platters of sushi and rare-roast-beef sandwiches, stacks of petit fours and slivers of cheesecake. I gained four pounds the first month, a victim of boredom. There really *was* nothing much *to* do but eat. I understood Mann's desire to keep Milch at arm's length, but he also refused to send us the dailies, so we were in the dark about how the script played. Our show had been hijacked, and we'd been orphaned.

The conclusion of the shoot came as a relief. We went back to work at Redboard and waited for Mann to deliver a rough cut of the pilot. Waiting was integral to the life of Hollywood, it seemed, along with gossip, money, and wretched excess. Finally, in April, David returned from the production offices clutching a DVD he'd agreed to watch only in the privacy of his own home—such were the security precautions enforced. A small group of us accompanied him to the house. There was a flat-screen TV available, but Milch couldn't operate the DVD player and was too tense to ask for help, so we huddled around a computer instead.

The first few minutes were stressful, especially for the maestro. The track jargon was difficult to decipher on account of a murky sound mix, but when the camera fixed on Kerry Condon—Rosie, the Irish exercise rider—astride Walter Smith's horse in full gallop, I could feel the adrenaline pumping. The moment was transcendent, capturing the elemental bond between horses and human beings so central to Milch's vision.

In the racing sequences, Mann's work approached the sublime. Thoroughbreds in action had never been photographed so beautifully or intimately. In terms of pure technique, he'd raised the bar very high indeed. He put the audience inside the fray, scraping along the rail with Leon Micheaux, the apprentice jockey, as he tried to find a hole in the field. Mann caught the color and the pageantry of the track, as well as the danger. The scenes of the horse breaking down were both shocking and elegiac.

The director had done a first-rate job. Nobody denied it. One could almost forgive Mann's imperial style on the set, but not quite. The howlers hurt, and the little dialogue changes stung Milch, even though he often remarked, about the delicate nature of collaborations, "You never get all your cargo to port." But there was still so much to savor—the low comedy of the degenerates, Escalante's ongoing battle with the English language, and the wryly tender exchanges between Bernstein and his consigliere, Gus Demitriou. "It adds up to a world, doesn't it?" David asked.

\* \* \*

After viewing the pilot, the HBO executives ordered *Luck* to series—eight more episodes—and put me on the payroll as a story editor. Though my duties didn't change, Milch was glad to have the network cover my salary at last. He'd been footing the bill for me and almost everybody else at Redboard through his production company. But no sooner was he out from under than he hired two new recruits for ill-defined jobs he invented on the spot, and they spent the better part of a year trying to figure out what they were supposed to do.

He was just as contrary when it came to script assignments. In a town where well-established writers would eat a spoonful of dirt to be awarded one, he chose rookies instead. He'd taken a shine to them, I guess, or glimpsed a hidden potential or felt obligated to do somebody a favor. Whatever the case, he seemed remarkably unconcerned about their inexperience, maybe because he knew he'd wind up doing most of the writing, or rewriting, himself, just as he'd done with my *NYPD Blue* episode so long ago.

In spite of *Luck*'s hundred-million-dollar budget and the tight demands of the shooting schedule, he continued to work in the same painstaking way, issuing the familiar commands to his typist—"Go back, go forward"—and finishing a scene or two a day, while an ever-increasing, mostly adulatory crowd looked on, with interns spilling down the hallway. At times he marched around like a general under siege. His sworn enemies were the production people with their ceaseless queries about when he'd deliver a script. Deadlines he regarded with dread.

Everything about *Luck* had grown in size. Now when Milch called an impromptu meeting, his office filled with fifteen or so staffers and their canine companions. The maestro's tendency to ramble became more pronounced—I remember a disquisition on *Benito Cereno* that lasted an eternity and put me in mind of the college classes I dozed through—but he was so good-naturedly self-deprecatory about his foibles that we all cut him plenty of slack. His employees invoked the word *genius* to describe him.

The sessions were more often useful. David vamped on story lines, and our task as writers was to flesh them out. That sounds simple, but he improvised so nimbly that the scene in question could rarely be improved. Even if you made it better— or thought you did—he'd hack away at your version and, with a few swift verbal strokes, take it to a higher level. To some extent this was a parlor trick, the result of long years at the craft, but I still found it frustrating and consoled myself with fantasies of locking him in a closet and not letting him out until he'd written a three-hundred-page book.

By my own lights, I believed I'd started to grasp the essence of screenwriting, a minimalist art compared to the kind of work I'd always done and one whose poetic component was signifi- cant, at least in Milch's hands. There was so much leaving out to be done, and so much left to the viewer's imagination. Nothing could be forced. You had to listen, breathe, relax, and let yourself be guided. I enjoyed a sensation of effortlessness when it went well, although that came, of course, only after lots of effort.

As we plunged ahead, Milch's relations with Michael Mann became more cordial, the tension no doubt leavened by HBO's strong support for the series. However belatedly delivered, the scripts were well received and studied with ardent interest. The directors Mann hired were impressed enough to stop by L.A. Farm to have lunch with David and explore the subtleties. Dustin Hoffman visited frequently, upbeat and unpretentious, meticulous about his lines, and Nick Nolte dropped off notes for his character, twenty or so single-spaced pages of scenes and suggestions Milch dutifully read and set aside.

In the absence of a meeting, he ate with us at a big central table in an atrium-like room with climbing vines and fire pits. Sometimes he was all business, but his mood could also be merry. In common with other former addicts, he harbored a rueful affection for his follies, awed that he'd managed to survive. His misadventures had receded far enough into the past to appear comic rather than self-destructive, but I wondered if his generosity and compassion might be a way of doing penance for any harm he might have caused.

At any rate, he had stories to tell. His days as a boozy Yale frat boy yielded some gems, although he was circumspect about George W. Bush, a classmate and fellow DKE, except to confide that he'd once been in a Texas duck blind with the Bushes and nearly shot George H. W. by accident. Had he talked with the former president recently? No, but Timmy Kissinger—Henry's son, another DKE—had contacted him a while ago and reported to David that George W. had recalled a number of Milchean escapades and concluded his account of each by saying, "And I barely escaped with my life."

Milch told stories about growing up in Buffalo, too, and how his father, the local mob's designated surgeon, regarded Christians as an exotic species. Elmer Milch wouldn't allow them into his house, but a goy playmate of David's once injured himself and required some patching up, so David broke the rules and rushed the kid inside. His dad made the necessary repairs and then proceeded to explain the arcana of Judaism to his befuddled patient. He'd hold up a fork and say, "This is a Jewish fork," before moving on to the knives and spoons.

Then lunch would be over, and I'd either step lightly or trudge back to the office, depending on the circumstances. If I had scenes to write, the hours flew by, but when we were in a holding pattern as Milch fumbled to discover where the story should go next, I endured the doldrums every writer ever hitched to Hollywood has bemoaned. In any event, David was exhausted by quitting time, rising woozily from the floor like a boxer from the canvas, hitching up his jeans, and heading for the Mercedes.

The writing took its toll, yet the labor was worth it. In the early spring, Mann sent us some DVDs of nearly completed episodes that lacked only a title sequence and credits. When I watched the first at home, I was unprepared for the emotional impact. A manuscript travels no great distance to reach the printed page, but *Luck* was evoked on a larger scale more vulnerable to human error. Against the odds, Milch's seed of an idea, planted in 2005, had blossomed into a work of art that amounted to more than the sum of its parts and stood in tribute to everyone involved.

A rising tide of expectation began to sweep through Redboard. The DVDs lent an actuality to what had been curiously spectral. Already we heard rumors about a second season, and maybe a third. The only sour note concerned a pair of horses who'd broken down during filming and had to be euthanized. The deaths were doubly upsetting because HBO had tried so hard to prevent such mishaps, adhering to a stringent four-page set of protocols the American Humane Society had devised to protect the animals.

The horses were forbidden from running on such widely prescribed drugs as Butazolidin, an anti-inflammatory, or Lasix, a medication for bleeders, and were tested at random to be sure they didn't. They submitted to physical and radiographic exams, and the vets had access to their full medical records. Still, as always, the deaths were haunting and symptomatic of the problems facing an industry whose attitude toward policing itself was lackadaisical at best.

Sadly, that was more true and damning than ever. Horses—primarily cheap ones—were breaking down at an unacceptably high rate around the country because trainers who were greedy or strapped for cash—or plain dishonest—entered their sore and injured stock in races. In many instances, the trainers were tempted by the money on offer. At tracks with a casino attached—"racinos"—the purses had grown fatter owing to the proceeds from slot machines and table games, so the incentive to cut corners and turn a blind eye had multiplied.

But nobody spoke of those issues at the wrap party Nick Nolte threw in Malibu. Fun was the order of the day. I'd just fished my first beer from an icy cooler when a jockey-size man in a broad-brimmed cowboy hat approached and piped up, "I'm in your book!" Sure enough, I located him later on page 8 of *Laughing in the Hills,* where I identified him as Jimmy Cuzick, an apprentice rider and fellow tenant at the Terrace Motel in Albany, California.

I'd spotted Cuzick strolling barefooted across the motel parking lot one afternoon. His mount, Spiced Falcon, had reared up in the starting gate, and Cuzick suffered a concussion and wore a patch over an eye. I'd hoped to talk with him about the accident, but he disappeared before I had a chance—racetrackers did that all the time, past masters at vanishing without any warning—and now, thirty-five or so years later, I'd caught up with him—Jamie, not Jimmy—in Nick Nolte's garden, a member of the *Luck* company who played Walter Smith's groom.

* * *

Another Hollywood lesson soon came my way. When the last script's finished, the writers are instantly laid off, and it's uncertain when or if they'll see another paycheck. Though I hadn't developed a "lifestyle," I still felt the pinch and tried to pin down Milch about what the future might hold, but that was futile. He can be an unreliable narrator. In his irrepressible urge to be kind, he's capable of telling people what they want to hear, even when it isn't in his power to make it happen.

"You'll be back to work in a month or so," he advised me.

Six months later, in October 2011, I finally did go back to work on *Luck*'s second season. The configuration at Redboard had changed again during our hiatus, with a new writer on staff—Waylon Green, an old pal of David's—as a coexecutive producer. Though Green's TV credits were extensive, stretching from *Hill Street Blues* to *Law & Order*, he was most famous as the author of *The Wild Bunch*. Amiable and ebullient, with a host of tales to tell, he seemed delighted with the job, reporting to the office just three days a week from his ranch near Santa Barbara.

Green was a favorite with the interns, who soaked up his yarns. At the drop of a hat, he had a story to match the moment, as in, "That reminds me of the time . . ." They were funny stories, too—a tequila-drinking contest in Mexico with the young Paul Newman, which Newman lost, or a catalogue of the pranks George Clooney had pulled on the set of *ER*. His anecdotes about the documentarian David L. Wolper, with whom he'd worked, were priceless. Imitating Wolper's high-pitched voice, he recounted how his old boss hated dialogue that measured more than "two fingers" on the page.

Green's assignment, we all assumed, was to speed up the delivery of scripts. Toward the end of the first season, with David worn out, the pace had slowed to a crawl, and at least one director had complained about not having enough time to prepare properly. So Waylon jumped right in and took charge, and Milch appeared to welcome his guidance and support. Green was almost as facile as the maestro, but he didn't bring the same emotional depth or psychological insight to the task, I thought. To be fair, few writers could match David in those categories.

In our first script for the second season, Green introduced a Russian oligarch into what I felt was a series already top-heavy with crime and criminals. For all I knew, he might've been heeding an HBO directive—adding more *Boardwalk Empire*-type material—but some of us feared that we'd stray too far afield from the track and the horses, and depart from *Luck*'s original premise. Yet we had no choice but to proceed and try to strike an acceptable balance. HBO wanted four scripts in hand before the filming started again in February.

Initially, Waylon seemed confident we'd meet the deadline. Even Milch bought into the fantasy, although he couldn't curb his habit of rewriting. He acted a little dispirited, not as energetic this time around, and no longer indulged in his loopy but entertaining lectures—no further mention of Herman Melville or Yale's Mr. Warren. Maybe the burden of writing ten new scripts, or roughly five hundred pages of text, weighed more heavily on him than we understood. "This doesn't get any easier," he once remarked after a grueling session.

He got more notes from various sources, too, and Michael Mann asserted more control, but he and Milch had difficulty finding common ground. Their goals as artists were at odds. Mann preferred fast-paced action, high drama, spectacular visuals, and conflict spelled out in capital letters—the very elements that had garnered his movies such praise. But he seemed to have no feel for nuance or ambiguity, or for the intricately wrought language and subtle grace that were the hallmark of David's best work. Mann's talent was operatic, while Milch dealt in chamber pieces.

In spite of the abundance of notes, David had scarcely rolled over. He stuck to his method and still roped us into idling for days on story lines he'd ultimately scuttle. He knew no other way to do it than by trial and error. Even with Green trying to ride herd, he'd veer off to improvise and come up with several tantalizing "what-ifs" that sent us off in a new direction. Here was the wellspring of his genius—an ability to conjure the miraculous from thin air—but genius pays no mind to the clock or the cost.

One afternoon, apropos of nothing, he decided he had to write a part—absolutely—for Joe Pesci, so he grabbed a phone and contacted Pesci's elderly attorney, who hadn't heard of David, *Luck,* or maybe even HBO. Milch and Waylon swapped some gossip about Pesci after the call—maybe not such an easygoing guy as Newman or Clooney—and raved about his gifts as an actor, after which Milch retired to his office with some pencils and a yellow legal tablet. Yet by week's end, Pesci had vanished as mysteriously as Jamie Cuzick from the Terrace Motel.

While we got lost on such sidetracks, HBO began to take the wraps off *Luck.* The pilot aired as a sneak preview after the last episode of *Boardwalk Empire,* but it failed to hold a significant portion of its lead-in audience. Undeterred, the network launched a massive publicity campaign before our official debut in January 2012. You'd have to live in Borneo not to hear about the show, and I often muttered to myself, "If any of my publishers had spent a fraction of HBO's budget promoting one of my books . . ."

In a relatively unprecedented move, HBO sent all nine episodes of *Luck* to the TV critics, acknowledging what we already knew—the show was a dense piece of dramaturgy that best revealed its charms and virtues over time. On balance, the reviews were quite good, with Milch's writing and Mann's camera work singled out for accolades. The only major dissenters were at the *New York Times* and *New Yorker*—the old "East Coast bias," somebody muttered, and perhaps that wasn't entirely wrongheaded.

Still, our mood was upbeat on the night of the premiere. It took place at Grauman's Chinese Theatre in Hollywood, no less, with a red carpet and a noisy gang of fans snapping cellphone photos of the stars. For the first time, I watched the pilot with strangers rather than friends or colleagues, and realized why some directors find such exposure so nerve-racking. Your carefully crafted work stands naked, and when a line falls flat or fails to get a laugh, you cringe inside. Is it your fault for being too cute or obscure, or is the audience just too dumb to grasp your intent?

From the reaction at the premiere, I suspected *Luck* wouldn't be a smash hit, at least not out of the gate. The crowd, though respectful, did not bubble over with enthusiasm, nor did the applause bring down the house. In an age of instant gratification, the show took a different tack and unfolded in the leisurely fashion of a many-layered novel. Milch never made it easy for his viewers. Instead, he introduced them to a shadowy, unfamiliar world, inviting them to set aside their preconceptions, tolerate a little discomfort, and trust that their forbearance would be rewarded.

Most viewers were unwilling to adapt, though, and the show did poorly in the ratings. Big stars or no, it was too challenging, esoteric, cerebral, or slow-moving—maybe all four—to attract the couch potatoes accustomed to a steady diet of predictable fare. Although the pilot scored higher in its Sunday slot than as a sneak preview, the Nielsens were still disappointing. But how could it be otherwise? In three of its first five weeks, *Luck* ran opposite the Super Bowl, the Golden Globes, and the Emmys, a trifecta of formidable blockbusters that always buried the competition. Surely HBO hadn't expected our series to buck the trend.

The lukewarm reception was still tough to swallow. In Milch's behavior, I recognized a syndrome I'd gone through myself upon publishing a book. After a spate of good reviews, you allow yourself to believe, however tentatively, you might have a hit on your hands—"cautiously optimistic," as the cliché goes—only to crash to earth when the reviews don't translate into commercial success. You're thrown into a tailspin and kick yourself for foolishly lowering your guard.

At the start of each week, David was anxious, on the phone to HBO to ask if the numbers had come in yet. There were hopeful moments—an uptick, say, that might signify a trend—but the following Sunday *Luck* would revert to form, and a gloom would descend on us again. Only with the last two episodes did the show hit its stride and begin to build an audience, but it was too late by then.

Though we'd finished only two of the four scripts HBO had requested, the cast and crew had already shot the first and were prepping for the second when a freak accident shut down the production. A horse from the *Luck* stable, being led along a path to the barns by a groom, got to feeling frisky, reared up, lost its balance, and landed on its head, injuring itself so severely it had to be put down. The groom was an experienced hand, and the horse hadn't been "performing," but the show was held accountable in certain quarters.

Within hours, TMZ and other blogs were reporting that *Luck* had "killed" another horse. The group called PETA—People for the Ethical Treatment of Animals—spread the disingenuous story, apparently happy to advance its own agenda at the expense of the facts. The story soon went viral, and even the mainstream media repeated it without bothering to investigate. It didn't help that the *New York Times* was about to print a stinging indictment of the racing industry's soft underbelly, either.

The sport was under attack, and HBO caught the backlash. Milch gathered his writers and, looking ashen, said flatly, "It's bad." He doubted the series could be saved. There was talk of using stock footage for the racing action, and of beefing up the crime angle even more, but those were improbable solutions to an insoluble problem. In spite of the AHA protocols, two horses had broken down, and—freak accident aside—no one could guarantee that a third wouldn't be injured while simulating a race before the cameras.

HBO had a valued brand to protect, of course, and the negative publicity hurt. David seemed resigned, but others in our camp were upset. The network had buckled without a fight, they argued. Our wranglers had done nothing wrong. Given the low ratings and the expense of *Luck,* one theory went, maybe HBO had seized on the accident as an excuse to cancel the show. I took that as sour grapes. The guessing game was academic, anyway. Two days after the horse's death we were all out of a job.

Everybody felt a little sick at heart about the cancellation, abused by fate and left with unfinished business. Whenever a film or a series wraps up and the curtain drops, there's a sense of loss, but it was heightened for us because the end came so abruptly. The greatest irony, and the one that rankled most, was that so many people on the *Luck* payroll loved horses, and not a few had given over their lives to caring for them.

Though I had legitimate credentials as a screenwriter now, I couldn't imagine churning out scripts on spec—the usual gambit for the newly unemployed—nor was I ready to look for another job. I doubted I could land one that suited me so well. As for Milch, I figured he'd be okay. He understood the vagaries of making art, and his devotion to the written word would keep him on an even keel. He was content on the floor of the writing room, and if a dog was close by, along with a couple of friends— for that's how David treated us—so much the better.

We never conducted a postmortem on *Luck,* but it scarcely mattered. The show belonged to the world, where its destiny would be decided. Someday an appreciative audience might rediscover it and celebrate its quality, although it might also wind up in the cabinet of curiosities reserved for those TV series too difficult for the medium. It made no difference, really, at least to me, since the pleasure resided in the work and the companion-ship, but if I were asked to place a bet on the outcome, I knew which horse I'd back.

*Narrative*, 2013

# Writers and the Movies: Joseph Mitchell

Why bother to make a movie about a writer's life? It's a fair question to ask. You'd be hard put to find a less dramatic profession, after all, unless you're talking in psychological terms, and the thrills can be few and far between. There are exceptions to the rule, of course. Lord Byron would light up the silver screen, leading the Greek insurgents while he recites heroic couplets and rattles a saber or two, but most authors are not as swashbuckling. Instead, they tend to be solitary when they're working and depressed when they aren't, and this, quite obviously, is not the stuff of Hollywood legend.

Still, the genre refuses to die, and every couple of years we're treated to a new literary biopic. The most recent is Stanley Tucci's *Joe Gould's Secret*, based on the work of Joseph Mitchell, one of the best and most self-effacing writers the *New Yorker* ever produced. Mitchell, in and of himself, would be a non-starter in the cinematic stakes, except that he became embroiled with Joe Gould, an extraordinary Greenwich Village character who considered himself the last of the bohemians and survived on donations from friends and strangers (the "Joe Gould Fund," to which Mitchell contributed, along with such stalwarts as e.e. cummings), while he purportedly labored on his epic narrative, *An Oral History of Our Time*. When Mitchell wrote his profile, in 1942, Gould's manuscript was already 12 times as long as the Bible (or so its author claimed), all of it scribbled in dozens of composition notebooks hidden in secure places around New York.

The profile, "Professor Sea Gull," is Mitchell's first piece on Joe Gould. He viewed his subject as an eccentric night creature, who wandered the city like the Ancient Mariner, asking for spare change, performing Indian dances at parties, and imitating a sea gull. (As a boy, Gould spent summers in Nova Scotia and kept a gull as a pet. He swore he understood the language of gulls and even translated poems into it. Longfellow's "Hiawatha" was a perfect fit, he insisted.) A chronic complainer, Gould suffered from the three H's—homelessness, hunger, and hangovers. Toothless, dirty, and exasperating, he lived on pots of cowboy coffee and heaping plates of ketchup ("the only grub I know of that's free of charge"). His tale is told in witty, beautifully cadenced prose, but when you read it, you feel that an element is missing.

It could be that Mitchell felt that way, too, because 22 years later he chose to tell the Gould story again. This time, he wasn't merely an observer; he included himself in the tale. As it happens, *Professor Sea Gull* proved to be a big hit with readers, and they sent Gould money and letters of support. In turn, Gould began using the *New Yorker* as his mailing address and frequently dropped in on Mitchell without so much as knocking. In the second version of their relationship, Gould isn't so charming and funny; instead, he's desperate and at times despicable, but he's also more human, and his plight is more touching. We learn that he does have real talent and was once praised by Ezra Pound. But his grandiosity and his airs are impossible, and Mitchell explodes and accuses him of being a fake. "There is no Oral History," Mitchell shouts. The grand project amounts to nothing more than a few notebooks, in which Gould obsessively repeats the same three or four themes.

"It exists in your mind, I guess," Mitchell says, "but you've always been too lazy to write it down."

Gould replies, in a low, indistinct voice, "It's not a question of laziness," before he turns his back and leaves.

The outburst provokes Mitchell's finest hour. As he calms down, he's ashamed of himself for pouncing on Gould. He recalls a time when he went around writing a novel in his head, one that never made it to paper, a Joycean saga he believed in so strongly that he could see it as a finished book, bound in green cloth and stamped with gold lettering—every would-be author's daydream, perhaps. "The recollections filled me with unbearable embarrassment," he writes, "and I began to feel more and more sympathetic to Gould." What if Gould had actually written the Oral History? The thought leads Mitchell to a key passage.

"It probably wouldn't have been the great book he had gone up and down the highways and byways prophesying it would be at all—great books, even halfway great books, even good books, even halfway good books being so exceedingly rare. When I thought of the cataract of books, the Niagaras of books, the rushing rivers of books, the oceans of books, the tons and truckloads and trainloads of books that were pouring off the presses of the world at that moment, only a very few of which would be worth picking up and looking at, let alone reading, I began to feel that it was admirable that he hadn't written it. One less book to clutter up the world, one less book to take up space and go unread."

So Gould, in the end, acquires a certain nobility for not having written a bad book. It's his secret that the Oral History doesn't amount to a hill of beans, but many of his cohorts and contributors still cling to the myth, as Mitchell once did; and when Gould died in a Long Island mental hospital, in 1957, they launched a search for the buried treasure. The search continued until Mitchell set the record straight in 1964, with *Joe Gould's Secret*. It would be among his last pieces of published writing and a fitting cap to his career, rich in metaphors about both the creative process and the human comedy.

Hollywood first approached Mitchell in the person of Michael Lieber, an L.A. producer, who caught a mention of the profile in the *New Yorker* and tracked down a copy. He tried to acquire the film rights in the late 1980s, but Mitchell politely declined to sell. Lieber pursued him for six years until Mitchell consented. Howard Rodman, a screenwriter, adapted the story, and Lieber shopped the script to directors. In his opinion, Stanley Tucci was an ideal candidate. Tucci's movie *Big Night* had the warmth, comedy, and intelligence of a Mitchell piece, plus he'd demonstrated his affinity for literary properties as an actor, too, with roles in *Billy Bathgate*, *Slaves of New York*, *A Midsummer's Night Dream*, and *Winchell*. If anybody could be trusted to faithfully convey Mitchell's vision, the production team thought, it might well be Tucci.

There are conventions to the genre, I soon discovered. The writer usually smokes, mostly cigarettes but sometimes a pipe if the part involves superior intelligence. It goes without saying that writers drink in movies, frequently to the point of total daffiness. They prefer hard liquor and knock it back straight from the bottle or flask when they're under stress. In addition, they have someone special in their corner, who makes their intolerable burden tolerable—a spouse, lover, friend or editor whose wisdom and sacrifice keep the furies at bay. And for some unfathomable reason, many writers in movies live or spend time by the ocean. Inspiration? Heavy doses of oxygen? Your guess is as good as mine.

I decided to watch a number of these movies in chronological order, beginning with *Beloved Infidel* (1959). The film is based on Shelia Graham's memoir of her affair with F. Scott Fitzgerald (the infidel, I assume, although he never utters a blasphemous word) while he was writing scripts in L.A. and hoping to get started on a novel about Hollywood. As played by Deborah Kerr, Sheila is a peppy, ambitious, pushy Brit devoted to celebrity gossip. (In the remake, you'd cast Tina Brown.) She meets Scott at a dinner party, and the sparks fly when they hit the dance floor to the tune of "Blue Moon." For all his boozing, Scott (in the person of Gregory Peck) still looks flawless. Even when he falls off the wagon later on, his only messiness involves a wayward lock of hair that slips down his forehead. "Stop, you're making me blush!" Sheila cries.

Scott may be flawless, but he's in trouble. He's been having a rough stay in Tinseltown, with four failed screenplays behind him and the studio chiefs trashing his elegant prose style. "We can't film adjectives," they tell him. But the saintly Sheila (it's her memoir, after all) is there to help, and she steps in as his lover/muse and sets herself the task of nursing him back to literary health. It won't be easy, because Scott is fragile and has his black moods. His books are out of favor, and he believes he's a forgotten man. In an early scene, he and Sheila, traveling incognito, drop in at a bookstore and ask the owner if there's any Fitzgerald in stock.

The owner, though kindly, is not encouraging. "Who reads good novels today?" he asks, unafraid to go after the big philosophical questions. "Now it's politics, yoga, cookbooks. Why, I've got a beautiful set of Balzac out back that the mice are enjoying!"

You can see what Scott's up against. His only ally is Sheila, and she urges him to ignore the studio and work on *The Last Tycoon*. She salts him away in her Malibu pad, where he smokes cigarettes by the ocean and writes in longhand on a sunny terrace. When he has four chapters done, he sends them to his agent back east to submit to magazines, but he's rejected everywhere, and it launches him on an epic bender. He pals around with some drunken swabbies, slaps Sheila, pulls a pistol on her and, in general, burns all his bridges. After some major apologies, Sheila agrees to forgive the old infidel, and Scott redoubles his efforts, but he dies of a heart attack before the novel's done. The End, as they say.

There isn't much in the film that's terribly unreliable, except perhaps the flattering portrait of Sheila Graham, but for a supposed tragedy, *Beloved Infidel* is remarkably untragic. Fitzgerald's soul-destroying despair is glossed over with a light touch. The movie shows an exceptional distance from its ostensible subject, and that's too bad since Henry King, the director, made some decent pictures. (In fact, his *Jesse James* offers a seminal moment in American cinema, in a scene where the James brothers are being pursued on horseback after robbing a bank. They escape by throwing stolen dollars at the posse behind them until the riders dismount and pick up the loot.) But King was probably tired by the time he took on Fitzgerald, since he started as a director in 1915. It was his next-to-last film; his last was *Tender is the Night.*

*Julia* (1977) is drawn from an autobiographical essay in Lillian Hellman's *Pentimento*, and it traces her development as a playwright, among other things. Hellman (Jane Fonda) is in a house on the beach as the movie opens, wearing a ratty bathrobe, typing, smoking and drinking whiskey neat. (Indeed, she sets a record for the most cigarettes inhaled in a single picture, managing to puff away even as she eats a sandwich.) Clearly, she's struggling, so when her lover/muse Dashiell Hammett (Jason Robards) returns home with a bucket of clams, she rushes out to meet him. But Dash is no Sheila Graham. He's tough and crusty. He's written novels himself, and he's not about to go easy on Lily just because she's young, pretty and worships the ground he walks on.

Her first words? "It's not working again, Dash. Falling apart again."

Guys love to hear that after a day of digging clams. "Put on your sweater," Hammett says wearily. "Drink some whiskey. I'll build a fire, and we'll start dinner. Don't forget the smokes."

"I'm not here to take orders. I want advice," Hellman shouts, but there's no response. "You're not a general habit, and I ain't the troops!"

Cut to a bonfire on the beach. They're both drinking whiskey now, and they should be nice and mellow, but Lily can't leave it alone. She's like a broken record. "I'm in trouble with my goddamned play," she says again, "and you don't care."

Dash is smashed, but he's a silly sort of drunk. No Scott-type violence here. "If you really can't write, maybe you can get a job," he tells her. "Be a waitress or a fireman. You could be a chief. It's not a bad idea, you know?"

Hammett belongs to the Joseph Mitchell school of lit crit—i.e., we don't need another crummy book—but his teasing only goads Lily to persevere. She smokes, strolls by the ocean and drinks more whiskey until she completes a first draft. Dash reads it right away. "You wanted to be a serious writer," he says, sober now and looking very Land's End. "That's what I like, that's what we work for. I don't know what happened, but you better tear this up." Long, solemn pause. "Not that it's bad, it's just not good enough." Long, solemn pause. "Not for you."

Tough love! But his criticism only goads Hellman, and so on. Of her second draft, Dash says, "It's the best play anyone's written in a long time."

"But are you sure?" Lily asks. She's sitting in the sand by the ocean.

"I'm positive."

And that's it. Enter fame and fortune from stage left. Soon Lillian Hellman is rich and a celebrity. Her play is on Broadway, and she brags about her skills as a fisherperson. Julia is a celebration of hard work, pluck and solid mentoring, with a tip of the hat to Dash Hammett, the Vince Lombardi of literary coaches, but at least it offers some action when Lily goes abroad and helps out in the battle against fascism.

There isn't much action in *Tom & Viv* (1994), alas. It's difficult to imagine the pitch for this vehicle. "T.S. Eliot is, like, a tortured soul. He's a Yank at Oxford studying with Bertrand Russell, who's a great dancer." The snooze factor sets in early, just as it does in the movie. Eliot (Willem Dafoe) proposes, more or less, to the wacky Vivienne (Miranda Richardson) in the first 15 minutes. "I never want to see the States again," he says, almost vibrating. "I want to live in Europe and write poetry. I love you. I love you more than life itself." Viv replies, "Oh, dear." But they marry, anyway, and spend a dismal honeymoon night in a seaside hotel, where Viv comes undone. While Tom walks on the beach and into the ocean, she drugs herself and tears apart the room. For a few tense seconds, it seems possible that her head might spin around, as Linda Blair's did in *The Exorcist*.

I figured the movie had to improve, but I was wrong. Momentarily, we're at a dance, and we see Eliot's eyes glaze over. He's in a creative trance and must get to a typewriter immediately, so he repairs to their flat and sits at a table before the keyboard, holding his head and groaning. Viv appears with a bowl of water and applies a compress to the back of his neck. "I never know when it's going to strike," T.S. complains, as if poetry hurt like a migraine.

"You write best when you're sick," Viv counsels him. "You make yourself sick, you know you do."

"Poetry is in my skin," Eliot says.

That was the last scene I could bear to watch before turning to the final movies, *Mrs. Parker* and the *Vicious Circle* (1994), whose director Alan Rudolph has often displayed a literary flare. The story centers on Dorothy Parker and her writer pals at the *New Yorker*, when the magazine was in its infancy and the fabled Round Table was in full swing at the Algonquin Hotel. Although Rudolph doesn't avoid all the traps—he gives us plenty of smoking, drinking, typewriters and even fornicating—he also supplies some true feeling, an element absent from the other films. In the lead role, Jennifer Jason Leigh's accent wanders all over the map, but her performance is still moving, because Parker is aware of her dilemma and unable to escape it.

She's a prisoner of the self she invented. People expect Dorothy Parker to be clever and biting, so she is always on. She and Robert Benchley, her friend/muse/unrequited lover, never say anything that isn't terribly snappy, nor do her chums at the Round Table. At first, the one-liners and the patter are funny ("Eddie," Dotty chides her husband, a first class drug and alcohol abuser, "you don't want to become the town drunk. Not in Manhattan."), but they never stop, and soon you have the sinking sensation that you're stuck at an endless cocktail party. Both Parker and Benchley wind up in Hollywood, where Benchley drinks himself to death and Dotty knits a sweater on the set of a picture she's written, paying no attention to the dialogue.

To her credit, Leigh looks awful at the close, puffy-faced from the booze and wobbly on her legs. There's a devastating scene on the studio lot, where an eager young gofer falls into step with her and gushes, "So many famous writers are from the Algonquin Round Table!" Famous, maybe, but not great, and Dotty knows the difference. She brushes him off by saying, "Ah, but no real giants. No Mermaid Tavern," and you feel the weight of a life gone out of control, along with its emptiness. The final moments find Parker alone at a hotel bar, where another young admirer stops at her booth and asks if he can buy her a drink. Sure, he can. The actor is Stanley Tucci.

Hollywood movies must entertain a mass audience, of course, so we may never get a picture that's sensitive to all the nuances of the writing life, but I'm still eager to see how Tucci fares with *Joe Gould's Secret*. Tucci himself plays Joseph Mitchell, while Ian Holm, who was also in *Big Night*, has the plum role of Joe Gould and the opportunity to be far more wacky than Miranda Richardson. There are cameos by Susan Sarandon as a painter, and Steve Martin as a publisher who tries to pry the non-existent Oral History out of Gould. The film had its premiere at Sundance, where it received generally favorable reviews. "The appeal of the story and milieu to sophisticated audiences suggest an OK box-office future in specialized markets," as *Variety* inimitably put it.

Will the movie explain why Joseph Mitchell, who died in 1996, quit publishing in the 1960s, except for some unsigned

"Talk of the Town" pieces? I wonder. Over the years, I'd heard many rumors to account for it—he was blocked, he had nothing more to say, even that the *New Yorker* no longer wanted to publish him—so I decided to check with one of his former editors. Mitchell still came to the office regularly, almost till the end of his life, the editor said, and worked on a long story about growing up in the South, but the story kept shifting its shape and gave him lots of trouble. His writing was so precise and lapidary that he had little margin for error. No final draft ever emerged, but Mitchell did leave behind some manuscripts, although it was as yet "unclear" if any of them would appear in print. Shades of Joe Gould?

*San Francisco Chronicle Magazine*, 2000

# Two Tales of Nigeria

**One Pound Sterling**

I'd only been at St. Andrew's College, Nnewi, for a few weeks when Paul Monike, my Nigerian friend, came down with a fever he couldn't shake. At first he suspected malaria, but when a dose of quinine failed to cure him, he changed his mind and blamed the lover he'd been seeing on the sly. She practiced juju, he told me, and there were any number of ways she could have made him sick, all to punish him for his refusal to marry her. But marriage was impossible, really. She lived on her family's yam farm, while Paul held an important post as a teacher of English. He couldn't yield to her wishes, any more than she could give up on her dream.

I held the same post as Paul, although I valued it a little less, partly because of G. B. Okoye, our headmaster. Okoye was a blustery type, loud and aggressive, who banged the ground with his walking stick and barked out orders. He considered himself an *oga*, or a man of power, and went to absurd lengths to prove it, driving his luxury Mercedes through the village at maniacal speeds. Paul couldn't help making fun of him. It was only a matter of time, he predicted, until Okoye crashed into a herd of the scrawny cattle that Fulani nomads, barefoot and in rags, guided to our abattoir.

"Principal will kill a cow," Paul said gleefully. "It will be a big, big incident."

Okoye could never pronounce my name correctly, so he quit trying and addressed me as "Peace Corps." If he was in a hurry, it sounded more like "Piss Cups." He enjoyed having me on staff because a young volunteer from America, however unskilled and naive, amounted to a status symbol, but he coped poorly with my actual needs. I'd been promised a house, for instance, but it wasn't finished when I arrived. The builders were holding out for a bribe, so for the moment I'd have to live in a toolshed. Okoye asked a servant to clear out the rusty spades and hoes, sweep away the cobwebs, and carry in a cot.

The shed was an agreeably spartan space. It gave me a curious sense of mission. The students were away on a midterm break, so I had ample time to write shocking letters to my parents about the deprivations I'd already endured. At night I sat up late with my shortwave radio and listened to ball games on the Armed Services Network, or read books until the college's generator shut down at ten, pitching us into a darkness so utter and complete I liked to step outside to admire it. Countless stars burned with an extravagant intensity against a black canopy of sky, and every noise was magnified—the buzz and click of insects, a bird's shrill cry.

St. Andrew's was an Anglican school. It used to employ a few Brits, but I was Nnewi's only white person now, so I merited a visit from anybody bold enough to come to my door. First was our local reverend, who wore an ill-fitting clerical collar and a threadbare suit coat. He had beady little eyes, vast enthusiasm for the gospel, and his own sense of mission. To my horror, he viewed me as a potential convert and grilled me about the nature of my faith, if any. When I mentioned this to Paul, he grunted and said, "That reverend is a fool."

I met next with an officer from the Benevolent Potters Guild, who asked for a small donation. When a Rosicrucian, too shy to knock, left some pamphlets by the shed, I boned up on the Knights Templar. Another well-wisher warned me not to sleep on the floor, because the concrete would suck the blood from my body. Word got around that I was from New York, so I had to verify the existence of snow and skyscrapers. A fan of Jim Reeves, the country singer, whose music was weirdly popular, valued for its syrupy sentiment, offered condolences on Reeves's recent death in a plane crash.

One day Okoye surprised me by taking an active interest in my welfare. He thought I might be lonely, so he forced Paul Monike to give me a tour. Paul didn't exactly jump for joy. I must have looked ridiculous in my button-down shirt and khakis, a poster boy for the ideals I was supposed to represent and only half believed in. Paul was in his early twenties, too, sharp and funny, with very dark skin and a broad nose that flared when he was angry. His voice boomed, echoing from a barrel chest. Though he never exercised, he was as fit as a middleweight contender, all muscle and no fat. I felt physically diminished in his presence.

"Come, come, make we go," he said, annoyed at the inconvenience. He led me across a soccer field and introduced me to the college's open-air classroom buildings. They were made of ocher-colored mudbrick and had corrugated tin roofs that drummed with a metallic splendor during a subtropical downpour, each drop of rain nearly as big as a dime. There were no doors or windows, so braying goats and squawking chickens wandered in, while lizards did push-ups on the ledges. Such challenges would test my ability as a teacher severely.

We walked to the village, just a stone's throw away. Nnewi had assembled itself in a haphazard fashion along a highway to Onitsha, the busiest market city in West Africa. The traffic was heavy, and accidents were common. A week seldom went by without a mammy wagon tipping over and spilling its passengers and cargo onto the roadside. I did many unwise things in Nigeria, but I never risked a ride in a mammy wagon. The prayerful mottoes painted on them were enough to scare me off—"Only God Knows For Sure," say, or simply, "Amen." Instead I traveled by Peugeot 404 station wagon, the elite form of transport, whose drivers were regarded as outlaws, both envied and feared.

I followed Paul into our own little market. It had a ramshackle glory, hammered together from plywood and bits of tin. The linked stalls resembled a shantytown born of ingenuity rather than advance planning. Vendors hawked their wares with a brassy exuberance, yelling to be heard above the traffic din and the highlife music blaring from transistors. It was all noise and color, and I loved it. Women balanced trays of oranges and bananas on their heads, and also buckets of water. Infants they strapped to their backs or their bosoms in a hammock of cloth, stepping around the sprawl of beggars afflicted with a crippled limb or some other deformity, each with a hat or a raffia basket for coins.

My notoriety had preceded me, of course. The traders were friendly but teasing, and they laughed appreciatively at the sight of me and called, "*Onye ocha, kedu*," or "One who is white, how are you?" If I replied with my few words of Igbo, "*O di mma*," or "I am fine," they howled. It was as if a stump had spoken, some emissary from the spirit world. The children asked to touch my skin and my blond hair, gathering in giggly groups to plead for some spare change, so I fished out some pennies. Known as coppers, they had a hole in the middle, and when I pressed one to a child's forehead, it stuck there like magic.

Paul rescued me. He shooed the children away, swinging an arm wide, but they only giggled some more. I was out of pennies, anyway. There weren't enough coppers in all of Nigeria to satisfy everybody who wanted them. We moved through the crowd and along the edge of a foul-smelling ditch piled with rotten fruit, trash, and excrement, all floating in an inch of murky water. High above, I noticed some vultures wheeling, a sign that more cattle had arrived at the abattoir. The cattle looked sick when they got to the village, their hides slack and their ribs visible as the relentless herdsmen, circled by flies, flicked at them with switches.

Paul stopped at a neat, orderly shop. A youth in his late teens ran it, and I was struck by his open face, lightly marked with tribal scars, and his gentle manner. Edwin seemed glad to welcome me, yet sophisticated enough not to make a fuss. His family must have owned the shop, but I never saw anybody else on duty. There was no need. Edwin was conscientious and meticulous, a born merchant. He didn't haggle over prices and could tot up a bill in seconds. Some traders inveigled their customers, while others were downright crooks, but Edwin never cheated. He had honor in his favor.

He set up a table and chairs for us, then brought out plastic tumblers and a quart bottle of ice-cold Star beer. In the heat and humidity, I was as thirsty as I'd ever been and drank the first glass almost at a gulp while Paul told me about himself. He came from a village nearby and had hoped to go to university, but he couldn't afford the fees and had settled for a lesser degree. He was content at St. Andrew's, he said. There were eight tutors in all, and only one was a fool. You could eat well at Nnewi, and Onitsha had good nightclubs. For some reason, he chose to trust me and talked about his lover, already a source of distress. "Top secret," he confided, glancing over a shoulder.

For my part, I confessed how nervous I was about teaching. I had no experience, but Paul thought the students, who were grown men, would be kind and tolerate me as a novelty act, or words to that effect. I was also anxious about the state of the country. Just before I arrived, a band of soldiers, whose leaders were mostly Igbo, had seized control of the government in a coup d'état, the bloodiest in West African history. Paul approved of the coup, if not the violence, but he worried that there would be reprisals. I'd been assured by Peace Corps officials that Nigeria was stable again, but I didn't believe it. Anyone with an ear to the ground, even a newcomer such as me, could hear the rumble of distant thunder.

I hadn't eaten since breakfast, so Paul ordered a plate of barbecued chicken cooked over a wood fire. The skin was crisp, charred, and delicious. I took a leg and greedily chewed the meat, while Paul did the same and then broke open the bone to suck out the marrow. In the midst of the feast, I felt a sudden need to pee. The beer had done its work, so I turned to Paul for advice, but he merely nodded toward the ditch we'd passed. This was my baptism by fire. Gritting my teeth, I unzipped my fly. I expected the traders to howl again, but they ignored me completely. In an instant I'd become that estimable thing, a natural man.

* * *

The builders, properly bribed, returned at last to finish my house. They were a vagabond crew in mismatched clothes that they'd snatched up at the market, where the contents of Care packages were routinely pilfered and sold. How else to account for a painter in a Michigan State T-shirt, or a carpenter in tattered Levis and a Cleveland Indians cap? All the street-savvy dudes affected this warped version of hipster style, and if their top clashed with their trousers, so much the better. Loud colors they also embraced, Day-Glo orange and candy-apple red.

The romance of the toolshed had faded, so I was thrilled to move in. Okoye had even splurged on a real bed for me, plus a mosquito net, a pair of armchairs with foam cushions in a floral print, and a two-burner propane stove. For fear of explosions, I installed the stove outside, near the shack that enclosed my one-hole latrine and cold-water shower. The latrine put me off at first, because I'd heard about a volunteer who sat down one morning and found a snake coiled in the muck below, hissing and flashing its tongue. It would be tragic to die in Nigeria from a snakebite on the ass, I thought, but in time I conquered my phobia and the constipation that went with it.

The house, H-shaped, had two small rooms on both sides of a common parlor. It was meant to be shared, Okoye told me—another surprise—but I protested when he suggested our geography tutor, who was also single, as my roommate. The geographer was a decent fellow, but he bored me stiff with his recitation of longitudes and latitudes. As a devout member of the reverend's flock, he did a fair bit of Bible-thumping, too, and never touched any alcohol. That was more than I could bear, so I lobbied instead for Paul Monike, who pleased me by accepting.

I slept well that first night in the new house. My net foiled the mosquitoes that had swarmed over me in the shed, and when I woke I could feel the cool concrete all around me, a welcome relief from the heat outside. Children passed by on their way to the primary school next door, carrying their books on their heads. Their uniforms were immaculate, washed and ironed almost daily. I could read the pride in each sharp crease. At the college chapel, the students sang hymns, an informal choir of 120 strong, and the words to such sturdy anthems as "That Old Rugged Cross" drifted toward me on a current of glad tidings.

The oil palm bush was another comfort. It seemed to enclose and protect the house, a living, breathing entity, its mysteries manifold. I understood why people believed the spirits of the dead congregated there. The oil palms, scrappy rather than stately, created a lush green barrier against the hubbub of the market and the village. Sometimes a voice would greet me from the crown of a palm, and I'd wave to a tapper extracting the juice to make palm wine. The wine could be very good when it was fresh and unadulterated, but if any water had been added, it not only cured constipation but could lead to a case of dysentery, at least for foreigners.

Paul and I got along well. The house, with its separate wings, allowed ample space for privacy. I never interfered in his affairs, and he didn't meddle in mine. If I heard his motor scooter start up after dark, I knew he'd gone to visit his lover in the bush, but I never brought it up. That was his business. I'd met the woman just once, and then by chance on a path, and I thought she was quite beautiful. She made me more aware than ever of my isolation. I was capable of feeling very sorry for myself in that department. I had no woman at all, not even an Onitsha bar girl, but I tried not to dwell on it and concentrated on my work instead.

The teaching left me exhausted. I felt like a poser in front of my students, who were older and more qualified than me. Some men had begun as teachers when they were just twelve years old. As the cleverest boys in tiny hamlets, they'd been sent to a city for their primary education, then returned home to open a school. Now they were doing a two-year course to improve their credentials and their pay rate. They were still hungry for education. They excelled at debate, leaping to their feet to praise a canny verbal thrust by crying, "Point!" Proud of their penmanship, they composed their essays in an elegant nineteenth-century hand. Rather than stick a pencil behind an ear, they planted it in their hair.

The classes gave me headaches until I realized I could do no good in Nigeria. My best hope was to do no harm, and once I recognized that, the teaching became easier. I saw myself as a sort of anti–Peace Corps volunteer, who belonged to a different organization, less arrogant and officious. The organization had some other members, too, guys who also subscribed to the "no harm" scheme. We kept in touch by mail and visited one another whenever we could, crisscrossing the country in 404s, although hardly anyone traveled to Nnewi. There was nothing to do except drink beer at Edwin's, or next to the pumps at the Total gas station, where the owner handed out free ball caps to white folks.

On the rare occasions when I had a visitor, I'd invite Paul to join us. He enjoyed the company, but he seldom stayed for more than a drink or two. He could be slippery like that, interested in Americans but not overly so. In the same way, he struck a careful balance between the rigors of his job and the delights of his sneaky affair. He also bounced between a modern view of the world and a belief in the supernatural that was deeply rooted in Igbo culture. For the Igbo, a god called *chukwu*, neither male nor female, was the supreme being, but that belief hadn't prevented most people from adopting Christianity, as well, when the missionaries arrived.

Christianity aside, I knew many Igbos who spurned the church in a time of doubt or travail and looked elsewhere for salvation. That was true of Paul when his fever began. He didn't take it seriously at first, because fevers were so common. When the dry harmattan winds blew down from the Sahara and almost buried us in fine dust, nearly everyone contracted a cold or the flu. My students hated the chill and dressed as if for winter in sweaters and jackets. Their throats were sore, they coughed and shivered, and they swallowed penicillin by the fistful. The dust was inescapable. It filtered past your lips and into your mouth. It flew into your nostrils, unless you covered your face with a handkerchief or a scarf.

When the fever persisted, Paul took his dose of quinine, but it had no impact, so he threw away the tablets. Though I urged him to go to the village clinic, he refused. I couldn't understand his stubbornness. He was suffering, and the suffering looked worse because of his superb physical condition. I never expected to see him stretched out bare chested on the couch, moaning and groaning, with a wet washcloth on his forehead. I absolutely never expected to find him staring at the ceiling for hours. He was morose and spoke not a word to me. When I tried to draw him out, he just brushed me aside.

"That woman," he muttered at last. "She has done it to me. I am finished."

The end of the affair, I assumed. He must be grieving. It was a normal kind of suffering, one I'd gone through myself. His lover must've dumped him, yet when I offered my sympathy, he got angry with me. This was no garden-variety fever, he insisted. He was the victim of juju. The woman must have spiked his food, or rubbed a potion on his lips as he slept. His strength was ebbing fast, and he needed to be cured. His attitude baffled me. He was an intelligent man and a college graduate, so I accused him of behaving like a child. We were both young and invested in certainties. Paul would no more dignify my version of reality than I'd bend to his.

"You don't know," he said wearily.

"Yes, I do. I do know."

"You don't know."

There was an Igbo word for the person Paul wished to consult, but I've forgotten it and, besides, I referred to the person in question as a "witch doctor" for the sake of argument. The arguing had a salutary effect on the patient, who rose from the couch to pace and waggle a finger in my face. An oracle was involved, he warned me, and that was no small thing. Insults hurled by accident could reemerge from the turmoil of existence to bite me on the ass, just like the snakes I feared. If I wanted to witness the cure, I could come along. I'd see the evidence, the hard proof that my youthful certainty demanded. He'd even wager on the positive outcome.

"One pound sterling."

I shook his hand. "Agreed. One pound sterling."

* * *

The next afternoon, I hopped onto the back of Paul's scooter. We were headed for the remote bush, a territory I'd never explored.

I imagined the vegetation would be dense and tangled, but I saw clearings and compounds everywhere, all connected by rutted dirt roads. There were farms where yams, corn, and cassava grew. We passed ancient, tattered men, who pushed heavy wooden carts laden with calabashes. They only moved a few paces before they stopped to rest. Their struggle was eternal, a ceaseless labor beyond the finite borders of time. Old women sat outside mud-brick huts with thatched roofs, naked to the waist, their breasts flat and sagging, as if an army of infants had sucked them dry.

Through the vivid splendor of the bush we rode until we reached the doctor's compound. Its size hinted at his prominence, even as the mudbrick walls, inlaid with shards of broken glass to scare off thieves, implied that there were valuables inside worth stealing. I brushed the dust from my clothes and tried to act nonchalant and inconspicuous, but again I drew a crowd. That irritated Paul. He was sick and sweaty, so he gruffly accosted a little girl and fired several rapid questions at her in Igbo, eager to hasten the consultation.

The girl escorted us to a hut by a grand house. A bolt of cloth hung over the doorway, and when the girl clapped her hands, the doctor ambled out. His mood was genial and cordial, due to the bottle of Spanish brandy that he gripped by its neck. He was a fleshy man in a flowing robe, big-jowled and stout of belly, and he wore an embroidered cap and had a leathery face dominated by a bloodshot eye, indelibly crimson. It glowed like a beacon. He seemed determined to hug me, so I let him. He smelled of tobacco and aftershave. It was as if I'd been gathered in by an entire continent.

The doctor spoke no English, but he talked to me nonstop. "America," he said merrily, and patted me on the head. I did my best to reply, concerned that he'd lose patience if I didn't and put a curse on me. After another titanic hug, he ushered us into the hut, a cluttered space adorned with the skulls and bones of small animals—monkeys, maybe, and porcupines. The air was hot and thick and fetid. I'd anticipated a spookier scene because of all the mumbo jumbo in Hollywood movies about Africa, but our host, apart from being fairly drunk, was a total professional. I thought he might require the brandy to attain an exalted state of mind. I could scarcely be critical, since I turned into a seer myself if I drank too many Stars.

He sat at a battered desk and gestured for Paul to sit opposite him, near a table where a blood-stained sheet covered a mound of something. When Paul produced a wad of money, he became even jollier. "Toast!" he shouted, pouring us each a large measure. We clinked glasses, and the doctor picked up an elephant-hair fan, the kind chiefs carried as a symbol of office. When he waved it, the air turned marginally cooler. He touched Paul's forehead next, and his eyes rolled back in his head. This happened so fast, and with such theatrical flare, I was convinced he'd had a seizure. I almost leapt to his assistance, but I decided to wait.

That was the right thing to do. He soon recovered. His eyes opened, and the bloodshot one glowed more brilliantly than ever.

The doctor seemed to be in a trance and stumbled to the table and put his hands beneath the sheet. The hut filled with an eerie sound of metal against metal, a muted screech. He might have been rubbing tin cans together, or scraps of tin. This was the oracle, Paul whispered. I listened to the screech until it stopped abruptly, and the oracle uttered some sentences in Igbo. I had no idea what was said, but the voice was so high-pitched and ethereal it might have belonged to a will-o'-the-wisp. I could barely hear it.

Paul sat transfixed, while I watched the doctor. His lips moved ever so slightly. I felt certain that he was a ventriloquist—another certainty. There was no other rational explanation, but I failed to understand I'd left the rational world behind. Perhaps the oracle had contacted an ancestor of Paul's, or perhaps an appeal had been made to a minor deity in charge of feverish lovers, but I couldn't tell. The doctor appeared to be drained, at any rate, and needed a belt of brandy before he could inhabit his mortal form again. From a row of apothecary jars, he mixed a remedy of herbs and powdered roots for Paul. He was very happy now and polished off the bottle.

I said nothing to Paul on the ride home. I was stumped about what to say, in fact. I believed the doctor was a sham, albeit a marvelously contrived one and well worth the price of admission, particularly if you factored in the free drinks, but I saw no reason to spoil it for my friend. He was overjoyed with the meeting. He already looked healthier and more robust, and promised never to see the woman again. He had the survivor's tic of making resolutions, every day a new beginning and so on. Our adventure should have ended there, except for the wager. Paul wanted to collect his money, adamant that he'd won.

He sang the doctor's praises and made the mistake of asking my opinion. I made the mistake of answering. The doctor was a terrific performer, I said, but he was a phony. He relied on trickery. When Paul bridled, I got a dictionary and showed him the definition of a ventriloquist—"an entertainer whose voice seems to come from a dummy or an animal." This was a setback for him. He was familiar with the concept, he admitted, but that didn't mean the oracle was a fraud. The universe was complex, even unfathomable, so oracles and ventriloquists could exist side by side. Only the doctor knew the truth, and he was sworn to secrecy.

I paid one pound sterling. Paul accepted it sheepishly, like someone who scores a tainted victory. We must go to Edwin's soon, he told me, because his fever would pass, and we must celebrate its passing. I agreed, of course, and felt guilty about dragging out the dictionary, but the certainty of youth isn't easily dislodged. I wondered later, too, if I'd been wrong to dismiss the doctor. Perhaps he had a touch of real magic, even a gift for healing. Of all the lessons I learned in Nigeria, the most lasting was how little I knew for certain.

*Narrative*, 2009

**Houseboys**

Even before I arrived in Nigeria, I took a solemn vow not to hire a houseboy. True, you could employ one cheaply, but that would be exploitative and a dreary echo of colonial times. As a young, vaguely idealistic American, I hoped to set a better example than the Brits and show a democratic regard for an individual's self-respect. I might have made good on the vow, too, except that I underestimated the number of houseboys around. Any white man without a servant was presumed to be in need of help or desperately eccentric, and since my eccentricities were still under wraps, the applicants kept flocking to my door at St. Andrew's College.

They came from all over the Eastern Region, sometimes traveling forty miles by mammy wagon on the breath of a rumor. Usually they were grown men rather than boys, and often twice my age. The most serious candidates, who had some actual credentials, presented letters of recommendation from their last employer, fondly recalled now that he'd left West Africa and retired to Bournemouth or Surrey. They recited a list of the "European" dishes they'd been taught to prepare, a Yorkshire pudding or a beef Stroganoff the brigadier's wife had been fond of, but I turned them away, one after another, until I realized houseboys would rain down on me forever unless I reneged on my vow.

Dominic was the lucky lottery winner. He showed up just as my patience was running out. His credentials weren't vastly superior to the others I'd rejected, but he didn't feel that way at all. He took pains to introduce himself as a cook steward, not a houseboy, and related the important duties he had performed until recently for an officer at the British Council in Enugu whose house, he noted, was much grander than my humble Peace Corps digs. "Very, very big, sir," he bragged. Dom's English was quite good, although crippled by the honorifics his former master had drilled into him. He had also finished primary school, another feather in his cap, and could both read and write. As an actor, he was supremely gifted. Tears flooded his eyes when he told me about the misery he'd endure if I failed to choose him. This was both touching and sneaky. I gave him credit for being inventive and awarded him the job.

Dom made a trip to his home village to collect his things, and returned on a bicycle with an old leather suitcase strapped to it. He would be quartered in the converted toolshed I'd once occupied. That was no hardship, he let it be known. He had a roof, a bed, a chair, and a table. With his starting salary of about twenty dollars a month, the going rate and all I could afford, he'd have enough cash left for a radio and the batteries to run it, a luxury every Igbo craved. As for food, he never spent much, subsisting on a diet of garri, or cassava root, and stews with a bit of meat or stockfish tossed in. He was as lean as those Kenyans who enter marathons, and looked as if he could sprint for miles without getting winded. Only the wealthy packed on weight in Nigeria.

My house was very basic. I had no toilet or indoor plumbing and no kitchen. Instead I cooked on a two-burner propane stove outside, right at the edge of the oil palm bush. Dom was depressed by the sight of it. His face collapsed, but there were no tears at least. Probably he'd become a little spoiled in Enugu, the capital city, but he was cheerful by nature and soon recovered. A bad job was better than no job at all, so he adapted and began to serve me three meals a day. Only dinner required much effort because I ate lightly at breakfast and lunch on account of the heat. My energy flagged on a full stomach, so I stuck to fruit and sandwiches until the early evening.

Dom had a large and varied culinary repertoire. His signature dish was an elaborate chicken curry with lots of garnishes, little side plates of peanuts, orange segments, raisins, and diced bananas and tomatoes. The first time he prepared it, he wondered if I liked chilies, and when I told him I did, he looked at me strangely. "Would you take it as we do, sir?" he asked. "As many as an Igbo man?" He meant this in all innocence, but I interpreted it as a challenge. The words "Igbo man" were loaded and implied an ideal, one that was felt but never wholly stated. If I lived up to the ideal, or even came close, I could expect a high compliment, but when I fell short I demonstrated what some people already assumed, that I was a lesser being marooned on a continent where I didn't belong.

"Same as you, Dominic," I replied. This was a long time ago, before I could tell a habanero from a jalapeño, so I had no idea of the punishment that lay in store. Hours later, my tongue still burned, along with the scorched roof of my mouth, and I would pay a further price when I visited my latrine the next morning. Dom tried, but failed, not to laugh as I chugged down cold beer and flapped a hand in front of my mouth in a doomed attempt to create a healing breeze. An Igbo man required seven or eight chilies in his curry, it seemed, seeds and all, so I had failed another test.

Although Dom was proud of his heritage, he took offense when I asked him to cook some pounded yam and bitterleaf soup, a stew with tart greens I'd enjoyed at the market. He believed I shouldn't eat the local chop because it was beneath me. I liked yams, though. They had a thick bark and looked as inedible as firewood, but once they were peeled and boiled, they could be as tasty as new potatoes. If you added a little water and pounded them with a pestle, they became as pliable as pizza dough, and you rolled some dough between your fingers and dipped it into the soup.

I thought this was a fine way to eat, but Dom felt my behavior was inappropriate. He warned me not to go "bush," or native, as if too much bitterleaf might cause me to strip off my clothes and dash naked through the jungle. Yet the truth was that he hated to pound yams. It was laborious and old-fashioned, an insult to the skills of a modern cook steward—women's work, really.

Dom also watched over my social life, as finicky as a maiden aunt when it came to my choice of friends. He approved of Michael Ofokonsi, our postmaster, who was respected for his stock of traditional wisdom, often expressed in proverbs. "It is little by little a bird builds its nest," Ofokonsi might say in praise of hard work or, to promote cooperation, "One finger cannot remove lice from the head." His attitude toward me was paternal. He could see how overwhelmed I was at times, so he offered advice and guidance and invited me to his compound for barbecued goat and palm wine.

Almost every day I stopped to chat with him at the post office, a mud-brick building with pigeonholes for letters and a ceiling fan that created a quiet rustle of paper. Ofokonsi was a good influence, Dom told me, but he worried that Fred, the village photographer, a gap-toothed hustler who ran with a fast crowd, might lead me astray.

But Fred was OK in my book. He operated from a fancy market stall that was always jammed with customers. Nnewi people loved to be photographed and valued the results. Whenever I visited someone, I could count on being shown an album of pictures or a special family portrait. Snapshots didn't exist in the village in 1966, so a fixed image, particularly of the dead, had enormous import. Fred used an old-fashioned box camera on a tripod, big and cumbersome, and arranged his subjects before a blank or painted backdrop, then rushed to his station and ducked beneath a black cloth to expose the negative. His subjects were not supposed to move, so they looked stiff and somehow timeless, like figures in a daguerreotype. Often they adopted a noble pose with a finger beneath their chins to suggest a studious nature, or tilted their heads slightly to gaze at the horizon, where a glorious future loomed.

Whenever Michael Ofokonsi dropped by, Dom hurried to provide refreshments, some sliced papaya and an orange Fanta, but he hid out when Fred arrived, and I had to shout at him to do his job. With a wounded air he'd comply, lingering long enough to give Fred the evil eye. Again it was a question of etiquette. Dom thought the photographer was rude compared to most other guests, who were stultifyingly polite, but that was mainly because they hadn't been invited. They just turned up cold, so that they could boast they'd been inside a white man's house. It had become a thing to do, an accomplishment of sorts. However halfheartedly, I had to admit them, and as they sat speechless on the couch, frozen by their own boldness, I took on the thankless task of trying to make conversation.

The uninvited guests were careful not to disturb the furniture, whereas Fred swept in with the abandon of a favored talk-show guest and sprawled into a chair as if he owned it. Never at a loss for words, he talked a blue streak and had an opinion ready on any topic. Dom objected to his casual disdain for the formalities, and I was a little shocked myself until I accepted his brazen manner for what it was, the very quality he'd translated into his business success. No Igbo forged ahead by answering a want ad. There were no want ads. What mattered was energy, ingenuity, and jive. Everybody had to scratch out a living from lean earth, so your power to imagine was the equivalent of start-up capital. If you created a bankable self, as Fred had done, so much the better. It was no accident Nnewi had produced the first Nigerian millionaire.

Fred's interest in me began when he noticed me drinking a Star beer at a market shop, an activity he endorsed. He consumed a fair amount of Star himself, he reported once he had decided to adopt me, especially on the nights when St. Bottles Society, his men's club, convened. The club was every bit as heretical as its name implied, and dedicated to offending the conservative citizens who frequented our Anglican church. Rarely did St. Bottles induct a new member, Fred went on, but they would let the rules slide in my case, and he laid out the requirements. They were very simple. A candidate had to be able to drink beer and sing, and though I wasn't sure about the singing part, I couldn't refuse the honor.

Fred collected me before the next St. Bottles session. We walked through the bush to a jolly bar and sat at tables outside under a new moon. My sponsor introduced me to a half-dozen men with his usual swagger and exaggerated the benefits I would bring to the club, such as increased visibility and notoriety that would lead, in turn, to free beer. I wanted to issue an immediate denial, but before I could, the group's president rose to address me.

This was Andrew Marcellus Okonkwo, whose appearance can only be described as baleful. His father, a teacher of classics, had called him Marcellus after the Roman general, hoping to imbue him with a strong character, and Okonkwo carried himself with such pomp and authority I guessed he must hold a significant position, possibly in the civil service, when in fact he tended to avoid work and survived on the proceeds of various schemes.

His haughty demeanor affected the others profoundly. When he assumed his orator's stance, a Napoleonic hand thrust between the buttons of his shirt, they all fell silent except for Fred, his loyal accomplice, who yelled, "Speech!" Okonkwo nodded happily, as if to acknowledge the acclaim of the crowd he must have heard cheering in his head. He was tall and fierce-looking and spoke with surprising eloquence, clearly an educated man. His fluid voice was rich and deep and ranged over the octaves in a musical way. He celebrated me as a harbinger of better things, the first but not the last of my kind to join the club, and he promised that someday there would be branches of St. Bottles all across America. I was a pioneer, a bridge between cultures, a gentleman and a scholar.

Okonkwo was awfully good, and when he concluded after fifteen minutes or so, wiping his brow with a handkerchief, his mates applauded. "Toast!" Fred cried, and a small boy brought out a cardboard carton of beer in quart bottles, followed by a tray of plastic tumblers that the men filled and emptied with alarming speed. I couldn't keep up, but I participated in the many toasts to friends and neighbors; to the revered highlife performer Cardinal Rex Jim Lawson; and to Major General Johnson Aguiyi-Ironsi, an Igbo and the current head of state, a leader of the recent coup.

As instructed, I poured beer on the ground as a libation to departed ancestors, too. "If you go back, we leave you behind!" Okonkwo roared. That was the club's motto, and we repeated it several times to ensure the forward progress of St. Bottles.

The singing began around midnight. The lyrics were in Igbo, but I had drunk enough to be relatively loose and could catch a glimmer of meaning if I listened attentively. One peppy song was an obvious tribute to the club, perhaps even its anthem, to judge by the men's fervent rendition, their arms around one another's shoulders as they swayed, while another provided an ironic gloss on the coup. Its chorus consisted of the names of the political leaders assassinated during the bloodshed—Sardauna of Sokoto, Samuel Akintola, Tafewa Balewa, and Festus Okotie Eboh. Black humor was an essential feature of any St. Bottles' gathering. The members laughed in the face of disaster until disaster moved closer to home.

I had classes in the morning, so I excused myself after a few songs and held out some money for the beer, but Okonkwo brushed it away. We weren't expected to settle the bill, because the bar's owner was thrilled to have our patronage. When the word got around that we had endorsed the place, it would be a huge boost for his business—a blessing of sorts that could just as easily have been withheld, Okonkwo implied with a satisfied grin. As the author of this gambit, he had also been its salesman, and it was his talent for flattery and manipulation that granted him such esteem in his circle. Whenever a new bar opened around Nnewi, he pulled the same caper. He had the clout of a newspaper critic who can kill a restaurant with a single bad review. Brilliant and lawless, he would still be singing at dawn.

\* \* \*

I became a student of houseboys over the next few months. My Peace Corps friends had also hired some help, and I was fascinated by the different styles. Lawrence in Onitsha, who worked for Russ Jones, was flamboyantly gay, for instance, and camped it up in the kitchen with his lover. The Cartwrights in Owerri had a gorgeous housemaid I flirted with unsuccessfully. Lying in their guest bed, I'd conjure up Eucharia's face and breasts and will her to come to me, but she never did. I lacked the necessary magic. Once I crossed the great bridge over the Niger River to see Bob Royer in Benin City, whose houseboy, Felix, had culinary pretensions that surpassed Dominic's. As a special treat, he grilled us a piece of meat we couldn't identify. "Grasscutter," Felix beamed. We'd just eaten a porcupine.

When it came to being cool, no houseboy matched Francis, who served Mike Higgins in Port Harcourt. We all envied Higgins's setup. He'd landed at a well-to-do college and had a house with a grand front porch and also a real bathroom, although the toilet wasn't plumbed. Instead the waste dropped into a bucket, and night soil men collected it after dark to sell to farmers as fertilizer. They were competitive and territorial, and if they caught an intruder stealing a bucket on their turf, a knockdown fight was likely to ensue. A pair of night soil men once did battle in the city streets, flinging insults and shit at each other, and it made the front page of the local paper.

Higgins led a charmed life. He'd grown up in San Bernardino, the first true Californian I'd ever met, and he had an effortless, laid-back grace. I couldn't imagine him breaking a sweat, even in Nigeria. He still dressed as if for a trip to the beach in a T-shirt, baggy shorts, and low-cut Converse sneakers, and so did Francis. In essence, Mike had transformed his houseboy into an African surfer dude. Francis used the same slang expressions as Higgins and spoke the lingo of the coastal meccas where Mike had once ridden the big waves. I almost fell over when I heard Francis say "gnarly." He wore a trendy little cap with its brim turned up like a bike racer's and whistled Beatles' tunes from *Revolver*, an album his master played endlessly. When I stayed with Mike, I could be certain he'd wake me the next morning with a blast of "Good Day, Sunshine."

What Higgins had re-created in Port Harcourt, of course, was a scrambled version of Southern California. You'd never find any pounded yam or bitterleaf soup on his table. Instead, Francis had learned to cook the sort of down-home grub you'd eat in a funky café on the Pacific. He did quarter-pounders with fries, steak-and-eggs, hot dogs, and even tacos. That was only possible because PH, as Mike called it, was a boomtown that catered to expats.

At its air-conditioned supermarkets, you could buy Rice Krispies, frozen pizza, Jack Daniels, and cases of Schlitz, along with tortillas and decent ground beef. Its nightclubs were the jazziest and its bar girls the classiest. All this was due to the oil money flowing into the city, scads of it. After years of exploration, huge deposits of petroleum had finally been discovered in the Delta, so reps from Shell-BP, Gulf, Elf, and Phillips had made the scene and were salting Nigerian pockets left and right to gain an upper hand.

Wherever we went in PH, we met expats. We saw them at the Hotel Presidential when we'd go for a swim, taking a shortcut from Higgins's house through the bush. It was a good, clean, generally snake-free path, but you had to watch out for army ants, a silent menace. If you walked through a colony, they crawled up your legs and began to sting you. In the midst of an attack, I always remembered Humphrey Bogart and the leeches in *The African Queen*. The ants caused the same type of shuddering revulsion when they invaded our crotches and armpits, seeking out our privates. If they massed on the frontiers of flesh you couldn't reach yourself, they could be hard to get rid of, and once Higgins had to pluck them off my back in a restroom at the Presidential, leaving me with a myriad of tiny red welts.

The hotel pool was Olympic-size. Chaise lounges were arrayed around its perimeter, and the wives of oil men, diplomats, and spies, both British and American, occupied them. They were a bored-looking lot, although not bored enough to be interested in us. My fantasy of a blazing affair in the jungle died quickly. In fact, the wives could be hostile, suspicious of anyone who'd travel to Nigeria voluntarily. They made it clear that they were in PH under duress, as prisoners of their husbands' desire for a big payday, and some projected a barely disguised contempt.

You could see it when they summoned a waiter. They were curt and dismissive and avoided any eye contact. The waiters, elegant in crisp white tunics with *Presidential* stitched in green script over a pocket, bristled with anger and fought to control it. They took their revenge by subterfuge and talked too loudly, their voices rising, yammering, even seething, and also by being slow to deliver drinks.

There was tension almost everywhere expats convened. Nigerians were too noisy, they complained, too animated and brassy, so they erected barriers and called for more gin. Pimms Cup was also popular, along with games of snooker and tennis. What most expats really enjoyed was having servants, the same as we did, although they kept a distance from their staff, while we were naive enough to regard our houseboys as comrades. That didn't make the expats unkind, just chilly, and their servants felt the chill.

"I couldn't live this well at home," a British functionary confided to me once. "Why else would I accept this bloody awful post?" The only expats who seemed excited by the raucous street life and its way of grabbing you by the lapels were the roustabouts who worked in the oil fields and at the country's lone refinery outside PH.

We bumped into them at such wild nightclubs as the Crystal Palace. From Higgins's compound, we rode there in a little Morris Minor taxi, black as a bug, careful to haggle over the fare because to do otherwise would be insulting. If you paid the asking price without protest, the driver thought you didn't take him seriously. It was de rigueur to accuse him of cheating. That restored his dignity and meant he wasn't invisible.

"My fran," Mike would say in pidgin, maybe shaking a finger for effect, "why you go do dis type of ting?" The driver, satisfied to be on trial, would deny that he'd been dishonest, although he often was, and an agreeable row would follow. We'd chip away at the fare until we whittled it down to a reasonable sum and then, with an affirmation of our common bond, a handshake or a clap on the shoulder, we girded ourselves to run the gauntlet of touts outside the club.

The touts couldn't imagine a more potentially lucrative sight than two young white guys in search of adventure. They converged on us in a pincer movement, either begging for coins or jabbering about the black-market goods they could supply, yet there was no danger until late at night when the criminal types lay in wait for drunks and rolled them in the alleys. The touts' expectations were actually very low. They dreamed of a gigantic score, of course, but they'd settle for a cigarette. If you decided to purchase some marijuana, they considered it a bonus.

The only sin you couldn't commit was to push them away. If they felt your distress, your dread of any bodily contact, of the occasional lesions on their skin or their ripe odor, they turned ugly and the banter ended. A tout might spit at you or lie about what you'd done to him, riling the crowd. It was a bad mistake to reject them. You were rejecting poverty, and poverty has its own dynamic.

The touts couldn't get past the bouncers at the Crystal Palace, so they receded like the waters and squatted in the dirt until the next taxi pulled up with its possibility of deliverance. Inside, we bumped into the roustabouts, who ran in bunches. They were loaded with money and overjoyed to spend it on women and booze. They had the reckless attitude of cowboys after a long trail ride, determined to tear up the town and start a little trouble. Whereas the bored wives thought we were demented, the roustabouts took pity on us for being so broke and stupid, and they always picked up our check. One night a fellow from New Zealand, so wasted he couldn't stand up, hired a taxi to tour all the best clubs and insisted we come along. He paid for everything. Our only duty was to carry him in and out. It was like drinking with the corpse of John Barrymore.

When the band began to play highlife, the dance floor came alive. You could smell a change in the atmosphere, a mingling of sweat, perfume, and desire. Everybody took a turn going around, even the clumsy and the flat-footed. The music seemed to act as a binding agent, holding together the opposed and opposable forces for a brief, transcendent moment. That's how it felt to me, at least. I was happy at the Crystal Palace because I had blind faith in the future. If anybody had told me the oil and the money would lead to catastrophe, I would have expressed my doubts. I still believed in the essential goodness of human beings, in their ability to do the right thing. I didn't know how deep, bitter, and irrational hatred can be. All I heard was the melody, not the drumbeat, as I danced.

* * *

After a trip to Port Harcourt, I was always glad to get back to Nnewi. The partying, though exhilarating, left me exhausted, and I missed the sleepy village, my students, and even Dominic. I was grateful for Mike's hospitality, but I liked the way my own life had become compact and confined to an area of cleared land bordered by the oil palm bush. In truth, I had almost everything I needed in Nnewi, and that surprised me. As an American, I'd been taught to define my needs in material terms. The Igbo offered me constant correction. What Americans labeled primitive might also be called essential. The word *enough* acquired new meaning, and I felt a reverence for simplicity I'd never experienced before.

My days acquired an easy rhythm. Even the teaching became easier as I adjusted to the climate. The paralytic anxiety I'd endured at first, certain that I'd reveal myself as a phony, undereducated and inexperienced, vanished when I understood how eager the students were for what little I had to give. In literature class, I began to enjoy the discussions, finally able to elucidate the parallels between Igbo society and the required texts.

*Pride and Prejudice* was a case in point. I had worried that Mrs. Bennet's struggle to marry off her daughters would seem remote or antiquated, but there were matchmakers active in Igboland, and a debate evolved between the pro-Bennet group, all loyal to traditional values, and the anti-Bennet modernists, who thought it old-fashioned for a mother to meddle in her children's affairs. Neither side would surrender, so we resorted to a soccer match to resolve the deadlock, with the pro-Bennet side winning on a free kick.

To be considered modern meant a great deal to most Igbos. It was an aspect of the same bright future I believed in. My students read any magazine they could get their hands on and passed along newspapers until the pages were in shreds. They asked for my old copies of *Time*, too, but I dared not share my *Playboy*s. I let a student browse through an issue once, and he walked around for days with a glazed look in his eyes, trying to readjust his notion of reality. The men were also devoted fans of television and gathered before the college's only set to watch *Okonu's Club*, a weekly dance program broadcast from Enugu, whose jovial host, Okonu, cautioned the dancers against any "bone-to-bone" friction.

They were equally attentive whenever Major General Johnson Aguiyi-Ironsi addressed the nation. When he took over in January, the country's mood was hopeful because corruption was so widespread. Any change, even if accomplished violently, was presumed to be for the better. The prevalent attitude was wait and see. My Nnewi friends still trusted and respected the new government, but it was May now, and the Islamic Hausa and Fulani in the north were disappointed in their new leader. The dead politicians in the St. Bottles song were primarily Muslims, and though Aguiyi-Ironsi had the assassins in custody, they had not been sentenced. Moreover, he talked about Nigeria becoming a loose federation of states rather than a republic. That would put the oil in Igbo territory, so the northerners and others were wary of the plan.

For the moment, though, village life appeared to be normal. Hausa traders still sold moonstones and leather hassocks at our market, and Fulani nomads still drove herds of scrawny cattle to our abbatoir. When I mentioned this to Dom as a positive sign, he merely shrugged. Politics was not a subject he'd discuss. It was too risky and might cause offense. He was odd that way, secretive about his views and his private life. He never felt entirely comfortable in Nnewi, I believe, since his home was elsewhere. He had no family nearby and no close friends. The Igbo could be clannish, so Dom concentrated on his work. He washed my laundry in an aluminum tub, transported cartons of Star to my house on a bicycle, shopped for groceries, and swept and dusted almost daily. At times, he must have been as lonely as I was.

Teaching held together my days, but the nights at St. Andrew's could be difficult, particularly when the reception on my shortwave radio went bad. If I couldn't pick up a few innings of baseball on the Armed Forces Network, I got fidgety. The familiar sound of an announcer's voice suggested a continuity I needed. It proved that America hadn't vanished just because I was in West Africa. At first I had relied on reading to fill the listless hours, but I'd finished all the paperbacks the Peace Corps had supplied. As for the novel I'd started to write, mildew covered its six pages.

Beyond the literary realm, I tried to entertain myself by sampling the drugs in my Peace Corps medical kit. They failed to yield a decent high, although the powder for crab lice proved beneficial after a trip to Port Harcourt and the Crystal Palace. You sprinkled it on your pubic hair, and the lice scampered out in a panic, as if they were fleeing from a forest fire, but they were too small to swat, unlike the sausage flies I slaughtered in periods of terminal boredom. The flies were about the size of a thumbnail, and when they flew into a room, they reacted poorly to the light. It blinded them temporarily, and they banged into one wall after another, loudly buzzing in protest. I tracked them with a rolled-up paper and kept a tally of the corpses, always hoping to set a new record. My behavior seems to me now a symptom of the underlying malaise that affected us all.

One afternoon Dom asked to confer with me. He looked very serious and confessed he had a problem. It involved his nephew Ethelbert. The boy's family could no longer provide for him, so Dom wished to take over. Ethelbert wouldn't be any trouble, he assured me. The boy would live with him, sleep on a raffia mat, and attend our primary school. I told him he'd have to clear it with the college's principal, and when he got permission, he was delighted. Maybe he thought Ethelbert could cure his loneliness, but I wondered if the boy was really his son. With his secretive nature, Dom could easily have been married. I was curious about the boy, too. Ethelbert would be a tough name to bear, even in a country where girls were routinely called Patience, Prudence, and Charity.

Ethelbert traveled to St. Andrew's by mammy wagon, all by himself. I happened to be sitting in the shade and grading compositions when he arrived, and I looked up and saw a tiny figure crossing the dry brown weeds of the soccer field and knew in an instant it was him. He had no luggage, just a satchel such as hobos carry, and he dragged his feet and walked with the slightly dazed gait of the uprooted, as if to resist whatever fate had in store for him.

His manner toward Dom was indifferent. If he felt any affection for his uncle, he refused to show it. Instead he wriggled away from a hug. With me, he was sullen and remote. I guessed he must be about seven, but he was nine, a fact I had to pry out of him. He rebuffed our questions and couldn't be coaxed into a smile. Ethelbert was the saddest child I'd ever met. He must miss his parents terribly, I thought, but the sadness was there the next day, and the day after that.

Ethelbert became a shadowy presence. When he wasn't at school, he followed Dom around. At odd hours, I'd find him asleep on the floor of my house, curled up in a ball. If he helped with a chore, I gave him a few pennies, but the money failed to cheer him. He was so sulky I figured he might be sick, so I asked Dom to take him to the village clinic. It was a well-run facility, although you had to stand in line for a long time in the hot sun before anybody examined you.

A doctor diagnosed a mild case of anemia and gave Ethelbert some pills, but his mood did not improve. The boy's embrace of melancholy was absolute. He never played with any other children, never laughed or cried or got angry. His one pleasure was to sit on my back steps, his chin resting on his fists, and stare into the oil palm bush.

Toward the end of May, I collected my mail one morning and found Michael Ofokonsi, ordinarily unshakeable, in an agitated state, cursing under his breath as he filed letters in pigeonholes. He was frantic about the welfare of his brother, a civil servant in the north, whose phone had been disconnected. He'd heard a report on the radio that some Hausa and Fulani rioters, furious with the Aguiyi-Ironsi regime, had launched attacks on Igbos in several cities including Kano, where his brother was based. The mob, armed with clubs and machetes, had gone from house to house through the *sabon garis*, districts reserved for strangers to the region, and carried out a campaign of ethnic cleansing. Muslim soldiers were rumored to have participated. Nobody knew how many people were dead.

I listened to the reports at home, but they were sketchy and conflicted. Only when the first refugees trickled into Onitsha and later Nnewi did we learn the true extent of the horror. The refugees were sometimes wounded, missing a finger, a hand, or a limb, and they told their stories in quaking voices. The mob had spared no one. Pregnant women were cut open, their fetuses cast into gutters, and children were murdered by the score. The killing went on for days, with houses in flames. Some people were still in hiding, afraid to show themselves, even though the cities were relatively quiet again. All the while Ethelbert sat on my back steps and stared into the oil palm bush. He was possessed by visions, I think now, and what he saw accounted for the enormity of his sadness.

*Narrative*, 2007

# San Francisco: Haight-Ashbury Days

**True Believers**

As a young man I wanted to be a poet. I couldn't think of a higher calling, so when I headed for San Francisco to pursue my goal, it was probably inevitable I'd fall in with Buster Farrell, who ran a print shop that doubled as a literary salon. Buster wrote poems himself, and they were good enough to appear in journals other than *Wooden Leg,* the little magazine he edited and tried to publish quarterly, although he seldom met his deadline. That was no hardship for his subscribers, really, since they were all Buster's friends and aware of his financial difficulties, but he still felt the pressure and would pick up the pace of his beer drinking, an activity he began before lunch and often continued long into the night.

Buster lived in a flat above the shop with his wife and infant daughter. Zoe Farrell was a gentle soul, blond and plump and forgiving. She tolerated Buster's money problems and also the impromptu parties that gathered steam down below and wound their way up into her kitchen. Zoe was always throwing together a cheap meal for three or six or ten uninvited guests, while her husband held little Rachel on his lap and discussed subjects of poetic importance. Deeply opinionated, Buster was a native Oregonian built like a lumberjack, with a springy black beard and Trotsky glasses. In debate, he could be intimidating. He'd bang a fist on the table and spill some beer, and I'd notice the inky hands and nails he could never get clean for all the scrubbing he did.

No matter how late the party ended, it never interfered with Buster's routine. He was a pro, back on duty at eight in the morning. His shop was no more than a glorified basement and cramped with the tools of his trade. It could be as dark as a tunnel down there, but for a fine printer to stay afloat at all was a miracle, as Buster liked to remind us. He conducted tutorials on the job, lecturing on the origins of Bodoni Bold, say, or the visionary element in the poetry of Robinson Jeffers. Even when his two big presses were operating, you could hear his voice above the clatter. The lectures slowed down his commercial work, though. To pay the rent, he printed fancy editions of literary classics for a book club and did a wonderful job, but his heart wasn't in it. As soon as he got a check, he invested in a publishing venture of his own that wouldn't earn a dime. That was Buster's great glory. He refused to put a price on beauty, but it cost him.

Without question, he was a superb craftsman. He had studied typography with the city's Old Master, a man renowned for his aesthetic purity and his bad temper, both traits that Buster shared. When he printed a poem on a broadside sheet, he spent hours picking over the proof copies. The process was in no way neat. He'd curse and kick a letter press, then stomp over to the corner bar to brood. Nobody dared to approach when he was in a foul mood, but eventually inspiration would strike, and he'd dash back and make a subtle adjustment to bring all the elements into line.

Ah, happiness! His big face beamed, and another celebration started. The broadsides featured such notables as Gary Snyder and Robert Creeley, so Buster could have sold them for some much-needed cash, but he insisted on giving them away. To be included in the loop was a hippie badge of honor, on par with growing your own pot or having the Jefferson Airplane's dentist fix your teeth.

I met Buster through a young poet friend, who had an actual chapbook to his credit and stood very tall in my eyes. My own "work," as I called it, was always elegantly typed on the page, but I knew how awkward it was and never bothered to send it out. The realm of literature was exalted, I believed, and I was desperate to enter it and gain access to its secrets and rewards. I spent most evenings browsing through the poetry books at City Lights, soaking up their essence for free. I sought out authors who were hooked on drugs or alcohol, since the idea of writing in an altered state held an enormous appeal for me. What could be easier or more fun? Whenever I was stoned, though, my "work" got even worse, less honest and more indulgent, and in my bleak hungover periods I doubted I'd ever write a meaningful word.

My friend, the published poet, invited me to lunch one afternoon. I was delighted and pictured a grand banquet with lots of wine and maybe women, but I had never seen the sort of place a published poet sometimes occupies. His apartment was small, messy, and cluttered with books, including a few from the Knothead Press, Buster's imprint. (All Buster's references to wood were a mock tribute to the mill town where he grew up.) In the fashion of the era, my host rolled a joint, and soon I was starving. When he went into his pocket-size kitchen, I fell victim to elaborate fantasies about the meal ahead—burgers, steak, could it be a leg of lamb?—but he returned with a loaf of bread, a can of tuna, and a jar of mayonnaise. I was stunned, but I managed to recover. If this was the standard poet's fare out west, I meant to do it justice and ate with good appetite.

After lunch, we took a stroll through the Haight-Ashbury. The year was 1969, and though the bloom was off the rose, the air still carried a hint of jasmine and patchouli oil—of innocence, you might say. "Let's drop in on Buster," my friend suggested. He opened the shop's door, and a strand of Tibetan bells jingled merrily. Inside, Buster sat cross-legged on the bare concrete floor, a needle and thread in hand, sewing together the signatures for the next issue of *Wooden Leg,* all sixteen pages. He had an assistant, an even bigger guy with a droopy belly, and the sight of those two giants doing such dainty work made us laugh. Buster gave me a finished copy of the magazine, along with a Ranier Ale, and when I saw it was his last one, I walked to the nearest market and, for the price of a six-pack, bought my way into the exalted realm.

\* \* \*

From that day on, I was a regular at the shop, where Buster welcomed anybody who cared about poetry and literature. His salon was informal, so he didn't hold forth from an armchair like Gertrude Stein, or post visiting hours like Maxim Gorky. The gatherings simply happened. People arrived at all hours and rarely called ahead. Buster was always very gracious. He'd interrupt his paying work to offer advice, criticism, and tips on book design. He received book collectors, student apprentices, political activists, artists, writers, and those who dreamed of being writers. The dreamers were the largest contingent by far. We came armed with our poems and notebooks, our half-baked fiction and jottings on bar napkins, and Buster, kind to a fault, took us seriously and made editorial comments. He never pulled his punches, though, so you had to be ready for the truth, or his version of it, anyway.

I delayed for weeks before I worked up the nerve to show him some poems I'd written. I waited until the early evening, when Buster was finished for the day and at his most mellow. He gave me a strange look when I handed him a manila folder, as if to ask, "What, you too?" then tilted his head toward a naked lightbulb dangling from a cord. He grunted and ground his teeth as he read, wrestling with the words on the page, and I had an urge to snatch back the folder and burn it on the spot. My fate, even my life, seemed to hang in the balance. Buster was wise enough to understand that, of course, and when he singled out a poem, rattled the paper in front of my nose, and said in his gruff voice, "This isn't bad," I felt as if I'd won a prize. He didn't invite me to contribute to *Wooden Leg,* the ultimate accolade, but it was enough for the moment to be "not bad."

If Buster thought somebody had real promise, he'd let the person set a poem or two in type and print them. I never reached those heights, but I watched others go through the drill. They were terribly self-involved and agonized over which typeface to choose, and whether or not it suited their sensibility. In private, I poked fun at them, but I didn't realize that a sturdy ego is essential if you expect to cope with rejection and win over an indifferent public. I still viewed the literary world as a meritocracy, where good writing always got its due, and I had no idea how easily the will to write can be broken. Those poems from long ago must be treasures to their owners now, a few scraps of a lost youth not blown away in the wind.

But I couldn't see any of that at the time. None of us could. We *were* young, and we were true believers. And who could blame us? We had firm evidence that lightning could strike and transform the merely mortal. Famous writers often turned up at the shop, especially Richard Brautigan, an old pal of Buster's whose whimsical novels had become bestsellers. Brautigan knocked them out in a matter of days at a café in North Beach. He was rich, gifted, and instantly recognizable. His photo graced the jacket of each book, in company with his current girlfriend. Tall and thin, with a Buffalo Bill moustache and a long tangle of blond hair, he'd descend on us from the heavens, toting a half-gallon jug of Red Mountain wine. Despite his fame, he seemed shy and sensitive, but I was too shy myself to talk with him. I listened at a distance and learned.

With such celebrities around, the salon grew in notoriety and attracted more hangers-on, and that further hampered Buster's ability to function efficiently. He fell behind on everything. He made an unwise decision, too, when he agreed to take in Marco Means, who'd been jailed for punching a cop at a peace march and was paroled into Buster's custody. Only nineteen, Marco was wiry and intense, with a Medusa-head of dreadlocks, the first I'd ever seen on a white person. He was a librarian's son from the Midwest, a rabble-rouser, a diabetic, a former junkie who suffered relapses, and a beer drinker to rival and maybe even surpass his benefactor. In his moral outrage, Marco was fierce and fearless, capable of almost anything, outstanding at injuring himself, and as in need of minding as a child.

Buster's reasons for looking after Marco weren't entirely altruistic. Though slightly warped, Marco was brilliant. His talent as an illustrator was unexcelled, and his medium was the linoleum block—an ideal complement to fine printing. He carved his intricate images into the blocks with a sharp-bladed Exacto knife, as precisely as a surgeon. Indeed, the spectacle of Marco in the throes of creation became a showpiece at the shop. Just as the arthritic fingers of Pablo Casals loosened in old age and allowed him to bow his cello, so too did Marco rise into himself. He was a picture of calm, regardless of how smashed he might be. His images often depicted a pitched battle between nature and the destructive forces of civilization, with unearthly flowers blooming in trash heaps and vines climbing over the rusted hulls of cars.

With Marco's illustrations, the broadsides became doubly beautiful, but his blocks demanded special attention, so the work took twice as long. The bills were stacking up, too, and poor Zoe's patience was wearing thin. Marco was scarcely a considerate lodger. He forgot to eat, failed to flush the toilet, nodded out, had no income, and everybody loved him. Everybody! When he fractured an arm in a fall, twenty well-wishers escorted him to the hospital.

One evening, when another party ascended from the depths, I saw how frustrated Zoe was. Balancing Rachel on a hip, she began flinging vegetables into a pot for soup, at her wit's end—not that anybody helped her. No, we sat and smoked and jabbered about poetry instead. When Marco used a coffee cup as an ashtray, Zoe lost it completely. She screamed at Marco, and Buster screamed at her, and Rachel started bawling.

The scene couldn't be more chaotic, you might think, but chaos knows no boundaries. To his credit, Buster got a grip. Drastic measures were needed if he hoped to survive, so he brought in a partner. This was Frederick Hayes, the linotype operator. His skills would add speed and flexibility, Buster contended, but Frederick was the ultimate harbinger of doom. He had no business sense and actively despised the concept of professional behavior. He was much older than us, nearly forty, and Harvard educated, with a long graying ponytail and an IQ that was off the charts. He regarded his linotype machine as he might a piano, cracking his knuckles before he sat down. Sometimes he wore a soiled ice-cream suit that he'd picked up at the Salvation Army. He resembled a maestro in ruins. Visitors watched in awe when he threw back his head and began humming, lost in a rhapsody only he could hear.

* * *

Frederick's presence boosted the shop's level of eccentricity to an all-time high. He had traveled the globe, spoke five languages fluently, and sprinkled his chatter with foreign phrases. I was never exactly certain what he'd said. As a sophisticated free spirit, he was also a sexual adventurer, and that rubbed Buster, with his small-town background, the wrong way. Where Buster had a curious nobility that derived from his mission on poetry's behalf, Frederick thrived on flamboyance, flirtation, and surreal jokes. Ask him to go right, and he went left. He admired rebels and outlaws, Burroughs and Genet, and willful obscurity thrilled him. If Frederick had a mission, it was to debunk and undermine, upsetting the status quo. That fit perfectly with Marco's anarchic streak, and soon they were conspirators.

Marco was seduced, in thrall, eager to do Frederick's bidding. Together they launched a series of side projects, leaving Buster to struggle. They created some phony stationery from the Department of Defense to be employed for mischief. Ever cheered by the prospect of disaster, they assembled a guide to earthquake safety. It offered such hints as "Get under a table and stay there for four days." In Chinatown they found a box of old linoleum blocks that had once belonged to a newspaper, printed dozens of them, and supplied absurd captions in English. There was no end to their madcap energy, and no profit from it, either, but they were irresistible, even to Buster's most loyal supporters. They were funny, playful, and unpredictable, while Buster was somber and stoic. Buster had the blues.

Before long, there were two salons uneasily occupying the same space. Buster felt outraged and betrayed. The free spirits were a threat to his livelihood. In response, he grew more dogmatic, and his opinions, never very adaptable, were set in stone. I once listened to him lecture on why Goudy, and Goudy alone, was the only typeface appropriate to a particular poem. He began the discourse around noon and finished it in the early evening. His beer consumption increased, and his temper got the better of him, too. He envied Marco and Frederick's liberty, although he disapproved of their antics. The attempts at compromise, and the brief flourishes of harmony, were destined not to last.

So we were all surprised when the feuding trio collaborated on Buster's new book of poetry. It wasn't a big book, only twenty poems or so, but he'd been saving spare change for two years to buy the paper. The Knothead Press would publish five hundred copies, some in cloth to be signed by the author, and try to sell it to stores and libraries, a first for Buster. There would be a huge party, of course, and the typeface would be Goudy.

For once, Frederick didn't snicker, and Marco outdid himself, giving up his usual obsessions to focus on the book's pastoral tone, evocative of Buster's childhood in the Northwest. He produced a powerful image of a hawk on the wing, and another of its prey, an oblivious field mouse in the tall grass. Taken together, the images captured the urgency beneath the calm surface of the poetry.

That was the final group effort. On the sly, Marco and Frederick planned to go into business for themselves, somewhere in the country where they could live cheaply. As for Buster, he sank deeper into debt. With his back to the wall and Zoe anxious about the future, he stooped to printing menus, leaflets, and wedding invitations. For a while, he even served as a vanity publisher of hideous novels and delusional memoirs. The awful prose gave him migraines, he complained, and I thought he was kidding until the afternoon I found him in the dark shop with a cold beer pressed to his forehead. His book was a letdown, too, despite the moving poems and elegant design. Not a single critic reviewed it, and it couldn't have sold more than fifty copies, judging by the cartons still on hand.

The salon limped along, stumbling toward its grave. Buster was too busy to read manuscripts or be convivial anymore. I lost touch with him myself, mostly because I'd faced up to reality and admitted I wasn't a poet of any kind, not yet. The hard truth hurt a bit, but I also felt a little relieved. Instead of staring at my navel all day, I got a steady job, and the regular paycheck did wonders for my mood. For the first time since I'd arrived on the coast, I had food in the fridge and enough cash to buy books rather than read them on the sly. I gained a renewed respect for Buster, too, and what he'd been willing to endure for his beliefs.

As bankruptcy loomed, Buster sold his presses and equipment to a liquidator. He and Zoe split up shortly after that. Ultimately, he left the city to find a new life. Where he landed I've never been entirely sure. According to one rumor, he remarried, moved to Maine, and teaches book design at an arts college.

That's the rumor I choose to pass along, remembering his kindness to us all. If anybody deserved a happy ending, or at least a second chance, it was Buster. I still have an inscribed copy of his last book, along with some broadsides and a few copies of *Wooden Leg,* and whenever I dust them off and show them to friends, I'm amused when somebody remarks (and somebody always does) that the collection must be worth a small fortune.

*Narrative,* 2005

## A Real Writer

All tales of reckless youth involve a large measure of folly, so I continue to be amazed that my brief career as a literary agent yielded any positive results. Whenever I remember those long-ago days, I see before me the dark, drafty, incredibly sloppy rail-road flat near Golden Gate Park I shared with Hank Daniels, my old roomie, who cooked up the plan to take the publishing world by storm. This was in the early 1970s, during the last gasp of hippie glory, when Nixon was unraveling and San Francisco still welcomed grand gestures destined for defeat.

Hank came west from rural Oklahoma, so he had no defenses against the city's magic. It sucked him in and filled him with ambition. In a few short months, he'd gone from being a humble bus driver's son to a first-rate seducer adept at picking up women. Handsome and charming, he'd even landed a good job as a west coast sales rep for a New York publisher. His salary might be modest, but it didn't cramp his style. He wore expensive snake-skin cowboy boots, drove an electric-blue Porsche, and slept on a king-sized waterbed, where he often dreamed that he could fly like Superman. Success and power, those were Hank's totems.

I had no totem myself unless you count confusion, although I worked in the book business, too, as a part-time stock boy for a local wholesaler. That's how I got to know Hank. He made regu-lar stops at our warehouse on behalf of his employer. When we first met, he was frazzled because he was breaking up with his high school sweetheart, who followed him to California. He was so touched that he bought her an engagement ring and moved her into his apartment, a maneuver he regretted the minute he realized it would curtail his nightly cruising. Advance planning was never Hank's strong suit. At any rate, he had to leave her. "I let her keep the ring, anyway," he told everyone, easing his conscience. Meanwhile, he'd found a new flat by the park and was looking for somebody to split the rent.

I was the ideal candidate. A weird green mold was creeping over the walls of my studio on Cole Street, plus I'd been robbed twice and owned almost nothing of value anymore, except the typewriter I relied on for banging out my stories and poems. The stuff was awful, and I knew it and never showed it to anyone, but I held a secret belief that in the Haight-Ashbury's utopian atmosphere, where human potential was supposed to be boundless, I might yet become what I wanted to be, a real writer. So Hank's pitch appealed to me. For an extra thirty bucks a month, I could have three rooms instead of one, all mold-free. Far out, I thought. I'll make the nicest room my study.

At the end of the month, I packed a suitcase, put my typewriter in its case, and walked over to my new digs. The flat was on the top floor and afforded us a fine view of Kezar Pavilion, where the roller derby matches ended with bottles breaking and the fans butting heads in bloody fistfights. Our landlord was Chinese and operated a tiny pizza parlor in a storefront down below. He took great pride in his pizzas, even though they didn't resemble any I'd seen before. His "special" involved bean sprouts and water chestnuts on top of a traditional tomato-sauce base. After a blast in the oven, the sprouts turned black and crinkly, but he regarded this as a culinary breakthrough, not a disaster.

Living with Hank proved to be easy. He left after breakfast to make the rounds of Bay Area bookstores, so I often had the flat to myself and passed the hours reading and daydreaming. Sometimes I didn't get up from my mattress on the floor until the early afternoon. My boss at the warehouse, a crusty old Socialist who harbored both confused hippies and draft dodgers, gave me a discount on his stock, and that allowed me to build up a small library. I browsed through the samples that Hank's company sent him, as well, but what really intrigued me was the pile of manuscripts stacked by his waterbed. They belonged to aspiring writers who hoped Hank would like their work, send it to the honchos back east, and recommend that it be published.

That was wishful thinking. Hank read very little and had no interest in literature, but he still felt guilty about ignoring the manuscripts. He was also clever enough to know that somewhere in those thousands of pages there might be a diamond in the rough, the next Richard Brautigan or Hunter Thompson. The publishing industry had lately embraced the hippie scene as a moneymaker, even hiring editors fresh out of college, who smoked a little dope. Why not open a literary agency that catered to the long-haired masses? Such was Hank's inspiration one evening when we were stoned ourselves. What a great idea! It would alleviate his guilt and maybe earn us some cash. Since I was addicted to reading, I could sort through the slush pile in search of gems while he did the wheeling and dealing. We'd be a perfect team.

I was forced to admit that his idea, while not really all that great, had some merit. Agents of any kind were scarce in town, and

I certainly had nothing to lose, but I still hesitated because I was an aspiring writer, too, and a terrible snob in the bargain, assuming a kinship with the immortals. In my arrogance, I thought the agent game was ruled by such brassy, cigar-chomping sharpies as Irving "Swifty" Lazar, who made headlines by selling trashy blockbusters for millions, so when I finally caved in to Hank's pressure—not for nothing was he a salesman—I insisted that we call ourselves Larry's Literary to suggest the oily nature of the trade.

I intended this as a joke, but it worked to our advantage. It generated a flurry of free publicity as the hippies tried to guess the identity of our silent partner. I did my best to feed the rumor mill. In one version, I cast Larry as a movie mogul from Los Angeles eager to tap into a fresh pool of talent up north; in another, Larry was a Berkeley philanthropist so crippled by shyness that he couldn't bear to meet an author in the flesh. Hank contributed to the buzz with his design for our business card. It featured a swirl of barely legible script as in a Fillmore poster, next to a drawing of a buffalo. That would be our logo, he said, and would certify us as pioneers. We were very pleased. Being an agent was a lot more fun than we had figured.

It was a sign of the times, I suppose, that anybody at all took us seriously. But we soon learned, much to our horror, how desperate some people are to see their words in print. As soon as we distributed our cards, the deluge began. Hank kept his job, so I ran our "home office," a spare room outfitted with a table, a filing cabinet scavenged from the boulevards, and my typewriter. Despite my initial misgivings, I experienced an odd contentment while I sipped my morning coffee and waited for the phone to ring, glad to have a purpose in life at last. No longer was I just another drifter. Now I could explain to my parents what I was doing in San Francisco, the very hallmark of maturity they were convinced they'd never see.

Dealing with our would-be clients was tricky. There were pushy callers who asked about our track record and wondered if we had the "muscle" to handle a masterpiece like *King: Sheepdog of West Marin,* but most others were anxious and a bit wary, accustomed to being rejected. If they wanted an honest opinion of their writing, a service I thought we actually could supply, I asked them to send a sample, but I disqualified some callers on the spot because I smelled trouble. One fellow warned me that he wouldn't accept less than $50,000 for his first novel, for instance, which was about (and I quote), "Man's inhumanity to man." Anybody who invoked Joyce or Proust as a model I also avoided, along with paranoids expecting to be cheated and poets who described their poems as "an exploration of self."

That may sound cold, but I was really being far too nice. Worried that I'd hurt someone's feelings, I listened patiently to monumental bores and towering egomaniacs. Often I traveled long miles to meet somebody who'd piqued my curiosity, usually by lying. Once I rode a Greyhound all the way to Fresno to chat with a scholar who claimed to be an expert on Buddhism. He served me green tea in a tiny cup and gave me a pamphlet about the Rosicrucians. Worse things happened all the time, most spectacularly when an ex-convict, recently released from San Quentin after doing ten years for manslaughter, knocked on the door, engaged my sympathy, and read aloud to me from the ripping yarn he'd composed behind bars. His performance held me captive for nearly an hour.

There were consolations. There had to be. Every now and then I came across a manuscript that woke me up and drew me in. It could be the writer's voice, the integrity of the subject matter, or a sense of emotional truth, but I could always tell when I was in the presence of genuine, heartfelt prose, and I soon became painfully aware that my dreadful stories and poems lacked those qualities. I simply made up my stuff (I once set a story in the Peruvian Andes) and imagined I was being creative, so the process of sifting through all those submissions and trying to separate the gold from the dross was an enormous help to me. Without knowing it, I was developing a tough critical eye I'd be brave enough to focus on myself someday.

While I was shoring up the office, Hank exercised his charm. He dusted off his credit card, flew to Manhattan to meet the young rebels in publishing, and sold two manuscripts, one on witchcraft and the other on tantric yoga. We were thrilled and celebrated for days, but our trendiness betrayed us. The rebels continued to snap up tracts on the latest hippie fads, but they passed on all our serious fiction and nonfiction—an insult to my taste, I believed, and to my aspirations—and I got so tired of hearing the phrase "a near miss here at Knopf" (or Scribner's or Simon & Schuster) that I promised to work even harder for Arthur Bendel, our star literary client, until I secured a contract for him with a first-rate publisher.

\* \* \*

Bendel was more than a client, really. He was my friend and mentor. I thought he had a touch of genius, and he didn't argue the point. For more than a decade, through a pair of failed marriages, he'd written three brilliant, difficult novels, all unpublished except as bits and pieces in little magazines. The novels were flashy enough to have attracted a big-time agent at William Morris, but the agent gave up after a year or so without a sale. Arthur was disappointed, of course, but he shrugged it off and started on his fourth novel. He couldn't be budged from his purpose. He had a monkish devotion to his craft and no other serious loyalties except to his daughter, Brianna, a precocious six-year-old, and the San Francisco 49ers, whose football fortunes affected his mental stability.

Like almost everybody else, Bendel reached Larry's over the transom. When his sample chapter arrived, I approached it with the usual ho-hum attitude, but I was soon in a state of high excitement. Man, could this guy write! Every sentence crackled with energy, passion, and wit. His language was also distinctive. It didn't sound musty or bookish. Instead, he captured the cadences of the street—American talk, our knockabout anthems. And how I admired his clarity! I never had to slog through a bog of murky prose to catch a glimmer of meaning. True, he got carried away and lost the thread of his story at times, but I was certain any skillful editor could iron out the wrinkles.

Bendel was a discovery, an original. Full of enthusiasm, I called him right away to heap on the praise, but he was curiously subdued. Though he had the grace not to say so, he'd heard it all before. Still, he invited me to visit him later that week to discuss our options.

For our meeting, I fished an old tweed sports coat from a closet to suggest how professional I was, and walked through the park to the Richmond District. I would take this walk often in the months ahead and always looked forward to it. It had such promise, such a bright expectancy of good times. While conga drummers in their colorful dashikis pounded out a relentless beat, young women fluttered around them like butterflies, and I'd breathe in the sharp, healing smell of eucalyptus, feel a bracing hint of the ocean on my skin, and believe in my innocent way that anything was possible.

Bendel lived in an ugly stucco building. Even on sunny days, it seemed wreathed in fog. When I rang his bell, an eye peered at me through a peephole, after which Arthur unlocked his many locks and stood before me in a rumpled Pendleton, baggy jeans, and carpet slippers. Like Auden, he preferred the slippers for comfort and even wore them for a stroll around the block. In his early thirties, short and stocky, with a long fringe of blond hair around his balding dome, he projected the distracted air of the literary elite. I could see in an instant that he didn't know who I was, or why I'd come. He blinked at me as a miner might do after several hours down a shaft, trying to adjust his deprived senses to the universe above ground.

When I reminded him of our appointment, he chuckled. "Absentminded," he mumbled. "Goes with the territory." He led me into his threadbare living room, where the only stick of furniture was a leather recliner positioned inches away from a big

Sony TV. He'd bought the set on credit to indulge his obsession with the 49ers. The recliner was Bendel's throne. His guests sat on the floor, or dragged in a kitchen chair.

I chose the floor and offered him a beer from the six-pack I'd brought as a token of my esteem, but he declined. "Too early," he explained. He never touched a drop of alcohol until he finished his daily stint around five, when he dived wholeheartedly into a half-gallon jug of Early Times, the bourbon that Walker Percy, his favorite modern novelist, was rumored to drink.

I had never met anyone as disciplined as Bendel. His entire life was arranged around his writing, and he never broke with his routine. While I was still snoozing, he ran five miles every morning and ate a nutritious breakfast of bran cereal and fruit. He swallowed vitamins by the fistful, too, so I took him for a health nut at first, but he was only hoping to counteract the effects of the booze. If he didn't have to report for work as a substitute teacher—that was how he paid his bills—he lashed himself to an IBM Selectric until quitting time, and then started on the bourbon. It eased his lonely evenings. On the romantic front, he had problems. His past marriages haunted him, and he was pursuing an African American woman, a fellow teacher, who deflected his every advance.

From the start, Bendel and I got along well. There was no point in sending out his old novels, he thought. It would be better to wait until he finished the next one. I agreed and fell into the habit of stopping by his place at the cocktail hour to check on his progress. While jazz played on the stereo, Miles or Monk or some other avatar of midnight cool, we talked about books and took them apart, a practice that was new to me. I'd never studied creative writing or even attended a workshop, so Arthur's way of analyzing a text was a revelation. Under his benign tutelage, I began to grasp what literature is and what it could be. Though I was a novice, he was kind and treated me as an equal. "It's promising," he said, when I had the courage to show him something. "But it needs work." Ah, work! That was the key lesson I absorbed from Bendel: writing is hard work.

Sometimes he reversed the procedure and visited Larry's in the late afternoon. Up the stairs he climbed in his ratty Navy peacoat, with a half-pint stuck in a pocket. If he'd achieved his goal of three decent pages, his mood was jolly, but any shortfall upset him. In either case, I was glad for his company. The liquor, though cheap, was warming, and I remember laughing a lot. About what? Laughter born of being alive, I guess, and realizing how fine we had it there in our boho paradise with the future still ahead—or so it seemed to me, Arthur's junior by seven years, someone who'd yet to take a serious risk in art or love. I remained blissfully unaware of the blows my friend had suffered, and the damage they'd done to his confidence.

If we were mellow enough when Hank got home, we joined him on his eternal quest for women. He called them "chicks," as if they were being hatched for his pleasure. Union Street was his chief hunting ground, where the fern bars attracted young office workers. Bendel and I were a poor fit in our thrift shop clothes, and the women confirmed it by glancing away. We further ruined our chances with our lofty literary talk, resorting to such dreary pickup lines as, "Have you ever read *The Magic*

*Mountain*?" Tubercular Hans Castorp cut no ice, so we retired to a booth and ordered more whiskey. Who'd want to make it with such stupid chicks anyway? That was our attitude, but we hoped a stupid chick would see through the mask and be sympathetic. It never happened.

So we moped and drank and watched in envy as Hank performed. Sure, he had looks and charm, but his success depended on his determination. Just as Bendel persisted in the face of rejection, so did Hank in his effort to get laid. He was an artist in his own right, a master of seduction. If a woman failed to respond to his patter, he hit on the next one down the line. Capable of opening with such banalities as, "Hey, that's a nice dress!" he kept it light and breezy until he connected. He never held out for a great beauty, either. He was a great democrat and liked women of all types, or so I thought when I felt generous toward him. At other times, jealous, I accused him of sleeping with trolls.

On the rare nights when Hank struck out, Bendel lobbied for a last stop at an African American club on Divisadero, where the object of his affection supposedly hung out. This was a mistake, and yet we committed it often. We'd hear the throb of Motown music as we pulled up, and I'd grit my teeth and follow the others inside. What nerve we had! We shone like beacons in that overheated, dimly lit room. I tried to look harmless, beneath contempt, not worth the price of a bullet. For Bendel, though, the club was a picnic on wheels. He slapped out high fives and danced the Funky Chicken. No doubt he survived because everyone assumed he was crazy. There were muttered threats and once a dust-up that left him with a fat lip, but for all his madness and bravado, he never found the woman he was seeking.

\* \* \*

Against the odds, Larry's Literary continued to flourish. We sold a book or so a month, enough to pay me a small salary, and when we were mentioned prominently in *Publishers Weekly,* the industry bible, Hank demanded that we clean up our act and move to more suitable quarters. He located a fancy Victorian for us on one of the Haight's prettiest streets. The owner, an academic, was so desperate to leave on sabbatical that he rented it to us without a quibble. In the lovely garden, where plum and cherry trees grew, we entertained bigwigs from New York, treating them to wine and marijuana and observing with delight as the California poison slowly seeped into their systems.

The new house improved our image, but it didn't affect the reception our most gifted clients got, the ones struggling to become real writers. After months on the job, I could define what those two words meant to me at last. A real writer was someone dedicated to expressing a particular vision of life in an absolutely individual way, through an attention to language that raised each sentence to its highest power. However backhandedly, and with plenty of gaps yet to be filled, I'd learned that much at least, so I was more bothered than ever that our best manuscripts went begging. There was too much business in the business of publishing. I was weary of rewarding witches and astrologers. What I craved, of course, was justice.

Yet my disillusion couldn't match Bendel's. I was so enthusiastic about his writing that he'd let a ray of optimism penetrate the depression that was always lurking, but as he battled to complete his new novel, certain it was a failure, his spirits sank. Contrary to our plan, I'd been secretly submitting an old novel of his, and when I showed him a laudatory rejection letter, he flew off the handle. "I've had enough 'encouragement' to last a lifetime!" he shouted. His paranoia, ordinarily in the high-normal range, cycled out of control. Convinced that his baldness was the cause of all his troubles, he ordered a wig by mail. It was a fluffy concoction fit for the male lead in a '50s beach movie. "How do I look?" he asked. The answer was, "Like a sorrowful Troy Donahue," but nobody had the heart to tell him.

I worried that he was losing his grip. He might have, too, if it hadn't been for Brianna, who spent the weekends with him and kept him steady. He drank much less bourbon and even carried out the empties. They played checkers and dominoes, and if the Niners had a game, they shared the recliner and watched it together. But here, too, Arthur was stymied. The team had left its former home at Kezar Stadium, exchanging a grass gridiron for the artificial turf of Candlestick Park, and that had led to a slew of knee injuries. For Bendel, every fumble, every dropped pass and missed field goal, seemed to echo his own stuttering fate. A vast conspiracy loomed, he implied to me, and at its core was betrayal.

Despite his distress, he soldiered on, and when the new novel was done, he presented it to me with a frown, as if to say, "Here's more water to pour under the bridge." I believed it was his best book yet, more dramatic and accomplished, and I fully expected to sell it, although I shouldn't have told him so. But I had no mastery over my wishes then—I wanted what I wanted. I sent the novel to Random House, where Bendel had an admirer renowned for his taste in literary fiction, and we sat down to wait. Only the most sensitive editors understand how time weighs on a writer, and how destructive a long silence can be, and this man wasn't among them. Ten weeks went by before he returned the manuscript to us, another "near miss."

It's true, as publishing lore holds, that some books are sold on the eighteenth submission, but that was never the case with us. After Arthur was rejected three more times, with each publisher citing reservations about the novel's commercial viability, I knew the worst and so did he. One editor asked him to consider a rewrite, and he was willing to try if they'd advance him some money—just five hundred dollars, a pittance, but they turned him down.

That broke him, I think. He got bitter and lashed out at the world. Who could blame him? All his solitary toil had come to nothing. Late at night, drunk and alone, he'd call Larry's and accuse us of a variety of sins, only to return to his senses in the morning and slip abject (but beautifully written) notes of apology through our mail slot.

This story should end unhappily, but it doesn't, not really. Arthur Bendel did publish a book eventually—three of them, in fact. He'd neglected his bank account for months and needed money fast, so he replied to an ad in *The Berkeley Barb* and started cranking out porn novels for a smut baron in the San

Fernando Valley. His pen name was Dick Drake, and his first venture, an offhand tribute to Hank, was *Waterbed Motel.* Next came *Jennifer's Awakening* and finally *Hellcats in Leather,* a classic of the stroke trade. Even as a hack, Arthur wrote so ferociously that it must have scared his customers a little. He claimed to be disgusted with himself, but the books were displayed on a shelf next to photos of Brianna, and he inscribed a copy for me.

His other novels, the blood of his labors, were stored in cartons. Could a committed editor have saved them? I'm still not sure, although I doubt it. Bendel had to find the missing element on his own since that's how he went at things, freestyle, with an exuberant faith in his work. I can't say what he might have done differently, either, except perhaps to be even tougher on himself, but that would be asking a lot. He'd done his best, after all. Dejected, he vanished for weeks to lick his wounds, then resurfaced in a brand-new suit. Hank and I were astonished. "I've got a job," Arthur said gloomily. He'd hired on as a computer programmer, and earned enough in his first month to settle all his debts.

On the other hand, Larry's Literary had hit a peak. We'd ridden the hippie wave to its logical conclusion and had crashed on the beach. I was bored with being an agent, anyway, and ready for a change, but Hank was still ambitious and negotiated a transfer to his company's head office in New York. He'd be closer to the Empire State Building, so he could hook up with Superman—that was our joke at his expense. Probably there were jokes about me, as well, but I had no regrets. In my semiconscious fashion, I'd absorbed many valuable lessons, and though I had to run smack into Bendel's brick wall of rejection before I was humble enough to heed them, my time at Larry's paid unexpected dividends when I began to write for real.

Hank failed to make his million in the Big Apple, but Arthur's stock soared. He attributed it to luck, and maybe he was right, because he got lucky in love, too, and met his wife, Belle, while he and Brianna were at a matinee of *Fantasia,* believe it or not.

They're still together and have a huge house on Lake Tahoe, the product of Bendel's early retirement. My old pal is portly now and walks rather than jogs. His wig is history. And listen to this—he has hobbies! He grows prize-winning tomatoes, fishes for Mackinac trout, and plays classical piano. After dinner, he'll pour you a brandy and tap out a Bach sonata for your entertainment. He swears he's perfectly content, and I have no reason to doubt it, but I can't shake a feeling that he has a ghost self somewhere, who sits alone in a room and types.

*Narrative,* 2005

# Travels

## An Innocent Abroad: Florence

I am on a cruise ship bound for Italy. I am 20 years old, a wayward student escaping from a small snowbound all-male college in upstate New York. I have never seen so much snow before, in fact. It starts falling in October and continues through the winter and into the spring. Our classrooms border a frozen quadrangle students must reach by hiking up a steep, icy hill. Only young men desperate for a formal education make the climb on a regular basis.

I am in rebellion myself, desperate to be educated but in a different, less punishing way. Maybe I can find out what I need to know by exploring, through trial-and-error. The world is big, and I want to see it. I imagine my future as a great romance. I have read too much Hemingway and not enough Dostoyevsky.

The sea has been very calm so far. I stand for hours at the rail and watch the wheeling birds and the spume-dappled water. There is nothing else to watch. We haven't seen any land for days, not since leaving Manhattan. This creates a curious sensation of being outside time, without a particular destiny.

When the Azores appear on the horizon at last, every passenger comes out for a look. The islands are hunks of rock in the ocean, nothing more, but everybody gapes and comments. One man even sighs. He will write a postcard home that begins, "Today we saw the Azores . . ."

Lisbon is our first port of call. A beautiful beach at Estoril, actual Portuguese people on the boulevards. That excites me. "Yes, I've been to Portugal," I say to myself, practicing. We stop in Morocco the next afternoon, in Tangier. Huckster merchants in fezzes ring the shore, shouting and waving. Oranges, parrots, a tempting strangeness. I wish I could follow them down a dank alley to taste forbidden pleasures, but I am too wary, still too American, unwilling to commit experience.

Not so Gregor, my roommate. I share a cabin with him and two other guys, all of us headed for Florence and a semester abroad. Gregor grew up in Brooklyn. He is hip to the streets, the first truly cool person I've ever met. He has a wonderful voice and sings wherever he is, performing gorgeous front-stoop doo-wop tunes. In Florence, he will sing to the swans in a park one evening, and the swans will rise up and flap their wings in tribute.

Gregor smokes marijuana. It is 1963, so he keeps this a deep secret. He will later turn me on in Arezzo, after our failed attempt to see some famous frescoes by Piero della Francesca that were being restored. I will ask him, accepting the joint at a crummy pensione, "Am I going to become an addict?" I am still too wary, too American, etc.

I don't know about the marijuana yet, not in Tangier. I do know that Gregor is unaccountably happy and singing his brains out as we sail away. He has made some friends among the crew, fellow druggies, and he invites me to join them at a party that night. The prospect thrills me. I, too, am dying to be cool and need all the help I can get.

The crew deck is down below. Gregor leads the way. As we descend, I hear dance music echoing from a portable record player, some kind of rumba or cha-cha. It's a merry scene, all right. The crewmen have hung colorful paper lanterns from overhead cables and put out a cut-glass bowl of punch. They have swapped their uniforms for casual clothes, Hawaiian shirts, and neatly pressed khakis. They dance with women in slinky dresses, who have elaborately styled hair and painted, doll-like faces.

I move closer and see that I'm mistaken. Those aren't women. Those are crewmen in wigs. In drag! I've been at sea for less than a week and already the scales are falling from my eyes. Life in its amazing fullness is reaching out to me, so I grit my teeth and try not to run.

Beer bottles clink, the engine rumbles. The indigo sky is alive with stars. When a tall sailor in a Rita Hayworth–style wig asks me to dance, I decline politely. I expect to be tossed out for being a spoilsport, but instead the sailor pats my cheek, calls me "honey," and urges me to enjoy myself. And I do.

This worries me a little. It goes against my upbringing. My mother, through her psychic powers, can probably see me now. I sense her disappointment. A man in a dress is supposed to be depraved, a monster. So why am I having a good time at a party where half the men are wearing dresses? Because it goes against my upbringing? Yes, it's possible. Fun may be had in new and unexpected places. That is the traveler's first lesson.

\* \* \*

The ship rolls on. We pass through the Strait of Gibraltar and along the Algerian coast to Naples, where we tour the harbor. Cobbled streets, the Tyrrhenian Sea blue and implacable. Sunshine, cottony clouds riding the breeze, a pervasive smell of salt. The city looks ancient to me, historic and filled with mystery. I am aware of barnacles and rotting wood.

The glassy-eyed fish at an open-air market are arranged precisely, as in a Dutch still life. The fat market women wear wedding rings, the shapely ones do not. Men huddle in doorways nearby and smoke cigarettes with a furious energy. They argue, they gesticulate, they stomp their feet and comb their hair. Their only job is to observe.

They are the fabled *ragazzi*, boys forever, even at the age of 45 or 50. They visit their mothers every Sunday unless they live at home, as many do. Priests—black crows—spook them. They're slow to go to confession. Their fathers work as barbers and listen to opera on the radio. The music drifts from shop windows, sublime arias I hear floating above the racket of the crowd.

I eat at a pizzeria. I eat a real Italian pizza—no cheese, a sauce of fresh tomatoes, herbs sprinkled on top. The red wine is raw but good. Gregor is still happy. He imitates Frankie Lymon and sings "Why Do Fools Fall in Love?" to a tattered bunch of urchins, who ask him for coins and pretend to steal his wallet. In England, the Beatles are busy being born.

We get off the ship for good in Genoa, dragging our bags behind us. In the morning, we will go by bus to Florence and settle in for the long haul. The thought of impending study fills me with dread. Professors, classrooms, dead air, responsibility—but there won't be any snow, at least. That's a plus, I tell myself. Meanwhile, we have a last night free to wander. I plan to make the most of it. I am a youth with a mission.

I walk from our hotel at twilight, into another ancient city that seems in a state of perennial decay. The colors are muted and faded, touched with an ashy pallor. Everything human has already happened here, I realize, and it will keep happening, infinitely repeated. The idea is new to me and comforting somehow. Genoa has already witnessed every mistake a young man can make. I count this as a blessing.

It's nasty out. The clouds open and rain batters the old stones, but I ignore it. My mission is to find a woman—a prostitute, to be more accurate. This, too, goes against my upbringing, but in Europe, women are part of the deal. It says so in every novel. The hero is always ducking into a bordello with some sleazy tart. I almost expect to see signs that read, "This way to the whorehouse."

Cafes, narrow alleys, the reek of gutters. I feel anxious and high on adrenaline, a thief about to pull off a crime. I check the railroad station and the waterfront without success. Maybe it's too early for the girls to be on duty. What do I know about the rules of whoring? Soon I am hopelessly lost. The rain drenches me to the bone. A driver hurrying home toots his horn and shouts at me, *"Cretino!"*

I am about to give up the search when I bump into a friend. It's Gregor, of course. He is also on a mission, same as mine. We laugh about this and order espressos at a bar, where old men in fedoras are playing cards for money. Gregor takes off the beret he bought in Lisbon and wrings it out. Water splashes on the counter, forms a tiny lake on the worn linoleum floor. You wouldn't think a swatch of wool could hold so much liquid.

Then we spot them, two hookers on their rounds. *Miracolo!* They are dressed alike, in tight red sweaters and short black skirts, and they carry shiny little purses of patent leather. Their stiletto heels click on the paving stones. Our mouths must be agape, because they pause by the bar and stare at us. The petite one is attractive in a hard-bitten way, but her partner is huge, built like a professional wrestler.

We have a problem, obviously. Gregor, being a man of the world, will solve it, I assume. He'll do me a favor and award me the petite one. But no, he wants her, too! We stand in the rain and debate the issue until he has a bright idea. How about a coin toss? OK, I agree. I flip a lira coin. I lose.

I'm sick at heart, reeling with envy. I watch Gregor disappear with my beloved, wishing I had a knife to stick in his back. The hooker has become immensely desirable in the moment, a prize, a trophy. Yes, I would gladly kill on her behalf.

The wrestler chews her gum and waits with her arms crossed, but I send her away. "I'm sorry, *signorina*," I tell her, adopting a forlorn expression and gripping my belly to show I'm indisposed. I keep an eye on her purse. For once, I'm lucky. She doesn't hit me with it.

\* \* \*

Our bus the next morning is a drab Mercedes. It rattles and belches as we motor along the coast. Suitcases are strapped to the roof, and the driver appears to be hung over. Firenze, it says on a little destination card above his head. Florence, the city of flowers, kingdom of the Medici, where we'll live with local families for the next few months and my new freedom will surely be compromised.

We follow a road that overlooks the Ligurian Sea. Fishing boats can be seen in the distance. The view is dramatic and inspiring, but I'm still upset. Gregor sits up front, his beret at a jaunty angle, as dry now as an autumn leaf. He even has the nerve to whistle, unconsciously celebrating his victory.

Portofino, a fishing village, is lovely. Houses in subtle tones of gold and rose-red, their window shutters closed against the heat. Balconies hung with laundry, a good clean scent of soap on the wind. America is all primary colors, a giant kindergarten. I prefer the softness of the Italian palette, the flaking paint, the disrepair, the palpable presence of the past.

The bus chugs up a hill, and a suitcase slips from its binding and lands in the road. The latch springs. Clothes go blowing about. Underwear, socks. *Che peccato*! What a pity! It's among the few phrases I know, having skipped the shipboard language lessons to stare at the sea. *Mi chiamo* Bill. Hello, I am a kindergartner from America.

We stop for lunch in Portovenere, on the Gulf of la Spezia. It's called Golfo dei Poeti, because so many poets have sung its praises, including Dante and Petrarch. Lord Byron once swam from Portovenere to San Terenzo, across the Bay of Lerici, to visit Percy Shelley at his rented digs. An incredible swim, really, for a wastrel.

Shelley's house, Casa Magni, still stands. It has an open ground floor and seven arches in a sort of loggia. The sea washes up almost to the front door. Shelley was mad as a hatter at the end, tortured by horrible visions. He died in a sailing accident at 29. His boat, a schooner, had lounge chairs and bookshelves built into it.

Casa Magni has a plaque to commemorate Shelley's stay. The plaque says, "Sailing on a fragile bark he was landed by an unforeseen chance to the silence of the Elysian Fields." Shelley did not write those words himself.

I'm touched, anyhow. I've never been to a village where poetry matters, where it has worked its way into the fabric of everyday life. Those British romantics lived like bohos, strumming their guitars and fathering children out of wedlock. I'm all for them. Am I not slightly Byronic myself? I believe there might be a poem or two in me, if I can just get them out.

Portovenere marches up a mountain slope, toward a fortress wall. There are olive trees, dark-green pines, and a bell tower with a clock. Tables are reserved for us at a trattoria by the harbor, on a vine-covered patio. We dine on pasta and roast chicken. The white wine comes in liter carafes and helps me to forgive Gregor. After two glasses, he's my bosom pal again, and we decide to chat up two women in our group, Jessica and Cynthia.

Jessica has the severe but compelling manner of a campus intellectual. She uses words like "deliquesce" and "ramification" and bites her nails. Her clothes are often black. She scares me a little, but Cynthia has the opposite effect. Blond and guile-less, she will be barefoot on Haight Street in a few years, her locks threaded with wildflowers and a curly-haired cherub on her hip.

We talk about literature, of course. Gregor quotes a line he swears is from *The Divine Comedy*. I think he's about to sing, but he doesn't. The wine goes around. Is it Jessica who mentions the famous grotto? The place where Byron launched his epic swim? We must visit this grotto, and right away.

Into the hills we go, without a clue where the grotto might be. Jessica speaks the best Italian, so we elect her as our leader. Byron, she asks? The swimmer? Heads shake, people give us strange looks. A big silence hangs over Portovenere. Most shops are closed. Lunch is over, the peasants are bedded down for a siesta.

The grotto remains elusive, but we don't care after a while. Our search loses importance as the wine wears off. The after-noon is bright and warm, and the bay is sparkling, so we tumble to earth on a grassy hillside, where Gregor promptly falls asleep.

Time passes. A lot of time, actually. We roust ourselves at last and stroll to the harbor, but everthing seems different. There are shadows where the sun once shone. The village is awake again, the citizens bustling about. The waiters at the trattoria have moved the tables from the patio, and it's as if we've never been there. We'd been erased.

"The bus is gone," Jessica says.

This is true. We've been left behind. We won't be in Florence when our families come to claim us. We're orphans and will have to pay a hideous price. Cynthia is crying. She worries that she'll be sent home to Delaware. What could be worse?

Gregor swings into action. We'll pool our money, he says, and hire a taxi. I throw in the ten-spot I hide in my wallet's secret compartment. There go dozens of espressi, bottles of Chianti, books of poetry and fateful assignations. We find a taxi stand and negotiate a fare. Thirty bucks, plus tip. The cabbie's a scoundrel, but there's nothing we can do.

In his little Fiat, we turn inland from the bountiful sea and race toward Florence on the autostrada. Cynthia has stopped crying and sits on my lap. That would be wonderful if we didn't have so far to travel. I feel her weight on my thighs. My feet are getting numb, and I'm tired and mourning the loss of my ten dollars. The literary life can be costly.

\* \* \*

Our taxi speeds toward the city center and the piazza where our college is located. We are late arrivals, bad students who have

342

missed the school bus. The director rolls his eyes at the sight of us. A fleshy, operatic man, he wears an ascot, leans on a walking stick, and affects a British accent. Probably he has read too much Henry James.

Cynthia is still nervous, thinking she might be expelled, but there's no way. The college has already banked our tuition. Instead, the director reprimands us—irresponsible behavior, detrimental to the group, blah blah blah. It's silly. In fact, my free-form education on the Continent is progressing nicely. In the last week, I've almost danced with a sailor in drag and almost made it with a hooker in Genoa. Who knows what I'll learn next?

In another room, Italian families are waiting. They will be our hosts, taking us in as boarders. They're dressed formally and look uneasy about the deal they've struck. To invite an uncultured young American into your home is no laughing matter. It's best to lock up the jewelry and the majolica.

Cynthia is claimed, and so are Gregor and Jessica. Finally, the director summons me and introduces me to an elderly woman with bright blue eyes—eyes that men must have fallen into, swooning, when she was younger. This is the marchesa. She has on a black dress shiny from wear, and her white hair is in a tight bun held fast with an elegant tortoise-shell comb. Her cheeks are round and rosy. She smiles at me in a serenely accepting way.

I am drawn to her immediately. Some people age with a special grace, without any bitterness, and the marchesa is among them. It's her smile that gets me. She can see right into my soul.

Absurd, yes, but I'm certain of it. It can happen like that at a first meeting—no barriers, no sense of opposition, a kind of purity. She knows I'm up to no good in Italy, but it doesn't faze her. What's youth for, if not for adventure?

I will bring her a dozen roses one day, and she will weep.

At twilight, we set out on foot for her flat. The marchesa limps a bit, favoring her left side. Still, she's cheerful. The walking is tough on me with a heavy suitcase. My feet are sore from the long taxi ride. Cynthia sat on my lap for hours, and she cut off the blood flow to my legs. How unfair! I've often wished for a woman on my lap, and when I get one it hurts.

It turns out the marchesa has fallen on hard times. Her flat occupies the ground floor of an old palazzo, where she has six cold, dark rooms hung with sun-bleached tapestries. Touch an armchair and you raise a cloud of dust. Ancestors in antique gilt frames loom large. They are brooding presences, distant and unfathomable. I can hear them whispering.

The marchesa calls for her family. They assemble in the parlor. Here's her son Aldo, a 40ish bureaucrat, who lives in the flat, too, along with his shy wife, Lucretia, and their son Giorgio, who's 13 and—incredibly—a baseball fan. He says to me, in perfect English, "Hello, sir. You are from New York. Tell me, please, how are the New York Yankees?"

I am thrown off-stride. The few responses I've mastered in Italian will not suffice. "Well, they need a starting pitcher if they hope to win the pennant next year," I say, also in English.

"And Mickey Mantle?"

"He's been injured. It's been a rough year for him."

344

Giorgio dashes to his bedroom and returns with his base-ball glove, scuffed and ragged. He keeps the pocket soft by rubbing it with olive oil. It could be a sacred icon, by his tender caress.

We sit down to supper. The marchesa serves thin vegetable soup, chewy bread and a stringy piece of boiled beef, but not a drop of wine. Hardly anyone speaks, mostly because of Aldo. Frankly, he's a pain. He imposes order. He reminds me of the hawk-nosed Florentine merchants you see in paintings, bent over a pile of coins. My soul is a blank to him and always will be.

For dessert, there is a special chestnut pudding. It tastes awful to me, but I don't let on. Instead, I kiss my fingertips and sing its praises, a gesture for which I pay dearly. Soon chestnut pudding shows up on the table almost nightly, until the stuff is coming out my ears. Only Gregor suffers a worse fate. He lands in a house with a family that worships fennel, and they feed him endless plates of it over pasta, sauteed, deep-fried, or raw in salads. By the end of the semester, he stinks of anise.

Classes start. It is a torture. Every morning around 7, the marchesa raps on my door and asks, *"Permesso?"* Sometimes I am awake and dressed, but more often my head is buried under a pillow. She sets a plastic tray on my bureau, always the same—a hard roll, butter, marmalade and a pot of strong coffee. Always, too, she is smiling. I envy her, really. I crave such equanimity myself, such a perfect balance on earth, but I fear I'll never gain it.

The streets teem with children in school uniforms. They tote books, they run in packs, they are adored by passing adults, who chuck them under the chin and pat them on the head. Kids are the true royalty in Florence, little princes and princesses whose every whim must be indulged. Childhood flies, after all. The madonna's glow? It comes from the glowing infant she clasps to her breast.

The traffic is intense. Diesel fumes, belching old buses, motorscooters that buzz like mosquitoes. I am forever dodging hellbent drivers and also soccer balls. The kids kick them back and forth, bouncing them off walls, cathedrals, monuments, and cars. No surface is spared from serving as a temporary goal, even the statues in the piazza across from my college.

Our school building has many windows, and that's too bad. I spend my classroom time staring at the piazza and wishing I were out there, where real life is going on. I watch the ancients seated on benches, their bodies bundled in overcoats despite the autumn warmth. Leathery faces, a white stubble of whiskers, intricate debates over who remembers what, and why. The sun shines on *bambini* playing in the dirt. All the young mothers are beautiful, even when they're ugly.

The professors drone on. They have an amazing capacity to block out our snoring. It's tedious to listen to a packaged lecture on the Renaissance, when the Renaissance is alive outside. I touch it almost daily. San Marco is near my flat, and I go there and sit in awe before Fra Angelico's frescoes. "The Mocking of Christ," "The Annunciation." He painted them from 1438 to 1445, but they could have been done yesterday. The frescoes are rich in emotion, in spirit, in longing—a longing I am beginning to share.

What do I long for? I want to be part of a civilized world, not the kindergarten of America. A world where art, literature, and music matter, where history is present and palpable. The old palaces in Florence, they alert me to how every human endeavor ends—chipped, battered, in debris. It's not so bad. I can accept it. That's what I think at the moment, but I am still young and not yet on familiar terms with grief.

Daydreaming again. There's a song running through my head, one by Rita Pavone, a pint-sized belter from Torino, who's a teen sensation. She rules every jukebox in town and will be mentioned in a Pink Floyd lyric someday and even perform on "The Ed Sullivan Show." We hear Rita when we escape into a café after class—*un bicchiere di vino rosso,* maybe a game of 8-ball if we can find a pool table.

In the cafés, we talk with astonishing energy. We cook up new theories about the nature of existence and advance arguments to celebrate our own brilliance. It's no use, though. The Italian guys put us to shame.

How sophisticated they are as they linger for an eternity over a single aperitif, their sport coats draped over their shoulders and their manicured hands free to punctuate their words. The only thing that disrupts their weary languor is a pretty woman passing by. Then they pant like dogs in heat.

I've concluded that cigarettes are essential to the pose. Sartre, he's always pictured smoking, isn't he? It must be imperative for a continental intellectual to be addicted to nicotine, so I spring for a 10-pack of Nazionale *con filtro* and fire up a couple every day. My eyes water at first, and my throat gets raw. I have coughing fits, but I stick to the program. Gradually, I do begin to feel smarter, although there's no objective evidence to support the claim.

A month goes by. The grapes are harvested, the Tuscan landscape flames with color. I buy a cheap bicycle and ride into the countryside. I ride along the turbid brown Arno and watch the fishermen with their long poles. The rains come in November, but the days are often still sunny, if bitingly cold. I go to the Mercato Nuovo for a new wool sweater and rub the snout of Il Porcellino, the famous bronze boar, for good luck.

But things are changing, the semester's winding down. Cynthia has an Italian boyfriend, for instance. It was inevitable, really, since those guys will pursue an American blonde to the ends of the earth. Guido isn't a bad sort despite his enameled hair and open-necked shirts. He's a pacifist guitar player, who lives in a ruined villa in the hills of Fiesole with his mother and two brothers, one a Marxist and the other subtly and sweetly loony.

We all take the bus up to visit one Saturday. Gregor sings to the other passengers. He's stoned as usual, on the last of the weed he bought in Tangier. Guido's mother is in her garden, plucking bugs from plants and polishing off a huge glass of Chianti. Blowsy yet seductive, the signora shows us around the villa.

I've never seen such wreckage, but she doesn't seem to mind. At an old cistern, she pushes a few rocks into the water. She knocks stones from a retaining wall with a backhand swipe. Let it collapse, she appears to be saying. Collapsing is our fate.

She serves lunch on a patio. Prosciutto and cheese, more wine, fruit in a wicker basket. Guido strums Joan Baez folk songs, while his Marxist brother offers criticism and correction. Politics in Italy are hopeless, a form of entertainment at best. Florentines care about the basics, good bread and olive oil, the closeness of family, the soul's ardor. Even the peasants know a little Dante.

After our meal, the loony boy excuses himself to chase small birds through the ruins. He loves the game. Here's happiness on the wing! His laughter echoes as he dashes down a hill, vanishing into a grove of olive trees.

I go for a walk with Jessica. I'm still awkward around her. She is intelligent, academic, and forceful in her opinions. Also clever and witty. I'm attracted to her mind, and that's a first for me. Thinking was not required of my high school girlfriends (or of me), but now I've entered an epoch of discovery and am eager to share my epiphanies. Jessica is the designated muse, whether or not she wants to be.

I light a Nazionale, cough, and tell her how lately I've been sitting on the loggia in Piazza della Signoria and writing in a notebook. It's pleasant there with the tourists gone. She doesn't blink, so I confess that I might want to be a writer someday. I realize she could slash me to bits at any instant, but she doesn't. Instead she's sympathetic. She listens. Soon we will be lovers.

By December, time has become my enemy. The days whip by, and I must face the distressing prospect of returning to my snowbound university. It makes me sweat at night, even in winter. I'm irritable around the flat, tired of Aldo and his clerkish routines. "*Va via!*" I'd like to shout. Get out of here, Aldo! The marchesa guesses the source of my moodiness and puts a chocolate bar on my breakfast tray.

Giorgio and I are still the best of pals, at least. He treats me as if I'm a weird older brother from a faraway planet. A crowd gathers whenever we play catch outside, and I make peppy chatter and embarrass Giorgio by saying he'll be the next Joe DiMaggio.

I bring the marchesa a dozen roses, and she weeps.

\* \* \*

The longing just gets worse! I skip classes to visit galleries and museums. I am devouring the paintings and sculptures, storing up impressions to nourish me in the dark times ahead. The guards at the Uffizi recognize me now and nod to me on their rounds. Are they laughing inside? Poor young American in love with art, he must go home to the land of Norman Rockwell.

Gregor and I plan a farewell weekend. We lie to our host families and say we're going to Rome by train to see the Pope. We go nowhere. We wallow in Florence instead, soaking up the city. We wander from café to café, get drunk and sappy, and find ourselves near Santa Croce at a medieval open-air bar jammed with grotesques. They're pounding grappa and eating roasted pig ears. We sleep both nights on park benches and wake covered with dew. Sunday we climb up to Piazzale Michelangelo and watch the sun rise over red tile roofs.

Our city, we cry! Gregor sings to Florence, and Florence applauds.

Next there's the gross nuisance of term papers and final exams. The hiss of radiators, those profs with hair sprouting from their noses. How can they dare to issue us grades when we've been studying the ineffable?

We throw a big party at the semester's end, but it's a hollow affair. Gregor, in his wine-soaked beret, will head to Paris and try but fail to be a painter. Guido proposes to Cynthia, then unproposes. She accuses him of being fickle, a Romeo. In his own defense, Guido shrugs. Cynthia will wind up in San Francisco, hiding her hash pipe on the fine leather purse Guido bought her on the Ponte Vecchio.

Jessica and I will travel to Switzerland, Germany, France, and England. We'll stop at many clubs and pubs and hammer many pinball machines, pretending our trip will go on and on. Rita Pavone is still on every jukebox, no matter what country.

But first I am in the piazza across from our college by myself—one more time, taking stock. Church bells toll, pigeons flap, doves are cooing. The sky turns pink. At that moment, I should be writing in my notebook, "Youth fades, the loving memories endure," but I don't have the words yet. They come to me years later, approaching with the speed of light.

*Salon*, 1998

351

## Barbados: All Right

It's an ordinary weekday morning in Speightstown, a little fishing village on the west coast of Barbados. The Caribbean is flat and clear, the color of turquoise, and the prevailing January trade winds push a procession of ever-changing clouds across a big blue sky. Already the local fleet has gone out to sea in pursuit of flying fish, except for a couple of ancient skiffs—*Elsie, Fondue II*—that are beached and bleaching in the sun by the Fisherman's Pub, where the lunch special today is macaroni and creamed potatoes. The pub is a cheerful, busy, rowdy spot, especially at night, so there are cautionary signs posted inside forbidding the use of obscene language and the theft of draft beer. The signs, it must be admitted, are frequently ignored.

Down the dusty Speightstown lanes come the married women of the village, off to do their shopping, immaculately groomed and dressed in bright dresses and fancy hats. They carry purses and comport themselves with great dignity even as they stroll past hardscrabble yards in which roosters crow and tethered goats munch on blades of grass.

The houses here are compact and made of wood, almost always freshly painted and resting on a foundation of concrete or coral stone from which they can be easily detached and transported. They're known as chattel houses—chattel being a person's movable property—and in the old days people routinely moved them from place to place, sometimes following the sugarcane harvest.

Radios are turned up loud in many of the houses, blasting reggae music and its Bajan derivatives. In one yard, a grizzled old man sits on his steps, nips at a bottle of Mount Gay rum, and talks nonstop to the clouds. It would be beneath the women to comment or take notice of him. Barbados was a colony of Great Britain from 1625 to 1966, and its most sophisticated citizens still have a reserve that's peculiar to the British, an ability to ignore any trace of unpleasantness and keep one's feet, as it were, on the imperial high road.

This makes for an orderly, polite society, largely untroubled by problems you might find elsewhere in the Caribbean. It shows in the demeanor of schoolchildren arriving on buses, each boy and girl in a spotlessly clean uniform, quiet, well-mannered, and respectful of their elders.

Other women, the wives of farmers in from the countryside, have set up along the town's main street to sell fruits and vegetables from baskets, carts, and tables. They are often elderly and weary-looking, their faces deeply creased. As they preside over beautiful displays of tomatoes, yams, breadfruit, green beans, and a half-dozen other treats, they banter with their customers in a melodious Bajan English, a form of pidgin that's so allusive and encoded most English-speaking tourists cannot decipher it. Their standard greeting, though, is intelligible.

"All right with you?" they ask, or, simply, "Is all right?"

I have been on the island for two days now and have learned a proper response. Whenever a trader lady calls out to me, I smile and say, "I cool."

I am in Barbados on holiday, obligated to live like a pasha on the west coast—also known as the Gold or Platinum Coast—which is the most striking, lush, and expensive acreage around.

The high season is beginning here, a time when wealthy Brits flee from the drippy grayness of another English winter to bask in brilliant, bone-warming sunshine such as they have never experienced at home. They are a curious sight, formal in their studied informality, half-naked in their bathing suits and yet still striding about the beach with the determined gait of financiers bound for the City, a ghost copy of *Finacial Times* under their arms. They love the heat of the tropics, but they resist its sensuality. I imagine them all to be related to the Royal Family and entertain myself by inventing whimsical names for them— Lord Demerol, Lady Smyth-Sonian, and the devilish Sir Tommy Shortpants.

My outpost in St. Michael Parish is a luxury resort a half-mile or so from Speightstown. I have a lovely suite of rooms ten yards from the sea. I go to sleep to the crashing of waves and wake to the sound of rustling palm trees and the fragrant smell of tropical flowers. Everywhere I look I see blazing primary colors, a welcoming world from which the concept of hard work has been banished.

At breakfast every morning I devise a recreational plan for the next 12 or so hours that involves swimming, snorkeling, tanning, reading, and at least one nap. It's a brutal, grueling schedule that would kill a lesser man. Always, too, over my tea and toast, I listen to the Caribbean Broadcasting Corporation's drive-time deejay, who delivers important news about cricket matches and impending calypso concerts.

This deejay is something of a comedian. Yesterday he put through a surprise phone call to a farmer outside Bridgetown, the island's capital. The phone rang about 20 times before the farmer finally picked it up.

"You sleepin' in your yard of your house?" the deejay asked him, in a comprehensible semipidgin. "Or you in that yard feedin' some pigs?"

"No pigs," the farmer replied, utterly unfazed to be talking to a stranger. "Just some sheep in a pasture. What I can do for you, mon?"

"Harry, we learn it's your birthday! You're plainly over 40! We hear you gonna marry that woman over in Christ Church Parish!"

"You never know, mon," Harry said flatly.

"Harry!" cried the deejay. "I go play a special song for you by Lesley Gore."

"Say by *who*?"

"*Lesley Gore*, mon!" Then came the tinny, nasal bleat of "It's My Party," a song that, like Dracula, will never die. I switched off the radio and hiked into town to buy some oranges and Banks beer, a local brew essential for survival.

At the Alexandra School, an Anglican institution, bountiful teenage girls were entering the grounds under the watchful, probing eyes of several young men across the street. The young men can always be found hanging around a wildly painted house, where their ostensible business is the repairing of "tyres." I think of them as the Tyre Repair Gang and believe that their actual purpose in life is to try and seduce the Alexandra girls. When the girls are in classrooms, the Tyre Repair Gang grow restless. They argue, joke, wrestle, and indulge in vicious games of dominoes. Sometimes they fall asleep under the palm trees in their yard, dreaming their fantastic dreams.

\* \* \*

Summer is the true rainy season in Barbados, when fierce hurricanes pose a threat to islands throughout the Caribbean. It isn't supposed to rain heavily in late January, but one morning we suffered through a cloudburst, one of those thundering tropical storms that saturates the earth with endless amounts of water in a matter of minutes.

In my living room I sat listening to the downpour and watching a little bananaquit bird, bright yellow, suck the residue of honey from the bottom of my teacup. I read the *Advocate*, too, a leading Bajan paper, and was distressed to learn that some readers felt the local calypso tradition was at an all-time low. One correspondent, Hal Hewitt, tackled the issue head-on.

"All that's necessary these days to make a hit calypso is to get a fairly good backing band," wrote Hewitt, "and repeat the following lines over and over: *Shake yuh bum bum; Jam in de party and Jump and wave.*"

Winter cloudbursts on the island are brief. By ten o'clock the sky was blue again, and Lord Demerol, whom I'd last seen nursing an after-dinner rum punch at the hotel bar, marched toward the beach as if to secure it, his snorkel tube in hand.

Two Bajan men, bare-chested and muscular, sped by the resort in a skiff powered by an outboard motor, Speightstown fishermen getting a late start. They reminded me of the men that Winslow Homer painted in the Bahamas, those stunning watercolors in which you can feel the artist's spirit taking flight in response to the very lightness of the atmosphere, so different from the oppressive chill of his adopted Maine.

My plan for the day was to go exploring. I had a rental car and had marked a route on a map that would allow me to cross the island to the Atlantic Ocean, where the scenery was supposed to be spectacular and the surf dangerous. Barbados is quite small, only 166 square miles from one side to the other, so the trip would take less than an hour if I remembered to stay on the left-hand side of the road. If I failed to remember, the trip might never be completed.

The really important thing was to have a loud, dependable horn. Bajan motorists blow their horns constantly to alert cyclists, pedestrians, cattle, cattle egrets, and small mammals in their path that they are approaching around blind curves, up steep hills, or along tiny, two-lane roads that provide no margin for error. Some roads, I discovered, are just one-and-a-half laners, and it requires some skillful calculation, or a silent prayer, to avoid an accident.

I set off around noon, drove through Speightstown, and climbed up a narrow road that flattened out after a few minutes and then ran through huge fields of sugarcane, a mainstay of the local economy for more than 300 years, although tourism has now surpassed it in economic value.

British colonials established the sugar trade here in the mid-1600s and imported slaves from Africa to do the backbreaking labor. By the end of the 17th century just a few plantation owners controlled the entire wealth of the island. They employed some white servants, but the black slaves outnumbered the indentured whites by about thirty to one. The slave trade was abolished in 1807, after which, very slowly, a period of emancipation began at last.

I went through the village of Belleplaine, then swung onto East Coast Road, a highway skirting the edge of the Atlantic. The landscape changed dramatically. It became less wooded and more open, offering broad vistas in every direction. I could see cliffs of exposed coral and a few trails worn into the grassy hills. The ocean was the same pellucid blue as the Caribbean, but the surf was foamy and pounding, far too rough for most swimmers.

A few surfers, both Bajans and tourists, were paddling about on their boards, the elite of a budding surfing scene. While the waves that day were not world-class, there was still plenty of space for everyone.

At Barclay's Park, a little café on the ocean, I ate a flying fish sandwich for lunch. The fish was delicate and delicious, dipped in batter, deep-fried, and popped into a soft roll. Another customer watched me with pleasure. He identified himself as Dexter from Bridgetown. Dexter was drinking a Banks, and it did not seem to be his first of the afternoon.

He chuckled to himself, pointed at my sandwich, and said, "You know that fish you eatin', mon? You ever see 'em fly?"

"Not yet," I said.

"Any fish like that fly in your country?" he asked.

"Not that I know of."

Dexter gave me a friendly clap on the shoulder and shared a cultural equation he formulated on the spot: "Barbados, we got flying fishes and the best in cricket. You people over there, you got NBA basketball and movies from Hollywood. Is so?"

"It's so," I agreed.

"All right, then," said Dexter, laughing and shaking my hand.

* * *

Sir Tommy Shortpants, the old rogue, was responsible for touting me on the horse races in Bridgetown. He was stretched out next to me on a chaise longue by the swimming pool, reading about them in the *Advocate*. They would be running on Saturday, at the Garrison Savannah under the auspices of the Barbados Turf Club.

I decided I would attend out of curiosity, to see what sort of spin the Bajans had put on the Sport of Kings. Their attitude toward gambling was somewhat contradictory. They were often religious and staunchly opposed to a current move to open Vegas-style casinos on the island, but at the same time they plunged mightily on the national lottery and indulged, as did the Tyre Repair Gang, in many petty games of chance, including checkers, darts, pool, and cards, along with dominoes.

"I like Passionata in the feature race," Sir Tommy whispered, serving up a tip. His skin, after a week in the sun, had turned the tawny color of a mahogany tree. "You won't go wrong with that filly."

"Passionata it is," I agreed.

"Jolly good!" He really said such things. "Well done!"

Bridgetown is a densely settled city of about 250,000, but I would guess that on a Saturday the number almost doubles. Bajans from the provinces travel long distances to shop in the big department stores and also to see and be seen, so the downtown streets are awash with people cruising, promenading, and gossiping. Neighbors bump into neighbors and cousins into cousins.

A "tuk band," a combo—bass, snare drum, triangle, and pennywhistle—that is unique to Barbados, was giving a concert in Trafalgar Square, passing the hat while six or so teenage girls were dancing. The girls shook their bum bums in a brazenly sexual way, as if to liberate the energies that they had to conceal while they were in school and in uniform.

Garrison Savannah is in a parklike area just outside town. Troops from Britain had once been stationed there, and a few buildings from the early 1800s still stand, excellent examples of Georgian architecture as practiced in the Caribbean. The racetrack itself was a standard oval with an old-fashioned, pre-electronic tote board. As I passed through an admissions gate, I heard Bob Marley wailing "Buffalo Soldier" through a pair of gigantic speakers.

The first race was about to go off, and I couldn't resist putting a few dollars on Brown Sugar, even though I hadn't yet opened the local version of a racing program. Brown Sugar, who proved to be eight years old, went down in defeat.

Most racing in Great Britain is carried out on the turf, and the same is true in Barbados. The grandstand was stuffed with a multitude of different types, black and white, all social classes. Women in hats fit for Ascot, aging doubles for the Queen Mother, were seated next to cheap-speed blondes who clutched the arms of Bajan men adorned in enough flashy gold jewelry to sink the Bismarck. The atmosphere was a happy combination of Jamaica Sunsplash and Santa Anita.

The second race brought me a bit of unexpected luck. My horse, First Home, acted up before the start, unseating her jockey, falling down, and rolling over. I felt doomed, but First Home managed to right herself and still had enough feistiness in her to nip Jumpjet at the wire, paying three-to-one. A groom paraded the filly before the grandstand like a debutante, and she received a muted round of applause and a few sighs of approval.

In the next race I made the mistake of letting my winnings ride on Yeltsin, a strapping gelding, but he fared as badly as his namesake has been faring in Russia. The only cure for it was a glass of Banks at a concession stand, where Bob Marley was now singing "Redemption Song."

By the time the featured race rolled around, late in the afternoon, there were as many Bajans outside the Garrison as inside it. Taxi drivers, coconut and pineapple vendors, children kicking soccer balls, a few dogs and cats and goats—they were all hugging a fence beside the track, both soaking up and adding to the growing excitement surrounding the big race, which carried a $30,000 purse.

I approached the pari-mutuel windows fully prepared to bet on Holy Smoke, a handsome gray gelding, but Sir Tommy's tip kept ringing in my ears, and I changed my mind at the last possible instant and put my money on Passionata, a horse that none of the island's handicappers had listed among their favorites. Passionata, alas, was not nearly passionate enough and faded from view long before the eventual winner, Loan Ranger, was unmasked.

\* \* \*

Edward "Budge" O'Hara, a Londoner by birth, and his wife, Cynthia, have operated a resort on Barbados since 1956, first as managers and currently, in company with their three children, as owners. In many ways their tenure mirrors the story of tourism on the island.

O'Hara is a tall, engaging, no-nonsense fellow whose service in the Royal Navy still shows in his bearing. An Oxford graduate in physics, he was wearing bermuda shorts with knee socks and a crisp white shirt with the resort logo on one pocket, as he explained to me over drinks one afternoon how he had strayed from the academic path.

The age-old fantasy of living on your own tropical island had helped to create the resort, O'Hara said. Another ex-naval officer named Ted Powell had decided after retiring that he'd endured quite enough of England's dour weather. Powell had an understandable craving for sunshine, so in 1949, on the basis of an ad in *The Times* of London, he bought a hundred-acre island in the British West Indies sight unseen.

The island, Calavini, was off the coast of Grenada and cost him $2,500. He stayed there for two years, but he began to fear that he would go totally native and absolutely bonkers. Calavini, Powell concluded, had to be sold. A member of the Cunard shipping family bought it from him for $12,500, and he realized enough of a profit to move to Barbados and start a little resort.

By 1956 the resort was not so little anymore. Powell needed to hire a manager, and a friend suggested Budge O'Hara, who, having drifted away from physics, was working at a hotel in the Cotswolds. After a bit of negotiating, O'Hara signed a three-year contract on blind faith and set sail for Barbados with his bride, Cynthia.

O'Hara still remembers his deep disappointment when the ship pulled into Bridgetown in a September drizzle. He and Cynthia simply didn't want to get off, and they waited until every other passenger had descended the gangplank before they accepted their fate. Things improved, of course, when the sun broke through the clouds.

"What were your guests like back then?" I asked.

"They were adventurous," O'Hara said, spiritedly. "Like pioneers, really."

A plane trip from Britain in those days took 21 hours, and you could count on a rocky ride. The resort had just 24 rooms and no air-conditioning. Yet it wasn't uncommon for guests to spend three months in winter. Diplomats, consular officials, affluent sun lovers from Venezuela or Colombia all came and stayed.

Barbados stood for high society. It had a flourishing gay scene, too, much of it centering on English stage designer Oliver Messel, whose fanciful touches still grace some of the most prized villas around. Agatha Christie also once visited. She set a mystery in the Caribbean and patterned the murderer after a young hotelier she'd met, someone not unlike Budge himself.

Even as the resort has expanded, O'Hara continues to be a hands-on manager. He and his family try to greet every new arrival, and he treats his staff as family, too. There are waiters, maids, barmen, and cooks who are directly related to employees he hired in the 1960s.

Guests can also be numbered in generations, island veterans of 20 or 30 years, some of whom return every February, at the height of the season. Such guests, Canadians and Americans now as well as Brits, are the most demanding, O'Hara confided, and they expect every detail of their stay to be exactly as it was the last time, and the time before that.

"What keeps them coming back?" I asked. "What's so special?"

O'Hara replied, "Barbados is a beautiful place but I think, really, it's the people here. They're polite and generous—it's the Bajans who make this island special."

* * *

A turquoise sea, a warm breeze, salt drying on my skin, those ever-changing clouds. I spent my last day in Barbados slowly walking and swimming along the west coast to Speightstown, passing beach merchants who wandered from resort to resort selling coral necklaces and healing pieces of aloe vera; some Bajan women carried kits filled with beads they used to braid the hair of tourists.

There were big coral outcrops to get around, each of them alive with tiny, skittering crabs. Sloops sailed by, and jet skis threw showers of froth into the air. Next to handsome villas and mansions were more humble homes, often hammered together from scrap wood and corrugated aluminum, their backyards stacked with fishing floats, broken oars, and battered dinghies.

I came to a scallop of beach where I saw Sir Tommy, darker than ever now, dozing in an oceanfront chaise longue, his body and soul apparently at peace. Finally, in Speightstown I emerged from the Caribbean tired and dripping, and I slipped into the soggy sneakers and T-shirt I'd carried in a little pack. They'd dry quickly enough, I knew.

I strolled the main drag and saw that Pizza Man Doc had some hungry customers outside his restaurant, while at Modern Technique Dental Studio, a few patients sat quietly in the waiting room. The Tyre Repair Gang's place was silent, with three young men asleep under the trees and another on a picnic table, all of them no doubt conserving their energy for the Friday night ahead.

From a causeway, I watched a skiff land. The four men inside hauled their catch up to the Speightstown Fish Market, a dark blue building that serves as a social center. They had buckets of flying fish and one big, bloody, beheaded shark that the youngest of the crew, smiling proudly, shouldered up to the market like a trophy. Women with sharp knives set to gutting and filleting the catch, and soon Bajans were lining up to buy flying fish, two for 50 cents, wrapped in old newspaper or dropped into a plastic sack.

I eased over to where one woman was working her way through a bucket and looked closely at the flying fish, all silvery blue and about 12 inches long, mackerel-like schoolers remarkably identical in size.

I hadn't seen any of them fly this trip, but it's true that they do, sometimes for several feet above the water. A typical flight goes on for ten seconds or less, but the fishes' wings—pectoral fins actually—don't really flap. The main force that propels them is their tail. They beat it in a sculling motion to attain flying speed. They fly, researchers believe, to escape from the dorado, or dolphin fish, that prey on them. So would I, and so would you.

Reggae music was pouring out of the Fisherman's Pub, and the bar inside was packed with Bajans celebrating the end of the week. I bought a pint of Banks and took it out to a deck over the water. A sunset ribbon of pink fluttered on the horizon. The Caribbean was so transparent I could see two skinny barracudas in the shallows.

As the sun dropped lower in the sky, Anna, the pub's waitress, scooped up my glass to replenish it. We had struck up a friendship of sorts. It was impossible not to be a friend of Anna's. She is round and upbeat and wears a paper cook's hat and always has a grin on her face. As a sideline she sells T-shirts—printed with Bob Marley or I Love Barbados—and I promised her I would tell everybody at home to go to the pub when they got to the island and buy one from her.

Anna blew me a kiss. "Is all right, baby?" she asked.

"Is all right, Anna," I told her. "I cool."

*Islands*, 1995

## Culebra: An Island Dream

There's a game schoolboys play on the island of Culebra. At recess, they hang around Banco Popular in Dewey, the island's only town, and try to sneak into the ATM cubicle whenever a customer emerges. The enclosed cubicle is air-conditioned, so the boys wave and laugh and make sure the students still stuck out in the heat (especially the girls) can see them cooling off and enjoying themselves. Sometimes they even open the door a crack to tease the stranded ones.

"Maria, look at me!"

"No, Josefina, you can't come in!"

I pass the kids on my way to the harbor, where the late afternoon ferry will soon arrive from Fajardo, a port on the main island of Puerto Rico. The ferry is a major attraction since Culebra is virtually undeveloped. It has no movie theatre, no fancy resort, no tennis court or golf course. There are no steel bands to greet tourists and no hucksters selling trinkets. The few shops in town are often closed for their owners' siestas. In Dewey you're lucky to find a postcard to buy.

The walking feels good, despite the strong tropical sun. Culebra is just seven miles long and mostly flat, so you're never far from the Caribbean and a quick dip. It's the largest island in an archipelago of 20 or so islands and cays, many of them part of a national wildlife refuge that provides invaluable habitat to thousands of seabirds and endangered sea turtle species—leatherback, green, Atlantic loggerhead, and hawksbill.

Yesterday I hired a boat to explore Culebrita, an outer cay. It was a smooth ride over, with pelicans diving all around us.

Once there, I climbed into a forest and sat for a while on a rocky ledge overlooking the sea, then clambered down and soaked in a pool as relaxing as a hot tub. Some visitors complain about the Culebran archipelago being boring, but I enjoy the distance from so-called civilization.

A large crowd has already convened on the ferry dock. The women and children rest in a shady plaza, while the men drink beer and talk. Beer is a staple here, as essential as rice and beans. Culebra has only 2,000 or so residents, but their thirst is mighty. All along the main drag, trash cans are filled with empties. For a poor town, Dewey is remarkably clean. The locals take great pride in it, because the streets are an extension of their homes, a communal parlor everybody shares. At the moment, Dewey is recovering from Hurricane Georges, which blew through at 110 MPH, destroyed more than 20 houses, and deprived many others of their roofs.

The ferry chugs toward shore and ties up. Fajardo has a new Kmart, so the returning daytrippers are loaded with treasures. I spot a Barbie doll, an electric fan, and a big Sony TV in a cardboard carton. Almost everything has to be imported to Culebra—furniture, building materials, the vegetables that won't grow in the flinty volcanic soil. Cattle once grazed in the highlands, but the herds are small now and beef is scarce. Nobody fishes commercially anymore, either. The government and a pharmaceuticals company are the largest employers in town.

The hardships of life on an isolated island don't seem to bother the Culebrans, though. They're used to scraping by, just as they're accustomed to the fury of hurricanes. The sea, the sun, the sky, the nearness of family and friends—those are the constants of their universe. Almost everyone seems lively and contented. Even the stray mutts look healthy and well fed.

* * *

My jeep is parked in front of a modest house on a side street, where an elderly couple sits outside in folding chairs to watch the passing parade. Their yard is a triumph of folk art, decorated with brightly painted fishing floats, rubber tires, and a menagerie of ornamental animals cast in cement, including a bunch of ducks. It's hard to tell if the couple believe they've created a majestic installation, or if they're only a couple of pranksters having a bit of fun.

"*Buenas tardes,*" I greet them. "Nice ducks."

The leathery-skinned husband grins and lifts a hand to salute. "Nice-a-ducks," he repeats. Most older Culebrans speak some English, but the younger ones tend to stick to Spanish on principle. They're Puerto Ricans first and Americans second. Not a few teenagers are eager to fly the coop and head for San Juan. They dress in big-city style, in Nikes, NBA jerseys, and flashy gold chains, and they specialize in attitude.

I'm on an important mission this evening, so I intend to proceed with caution. Driving on the island can be tricky. Only a handful of roads are paved, but they've got just as many potholes as the unpaved roads. More treacherous still are the storm drains that sneak up on you, metal grates as rattling as cattle guards. If you hit a drain in second gear, you fly up from your seat and your head smacks the roof. Away from Dewey, the roads are even worse, all dirt and deeply rutted. You must watch for roosters, cyclists, and water hazards. It's every man for himself.

My destination is Mamacitas Restaurant, the unofficial clubhouse for Culebra's colony of gringos, who make the most of a two-hour happy hour that often stretches into three. The gringos, seduced by the island's wonders, operate small businesses to support themselves—charter boats for diving and snorkeling, kayak rentals, freelance plumbing, you name it.

Mamacitas is the place to stop if you need something, but it has a drawback, as well. Nowhere else does gossip travel so fast. You can't sneeze at the bar without somebody five blocks away knowing about it. The flood of innuendo has ruined marriages and derailed affairs, upended careers and brought down the law. It's an authentic Culebran hazard like the mosquitos and no-see-ums that raise tiny red welts on your skin.

Tonight I'm looking for Chris Goldmark, who has a reputation as a first-rate fishing guide. I order an icy Medalla beer and ask after him. The bartender says Chris drops in most nights to get his messages, so I leave one with my phone number. There's no hurry, of course, and no pressure. Services here are delivered at a leisurely, not to say glacial pace. A man could probably live on Culebra, never accomplish a thing he'd set out to do, and not feel the least bit guilty.

The sky is streaked with pink and stacked with billowy clouds when I depart. I cross a bridge over Laguna Lobina, glance down at the clear blue water, and see some glowing orange coral and a baby barracuda. The warm, humid air washes over my skin as a full moon rises over the Caribbean. At the moment I, too, have no desire to accomplish anything. I am surrendering to the tropics, entertaining a fantasy about opening a kayak rental shop.

I drive on to join Bob White, a fellow I met on my flight over. There was a mix-up in San Juan before takeoff, and when the pilot dashed back into the terminal, Bob quipped, "I'll bet he forgot to key the plane." I laughed, because the plane was very small and scary, its six tattered seats patched with duct tape. The propellers made a deafening racket, and one passenger started whispering prayers the minute we taxied onto the runway.

Bob is a retired IBM executive from New York. He stumbled on Culebra during a sailing trip years ago, fell in love with it, and bought some property, as more and more northerners are doing. When I knock, he invites me into his house. It's the first time he's been back since Hurricane Georges; the house took a serious beating, two decks trashed and some power lines down. Sand covers the kitchen floor and sticks to the fridge in wet clumps.

I expect Bob to be upset, but he's philosophical about the damage, having adopted the laidback island attitude. The repairs will be completed according to a schedule he can't control, at a cost he can't predict. He had to wait ten years to clear the title on his property.

Bob and I have dinner at Tina's, a merry café not far from the baseball stadium. The tables wobble, and we can hear singing and clapping at an evangelical church nearby. The fried chicken sounds good, but Bob advises to me to order fish.

"It's fresh" he says.

"What kind is it?" I ask our server.

"Fish," she says.

The mystery fish is huge. Its head and tail flop over the edges of the plate. The skin is crisp, and the flesh flakes away in glistening chunks. The server brings bowls of rice and beans and a bottle of homemade hot sauce with dangerous little peppers steeping in it. I risk a couple splashes, and my tongue burns.

Chris Goldmark calls at eight the next morning. Yes, he has access to a friend's boat and can take me to the flats for bonefish. We'll meet that afternoon at Mamacitas, but first I plan to spend some time in the sun. Like the schoolboys at Banco Popular, I've been playing a game, trying to comb every beach on the island. Melones, Tamarindo, Brava, Resaca—I've visited them all. To my surprise and delight, they've all been deserted.

Only at Playa Flamenco have I seen other people, although never more than 20. And even then, Flamenco feels secluded. It's an unspoiled stretch of bone white sand that's curved like a scallop shell at the edge of the sea. Green hills surround it, and the offshore corals offer fine snorkeling.

I decide to hike from Flamenco to Carlos Rosario beach, where the snorkeling is supposed to be even better. The path follows a slight uphill grade into a tangle of gumbo-limbo, ficus, and mahogany trees. Thorny acacias, invaders from Mexico, grow with abandon and threaten to eclipse the native species. I pass some lizards doing push-ups and a kestrel on the prowl, then stop to watch a frigate bird soaring overhead, its great wings spread wide.

The day is hot. I soon work up a sweat. Mosquitos trail me in pesky clouds, along with sulfur moths. At the crest of a hill, I glimpse Carlos Rosario below. Nobody's there, of course. In minutes I'm in my snorkel gear and finning over some coral, my ears deaf to the waking world and my eyes glued to the one underwater. The fish are extraordinary—an electric blue tang, snappers with yellow tails that burn like candle flames, and a school of tiny silvery creatures as bright as newly minted coins.

I swim until my legs are tired and I've seen all there is to see, then walk back over the same path and bump into four horses on the loose, who lead me to Flamenco.

At three o' clock, I meet Chris at Mamacitas. He's from New Jersey and reached Culebra via San Juan. He holds a fly rod rigged with a new fly he wants to try, a Yucatan Special that originated in Mexico. Culebran bonefish are really big, much larger than those in the Florida Keys. We'll look for them on a flat off a reef in an intertidal zone, where they forage for crab and shrimp in the shallows.

A diveboat skipper drops us off at a spot called Dakity. It's a strange sensation to watch the boat pull away. I'm left standing knee-deep in the Caribbean, so far from shore only an Olympian could swim to safety. The flat is an undulating marl plain covered with gray-green sea grasses. The marl's in great shape despite the hurricane, Chris tells me, leaning down to pluck a conch from the sea floor.

"They'll be thousands of conchs here tonight," he says, "on account of the full moon."

We walk forward, stalking, almost on tiptoe. I'm so involved in scanning the horizons for bonefish I fail to notice a manta ray streaming toward me. When we see each other, I don't know who's more shocked, the ray or me. I nearly fall over, while the ray spins around and vanishes in an instant, spooking hundreds of glass minnows that leap into the air like a line of dancers.

We continue stalking until we finally see a bonefish about 70 feet away, nose down and tail sticking out of the water, grubbing for food. That's too far for an accurate cast, so we edge closer. The hunt demands patience. One false step and the bonefish will split as quickly as the manta ray. I need to put the Yucatan special directly in front of it, but a strong gust grabs my line and whips it to the left of the target, where the fly hits the water with a deadly splash.

So long, bonefish.

Other fish soon turn up, but the wind is giving me fits and tying knots in my line. Chris nudges a sea cucumber with his toe and lifts up another conch, tickling it from its shell.

"Hardly anybody catches a bonefish first time out," he offers kindly, aware that I'm about to prove him right, but for once I don't mind being skunked. It's enough to be standing where I am, while the sun sinks behind the clouds and fills the sky with rosy light.

\* \* \*

The next afternoon, I'm sitting at a picnic table under a big tamarind tree, looking out over Fulladoza Bay. With me is Teresa

Tallevast, a U.S. Fish & Wildlife Service biologist, who has been studying Culebra's marine life for 13 years. She works at a lovely compound near an aged desalinization plant that supplies the island's potable water. The plant resembles something assembled hastily, a batch of mismatched machinery held together with bailing wire and positive thinking.

This was the site of the first settlement on Culebra, but when the U.S. Navy arrived, shortly after Puerto Rico was ceded to the United States in 1898, the officers in command drove the natives down to the harbor and named the new town in honor of Admiral Dewey. Most Culebrans refuse to speak Dewey's name, though. Instead, they refer to the town simply as "Pueblo." Islanders have long memories.

I mention how tranquil the island feels, but Teresa warns me that's deceptive. In fact, there's a real estate boom going on. Much of the unimproved land across the bay has been subdivided into five-acre parcels and sold to off-island speculators. Sooner or later, they'll build houses and possibly resorts. Only the shortage of wood and other construction materials keep the market from exploding.

Even with development contained, the island has been deforested over the years (in part because the navy used it for gunnery and bombing practice from the outbreak of World War II until 1975), and Teresa has recorded the impact on the environment. She cites the fishing bat as evidence. It's as large as a crow and feeds on fish. The bat has no major predators, but its numbers are declining. It needs old-growth trees to roost in, and those trees have been cut down.

The health of Culebra's coral reefs is also in jeopardy. When the island's vegetation is removed, the topsoil washes down to the sea. The mangroves' shallow roots are supposed to trap the sediment, but the mangroves are also disappearing. They topple over in storms, and the locals clear them away to put up a shack or build a dock.

So the sediment is carried out to the reefs. The water becomes turbid, and less sunlight penetrates it, affecting—even covering—the coral, which requires plenty of sunlight to survive. The lack of sun affects the sea grass beds, too. The grasses turn brown, then wither and die. It doesn't take much to upset the fragile ecosystem and destroy a natural balance. The reefs on Culebra may someday be as damaged as most other reefs in the region.

"The system can handle a certain amount of sediment," Teresa says, "but once we go beyond that capacity, the habitat inevitably declines."

* * *

On Saturday afternoon, Dewey—or Pueblo—turns into a miniature carnival on wheels. People are hanging out on street corners and drinking beer at a speedier pace than normal. At Rosa's Bar, Jaime the bartender dispenses cold brews through an open window. Jaime lived in Brooklyn for seven years, but he came back to the island a New York Yankees fan.

"Who'll be the Puerto Rican champs this winter?" I ask, since baseball's season is about to begin.

"Maybe San Juan," Jaime replies, although not with enough confidence to send me searching for a bookie.

Hotel Puerto Rico is jammed with patrons, too. The bartender here plays a jaunty tune on his harmonica, one eye closed, his lungs pumping. He's transported. A police van circles the streets, but the cops only smile and chat. Probably they've got their own party to attend as soon as they're off duty.

I buy a Medalla at Romero's liquor store by the ferry dock. Romero has a heart tattooed on his right bicep. His three children were born on the mainland at a Fajardo hospital, he says, and he regrets it. There's a general feeling in town that something unique—a distinct Culebran identity—is slipping away as time passes and the future rushes in with all its changes, wanted and unwanted.

The ferry pulls into the harbor again, and I see more booty being unloaded—a spool of telephone cable, a wicker armchair, a table, some lumber.

"The Kmart ruined Fajardo," Romero sighs. "The small businesses can't compete."

I move on to Hart's Oasis, where the front door boasts a gaudy painting of a flamingo. Here the bartender has an actual TV at his command, and he's watching a World Wrestling Federation jamboree. Hart's may be a real sports bar someday, he brags. At a grocery store next door, the owner has posted a page torn from a tabloid. HEAVEN PHOTOGRAPHED BY HUBBEL TELESCOPE, the headline screams.

* * *

Sunday morning breaks with a familiar wash of sunshine, but Dewey is quiet now, its revelers still sleeping off their excesses. Culebrans are regrouping, preparing to return to ordinary life on Monday. Every church is packed. A preacher's voice rises at Jerusalem Methodist, where a little girl in a print dress, her hair in braids, darts from her pew full of mischief and escapes into a house across the way. Below the bridge over Laguna Lobina, the orange corals grow.

There is one last beach to visit before I leave. Soldado is hot and deserted, and the sand stings my feet. The sea is its usual elegant turquoise. I float on my back for a while, then put on scuba gear and chase some yellowtail snappers. What splendid isolation! It would be nice to preserve Culebra just as it is, beyond the grasp of developers and all those changes the future will bring. But that's not likely to happen.

Later I board the same rickety prop plane with the tattered seats. The engine kicks in with a roar, and we climb up from the airstrip and soar over the water. It seems to me then, as Culebra disappears, that my time on the island has the quality of a dream. Did I really stand on a marl plain and almost collide with a manta ray? The dream is a rich one, and I'll remember it pleasantly in the days to come.

*Islands*, 1998

## Cavagnaro's Bar & Grill: East Hampton

In the summer of 1980—the summer I adopted Cavagnaro's Bar & Grill as my local—I rented a house in the woods of East Hampton as a form of therapy. I hoped to recover the social skills I'd lost while writing my first book in near total isolation, in a dilapidated trailer in the Northern California wine country, where my only regular visitor was a seventy-five-year-old fishing buddy. Jack and I played cribbage for a nickel a point and drank Brown Derby beer with shots of Old Overholt back. I don't recall either of us mentioning books or literature.

All that would change in East Hampton, I assumed. With so many authors around, I'd be able to catch up on the literary shoptalk I'd been missing. I imagined long, boozy evenings discussing the latest controversy in the *New York Review of Books,* at the same taverns where James Jones and Truman Capote used to hold forth. I had just one contact in town, an old friend married to a columnist at *Time,* but she turned out to be very well connected and invited me to a Saturday-morning softball game for writers. Perfect, I thought, exactly what I had in mind—a lazy summer devoted to idle pursuits.

A lot of writers showed up that Saturday, some quite famous. I realized with chagrin I'd never read any of their books. They produced thick nonfiction blockbusters and plot-driven novels destined for the movies. Maybe the trick wasn't to live cheaply in a trailer and pray a publisher would like what you wrote. It might be better to come up with a marketable idea and sell it for a big advance before you'd put a single word on paper. Deals had probably been cut right there at second base. The scales were falling from my eyes.

The *Time* guy was the official scorekeeper and kept elaborate statistics. If you needed to know what Carl Bernstein batted last season, he could tell you. He rigged the game according to seniority. The writers who'd been around the longest—years in some cases—always got to play, but newcomers like me usually rode the pines even if they'd been (also like me) a high school hotshot. Everyone took the softball seriously, too, and they didn't bother with drinks afterward. Instead, they behaved as they did in Manhattan and rushed off to their next engagement. Clearly, I'd been deluded about the literary shoptalk.

Even if nobody else craved a postgame beer, I did and stopped at Cavagnaro's on the outskirts of town. It occupied the ground floor of an ordinary three-story brick building. I'd driven past it several times, but I'd never noticed any activity and wondered if it was still in business. When I peeked inside, the answer appeared to be no. The place was empty except for a short, stocky man of seventy or so sitting at the far end of the bar reading the *Daily News*.

He did not glance up from the paper when I entered. Instead, he buried his nose more deeply in it, determined to ignore me. That was Al Cavagnaro, who'd been on duty since 1951. His father had opened a restaurant and deli on the site in 1923. Al and his wife still lived in quarters behind the bar, and he cooked when he was in the mood to cook, which wasn't every day.

In spite of the chilly welcome, I climbed onto a stool. Cavagnaro's was a relic of the 1950s, a classic Italian joint with

Sinatra on the box and red sauce in the kitchen. I tapped my fingers until Al finally rose from his seat with an audible groan and tossed a coaster in front of me. "What're you having?" he asked warily, then brought me the beer I ordered and returned to his paper. That was fine with me. I felt comfortable in the quiet room with its the worn wood and vintage appointments. The bar offered a pleasant refuge from the glitzy nonsense of the Hamptons.

Al was a true Bonacker, I recognized—crusty, flinty, someone who didn't suffer fools gladly. The name derives from Accabonac Harbor, where the baymen and fishermen ply their trade. Most Bonackers regard the summer people with dismay or worse, as I should've guessed from Al's cold shoulder, but I respected him for not caring if he made a buck off the tourists. "See you later," I called as I left. Al spoke not a word.

When I came back the next day, he was watering the shrubbery out front. "You want another beer?" he asked. I nodded. "Okay, I'll open up," he muttered, handing me the keys to unlock the door. By such fits and starts, we lurched toward a conversation. After six visits, Al asked where I was from, and after my eighth, what I did for a living. He'd never had many writers as regulars, he told me, but the painters from Springs, like Jackson Pollock, used to drop in on occasion. "He'd pull up in his coupe with a babe on his arm"—not Lee Krasner, I gathered—"and hit the whiskey," Al confided.

Al didn't drink himself, but he had a terrible sweet tooth. He wasn't supposed to indulge it because the doctors had put him on a strict diet—they were treating him for bladder cancer—and his wife made sure he stuck to it. But he'd devised a strategy to get around her. Whenever she went out, he'd sneak into the deli next door for a pint of ice cream, then melt it in his microwave and slurp it down as fast as he could before she could catch him at it.

The bar was seldom crowded in the early evening. Most customers were Bonackers off the boats or in from the potato fields, still in their work clothes. They sold me freshly dug clams and taught me how to surf cast for bluefish. If they were hungry, Al might grill a burger for them, but he couldn't stand to cook all the time. He'd make lunch on Tuesday and be closed on Wednesday. I don't remember a menu. Once he boasted that he'd fixed prime rib, and I was sorry I hadn't ordered it when I saw the huge slab of juicy pink beef he served.

So Cavagnaro's became part of my summer routine. I'd write at home, then visit Al most days. If things had gone well at my desk, I'd celebrate with a bourbon or two, but more often I felt I deserved no better than a Beck's or a Heineken— microbrews and IPAs were not yet on tap in that distant, deprived era. Sometimes I sat at a table to read a book, and other times I joined in the ongoing conversation about the farms and the sea. Four months flew by, and my lease ran out and I got ready to move to London at the end of September.

Al's face fell when I informed him. He looked genuinely wounded, and I was surprised. I'd never seen him show any emotion before. He saw the makings of a Bonacker in me, apparently, and couldn't believe I'd decided to leave instead of settling down. It was as if I'd refused an OBE or declined some other honor. He bought me drinks and insisted on feeding me a platter of homemade sausages, worried I'd risk starvation in faraway Europe.

"You're one of a kind," he said, patting me on the back. That was a high compliment to pay a summer person, and I was grateful for it. He wanted a photo of us together behind the bar and enlisted a slightly tipsy customer to snap the picture. I still have it somewhere in storage. I'm holding up a glass of beer as though for a toast, and Al's smiling broadly. I sent him a post-card from London and later heard he'd beat his cancer and lived on into his eighties—still a curmudgeon, no doubt, and much admired by all who knew him.

*Narrative*, 2014

## A London Village: Islington

To arrive in London on a rainy autumn morning, straight from Heathrow on the express train to Paddington, is to find yourself transported into a canvas by Magritte. There I was, wheeling my new suitcase to a modest b&b, accompanied by travelers from France, Germany, Japan, and most other countries of the world, all wheeling their suitcases to modest b&bs. We should have been wearing bowlers, really, and floating a few feet off the ground.

Only when I stepped into the Dalton Arms and lost the crowd did I know for certain that I was in England. The desk clerk was reassuringly called Clive, the lobby walls bore framed portraits of various royals, and I was promised a hearty breakfast of bacon, baked beans, grilled tomato, toast, marmalade, and one egg. I didn't dare ask for two eggs, for fear I'd upset a subtle cultural balance that had been in play since the signing of the Magna Carta.

An old saw has it that London is a city of villages. I was returning for a longish stay in what I think of as my village, the Borough of Islington, north of the Thames. When I first lived there 20 years ago, in a fourth-floor walk-up on Myddleton Square without any central heating, it was considered a marginal and even unattractive place by many people, since it had no major museums, attractions, or high-end restaurants.

The look of it put off some visitors, too—largely Georgian with a few Victorian touches, featuring row upon row of nearly identical blocks of flats, all built of drab and weathered brick.

Islington was left-leaning, as well, and sexually tolerant and racially mixed, with lots of subsidized housing for low-income families. In other words, it amounted to a Tory nightmare, but to a San Franciscan, it felt like home.

Islington is no longer undiscovered. Myddleton Square has become an "address," where the price of flats is beyond the reach of ordinary mortals. On blocks that once were a jumble of pubs, chippers, corner groceries, and tradesmen, you find new shops with designer clothes in the window and fancy restaurants serving postmodern cuisine from all over the world. On Liverpool Road, I passed a storefront with a sign that read "Flotation Tank" and thought I might keel over on the spot, pursued by relentless California as poor Scrooge was dogged by ghosts.

But I was saved by the sight of another store across the way, painted a lush green and in perfect trim, its hand-lettered sign advertising "H. Crabb, Concertina Maker." In a sense, the contrast sums up London at the moment. Like most sophisticated European capitals, the city is going global, but there remains a quintessentially English quality at its core, although you may have to hunt for it now.

Still, after some diligent legwork and with the help of a realtor, I landed in a neighborhood that's relatively unspoiled, in a flat at Highbury Terrace in a block constructed in 1789. The flat has high ceilings and big windows that look out on Highbury Fields, a crescent-shaped park of some 27 acres, where you can always count on an animal lover to be walking an incredibly well-behaved dog. In the Georgian period, the area was favored because it was on a slight rise, above the clamor, soot, and smog of the city; gents who did business in London but wanted a more tranquil, rural residence were the first to move in.

At the same time, Highbury Barn—a converted farmer's barn—was notorious as a "pleasure resort," especially in the mild summer months, when you could participate in lawn bowling and trapshooting and consume strong ale by the hogshead. It hit its rowdy apex in the 1860s, when the owner built a music hall and imported famous continental performers— among them Blondin, a celebrated tightrope artist—but he ran into problems with his neighbors, now Victorian conservatives, who objected to the drunken behavior and finally denied him a license to operate.

Highbury Barn is currently our shopping strip. The barn, refurbished, still stands and serves as the local pub, where the habit-prone regulars repeat their ritual imbibing (and often their warmed-over conversations) on a daily basis. I've never seen the publican outside his establishment; he seems to live in a purgatory of cigarette smoke, recorded pop music, and flashing fruit machines, his right arm a little twitchy from pulling so many taps.

The strip has two news agents and also a pair of greengrocers, who appear to be waging a silent war. There's a great divide between them. The younger merchant, a tough, unshaven guy who doesn't radiate happiness over his earthly lot, allows customers to select their own fruit and vegetables; while the older fellow is a traditionalist and does the selecting for you. That may seem a small point, but it isn't among the English.

Our butcher, too, is traditional and dresses in uniform, always in a fresh white apron, a tie, and a butcher's hat. His meat is free-range, his eggs are organic, and he stocks a wide array of game—venison, partridge, pheasant, pigeons, and hare. Probably he is the barn's gastronomic king, although he gets close competition from the Parisian-style fromagerie, where the cheeses are made in-house and the duck legs rest obscenely in a vat of killer confit.

Given the amenities, it's easy to understand why some people never stray from Highbury, but I am not among them. To my mind, the virtue of the location is that it affords access to so many north London districts where you rarely meet another American, much less another tourist; indeed, it isn't possible to buy a picture postcard of Big Ben or Buckingham Palace anywhere in Islington, not that I've seen. Though I admire and appreciate the city's landmarks, what I enjoy most is the ability to wander freely and get lost.

Only on foot do you discover the subtle architectural variations that occur block-to-block, such as the changing color of the bricks as they go from rust to brown to gray. On foot, you sense a pattern in each neighborhood; the squares and churchyards adhere to a plan drawn up centuries ago. You're also aware of the natural world, of the cawing crows and the dove's coo. The blackbirds of fairytale are also around, distant relatives of the 24 unfortunates baked into a pie, as are the magpies that the English count for purposes of divination: "One for sorrow, Two for joy, Three for a wedding, Four for a boy."

I got lost in Dalston recently. It's only a mile away, but my Highbury friends couldn't tell me much about it except for Simon, who's a cricket fan. He goes to a Dalston pub to watch the important test matches on TV, because the West Indians there are so informed and enthusiastic. (In fact, the library proved to be named in honor of C.L.R. James, whose cricket classic, *Beyond a Boundary*, transcends the genre of sporting literature.)

So I was prepared for a Caribbean flavor, but what I encountered was something more polyglot and vital, a High Street alive with Turks, Cypriots, and Kurds, each with their own representative stores and cafés. I had baklava and a Turkish coffee, then turned down an alley devoted to Nigerian fabrics and food. All this was a mere prelude to the grand street market, where the various new Londoners bartered with Cockney traders in a rich mix of languages and a smattering of pidgin.

Islington, too, has its street markets, most notably Chapel Market for produce, fish, clothing, and inexpensive household goods, and the antiques arcade at Camden Passage, where you can buy a 19th-century door knocker or magnifying glass. The most famous market in the city, obviously, is on Portobello Road at Notting Hill Gate, but the crowds have been huge since the Hollywood Effect set in. Hard as it may be to believe, some tourists expect to bump into Hugh Grant stocking shelves at the travel bookshop.

I prefer the less trendy weekend market at Spitalfields in the East End, in the shadow of Nicholas Hawksmoor's Christ Church, one of 50 constructed by edict after the Great Fire of

1666. Though it lacks the fashion element of Portobello Road, it has pretty much everything else you might want—wonderful bakers, barbecue pork sandwiches at the Arkansas Cafe, obscure music on vinyl, throw pillows bearing the image of Che Guevara, and the weirdest burritos you'll ever eat.

From Spitalfields you can drift over to Brick Lane, the red-hot center of the Bengali community. Here you can engage in a game of three-card monte, or listen to the guy who plays excellent stride piano on a battered upright outside a warehouse. Smoked haddock is for sale, along with little cups of jellied eel.

On my first visit, I thought I'd have lunch at one of the many tandoori shops on the lane, but I wound up in a line of 30 at the Beigel Bake (open 24 hours every day) for a salt beef beigel, which bears only the slightest resemblance to the bagel as we know it. The item in question was smaller and spongier, and the salt beef was our corned beef. Sliced from the brisket in chunks, it was piled on a warm beigel and dotted with mustard—a simple yet altogether satisfying meal.

The saltiness makes you thirsty, though, so you might move on to Whitechapel Road for a beer at the Blind Beggar, the pub where Ronnie Kray of the gangland Kray twins shot a rival in 1966 for calling him a "fat poof." Kray went directly to prison and died there not long ago as a born-again Christian, although he asked his pastor to keep it a secret. "I don't want anyone to think I've become a Christian," he said, "just to get parole." There is, apparently, honor among thieves.

London, then—my London—is made up of such places and scenes. Any guidebook will lead you to the Tate Modern or Sir John Soane's Museum (and both will be worth the time), but it's what you discover in your accidental roaming that stays with you. Sunday is especially fine for exploring, since the city slows to a crawl as the English, bless them, still demand their day of rest.

You might consult your tube map, ride to an unfamiliar stop, and walk until you begin to tire, then buy a paper and read it slowly over a pint at a pub—around 1 o'clock, say, when the pubs are quiet and conducive to meditation. Soon you'll be hungry, so the trick is to locate a restaurant (there are hundreds) that does a traditional Sunday roast of beef or lamb. Don't worry about the calories, order the mashed potatoes and the Yorkshire pudding. You might even indulge in a glass of red wine.

Afterward, you'll feel sleepy, and it's best to return to the hotel for a long nap. In the evening, you'll require only a light supper and a good book or a glance at the telly where, if you're lucky, you might catch a darts match or a snooker tournament and know for certain you're in England.

*San Francisco Examiner Magazine*, 2001

# Reviews

---

*The World is My Home* by James Michener

In his new memoir, *The World Is My Home*, James Michener puts to rest the idea that there are no second acts in American lives. As the old saying goes, his life really began at 40, when, during World War II, he sat down in a Quonset hut on Espiritu Santo Island, lit a smoky lantern, and turned out the linked stories that became *Tales of the South Pacific*, which won him a Pulitzer Prize in 1947. This stroke of luck helped to transform him into James Michener, the best-selling phenomenon, and he has continued to live on the grand scale ever since, becoming in the process America's "best-loved" writer.

Michener's reminiscing doesn't have much in common with the usual literary fare. There are no drunken brawls, no brilliant seductions, no drugs, and precious little animosity. Vice for Michener consists of an addiction to the fine arts. When he discusses writing, he often does it with an eye toward the business end of things, offering cautionary advice to beginners. Above all, he comes across as a practical person, and his book has the flavor of another, pre-Elvis era, when issues of complexity could be mastered through grit, hard work, and positive thinking.

In choosing to call *The World Is My Home* a memoir rather than an autobiography, Michener alerts us at the start that he will not be terribly revealing about himself. We must ferret out the salient facts from chapters that are arranged according to subject—Travel, People, Health, and so on. He jumps backward and forward in time, and while this allows him the leisure to dwell on his strongest concerns, it opens gaps in the narrative that leave a reader scratching his head over the missing parts of the puzzle.

Michener had a difficult, scarring childhood. Orphaned at birth, he grew up in Pennsylvania, bouncing from one foster home to another. The homes were run by Mabel Michener, a caring, intelligent woman, who took in the wounded and the abandoned. Others in the Michener clan were not so kind and put it to young James that he was not a true Michener, and that gave him an independent spirit, as well as an emotional armoring, that molded his character. He became a Quaker and has always held the sturdy, unshakable values of the Pennsylvania Dutch.

In his teens, Michener took to the road, hitchhiking around the country and developing a love of exploration and adventure that never left him. As a scholarship student at Swarthmore, he was a classic high achiever. He enjoyed painting, poetry, and music, especially opera, but he showed no predisposition toward writing. Eventually, he went to work in publishing, and as his 40th birthday approached he found himself about to be drafted into the Army. He enlisted in the Navy instead and was stationed in the South Pacific, where the life-changing episodes began.

The chapters that deal with Polynesia are the stars of *The World Is My Home*. Michener's recollections are sweetly nostalgic and have a simple human happiness that is sometimes missing elsewhere in the book. He fell into an island paradise that was far enough removed from the war theater to pose no serious threat, and he was soon gifted with a writer's most precious possession—wonderful material. There were honky-tonks, colorful characters, a surpassingly beautiful landscape, and just enough weirdness around the edges to keep everybody on his toes.

Michener admits to being a bit of a Boy Scout, but the South Pacific seems to have loosened him up a little. In a distant, Victorian way, he describes the sexual dreamland in which many Americana GIs were living, invited by their hosts to take up residence with the most gorgeous young girls of the islands. So lubricious was the scene on Bora Bora that soldiers often didn't want to return to the states. Michener makes Polynesia sound like the Playboy Mansion, but he plays his cards so close to the chest that it's impossible to tell whether he was really only an observer, someone who liked to admire the naked bodies of the natives when they went skinny-dipping at twilight.

Observation has always been central to Michener's work. He has a vast curiosity, and his research and reporting provide the substance for his novels. Yet, by his account, he might never have written a word if he hadn't almost died in a plane crash while landing at Tontouta Air Base. His brush with death gave him the willies, and during a long night of soul-searching he realized that he was dissatisfied with himself. "As the stars came out and I could see the low mountains I had escaped," he says.

"I swore: 'I'm going to live the rest of my life as if I were a great man.'" It's the *as if* that matters here, for Michener is essentially a modest soul. From that moment on, though, he would ask the best of himself.

It takes an idealist to make such a vow, and Michener is idealistic to the core. He confesses that he would have made a good minister if he had more religion. But it was his fate to hole up in his Quonset hut and transcribe as accurately as possible his vision of the South Pacific. When the manuscript was finished, he submitted it anonymously to Macmillan, where he had gone back to work as an editor, and the company published it to scant critical praise and indifferent sales. The cheap, ugly dust jacket remains an object of scorn to Michener. On the basis of his reception, he had no intention of quitting his job, but then, out of the blue, he won the Pulitzer, and his transformation was complete.

Well, not quite. *Tales* went on to sell many copies, but Michener earned his first megabucks from the Broadway adaptation, *South Pacific*, a Rodgers and Hammerstein collaboration. For a time after his success, he struggled with his identity as a writer until he hit on the sort of formulaic "big book" that has become his stock-in-trade. The formula allowed him to travel widely, and Random House provided him with a well-oiled editorial machine geared to getting his manuscripts in shape and between covers in a timely way. Michener views himself as an old-fashioned storyteller and claims not to be affected by critics—a claim his fellow writers might doubt. But there is no doubting another claim of his, that he has pleased a huge international audience.

In a crucial sense, the ability to please readers is only half the battle of literature. To be "best-loved" at anything, you have to dance around the darkness. In *The World Is My Home*, it is the darkness that Michener avoids, seldom delving below the surface. He doesn't seem comfortable with intimacy or emotions, and one suspects that this must go back to his earliest days as an orphan, when he had to steel himself against the world rather than embrace it. Although he has gone through two painful divorces, he mentions them only in passing. His current wife is barely alluded to, and we get so little information about their relationship that we wonder at the intensity of Michener's privacy.

His public adventures are much more fully recounted. We are offered glimpses of Michener as a liberal politician, as a goodwill ambassador for the United States, and as a fortune-teller whose prescience astounds the residents of Doylestown. He sprinkles the book with famous names, but there is seldom anything surprising in the anecdotes, and we must be content to learn that he has palled around with singer Ezio Pinza, Walter Cronkite, and Art Buchwald, and that he lobbied to get Robin Roberts, the old Phillies' pitcher, into the Hall of Fame.

The portrait Michener draws of himself shows us an honorable, driven, high-minded man who hangs onto his optimism at all costs. His generosity to universities and to other writers is well known, and he may have no peer as a knee-jerk liberal—to Michener, that's a term of praise. Where his work will ultimately land is up to posterity, of course, but he has a right to be proud of his output, since writing one book, much less 34, demands respect. In contrast to most immensely popular novelists, he has picked themes and topics that are challenging and sometimes politically sensitive, and he has never indulged in the cheap shot.

In the end, *The World Is My Home* most resembles a Horatio Alger story, in which all the traditional American virtues lead to a triumph on the grand scale. It is an entirely American document that could not have come into existence without being nurtured by the Puritan taproots of the country. Michener's memoir is high-strung, entertaining, occasionally funny, and curiously touching in what it omits. We admire the passion and the energy he brings to the task, especially at the age of 85.

*Los Angeles Times*, 1993

## *James Thurber: His Life and Times* by Harrison Kinney

The obsession that led Harrison Kinney to write his epic new biography, *James Thurber: His Life and Times*, began when Kinney was a seventh-grader in Maine and stumbled on Thurber's work at his local library. He seems to have been both awe-struck and star-struck by it. He went on to write a college thesis on Thurber, tracked down his hero at the *New Yorker*, landed a job there as a reporter under Harold Ross, the magazine's legendary founding editor, and spent more than 40 years compiling the material that forms the substance of his exhaustive but ultimately winning book.

In Kinney's portrait, James Thurber comes across as a gifted, troubled, and often disagreeable man. Born in Columbus, Ohio, the town he made famous in his writing, he suffered a childhood mishap that marked him for life when an older brother accidentally blinded him in one eye with an arrow while they were playing a game. Thurber was shy by nature, and the accident increased his shyness and caused him to be clownish and awkward at times. He blamed his parents for not rushing him to a specialist and trying to save the damaged eye, and this perceived slight, Kinney writes, later became the focus for all his tumult and grief.

In high school, Thurber fell in love with the English language, acquired a reputation as a wit and turned into an avid reader, but he still showed no sign of his enormous talent as a writer. He washed in and out of Ohio State University and began to think that journalism might be his metier. Of particular interest during this period were his relations with women. He idealized them and remained a virgin until he "stepped aside" while traveling in France at the age of 25. His sexual initiation seems to have been traumatic, Kinney writes, and induced in him a form of nervous breakdown.

Within two years, Thurber was married and had embarked on what Kinney calls his "mockery of the female sex, developing a prejudice he would keep for a lifetime." Thurber presents himself in print as a highbrow Archie Bunker. "A woman is a person who will advise you tragically, on any and all occasions, that she can't take her hat off because her hair is a wreck," he wrote at the time.

To the good, he was also cultivating a prose style and learning from such masters as H. L. Mencken and George Jean Nathan. He went to France once more, got a job with the Paris edition of the *Chicago Tribune* and found a literary agent in Manhattan to circulate his freelance pieces, starting down the road that would eventually lead to his triumphant career at the *New Yorker*.

In this multimedia age, it's hard to imagine how powerful the magazine was in its first incarnation. It set standards, spotted trends and served as an emblem of sophisticated urban life. It was especially valued for its beautifully written light humor. Thurber had a knack for that, but he didn't break in easily. His submissions came back so fast, in fact, that he "began to believe the *New Yorker* must have a rejection machine." But he soon understood what Ross wanted—short, sharp features done in the chatty tone of a personal letter—and he was hired as a staffer in February 1927 with the help of E. B. White, who became one of his champions and dearest friends.

Ross had a genius for creating a psychological environment in which his maverick, brilliant, tormented and frequently drunken writers were allowed to flourish. Such key players as Thurber, Dorothy Parker and Robert Benchley had the status of Broadway stars and comported themselves accordingly. Drink would contribute to the death of many of them, including Thurber.

On the social background of the *New Yorker*, Kinney is very good indeed. He managed to interview virtually every important staff writer of the era, and his cross-cutting from one point of view to another provides a fresh look not only at Thurber but at the inner workings of the magazine. He is excellent, too, at tracing Thurber's evolution into a first-rate humorist and recounting his successes.

Among the most charming aspects of Thurber was his skill as a draftsman. The drawings reproduced here hold up wonderfully. He did them with a minimum of fuss on whatever surface happened to be handy—a menu, a scrap of paper, a restaurant wall. (The Smithsonian Institution has preserved a wall fragment from the *New Yorker*'s old offices with a Thurber drawing on it.) His artwork suggests a world glimpsed in outline, in fleeting glances, a world of the half-sighted, and he gets a remarkable amount of energy into a few minimal pencil strokes. He was a deeply insecure person, but the drawings give no indication of that. Instead, they have a deftness and surety that must have gratified him.

Thurber earned a decent living on his articles, but the big money finally rolled in when his plays were produced and Hollywood came calling. He had divorced and remarried by then, and his one good eye had started to go bad. He was also plagued by a syndrome that affected many of his peers at the magazine—they tired of doing the sort of writing that they were known for, their trademark stuff, but they were too fixed in their ways to extend themselves. The *New Yorker* specialized in small, well-made prose pieces and in gem-like stories that did not rock the boat. Its editors shied away from any dark or upsetting vision and generated in consequence literature that was admirably done but, as one critic has put it, inevitably minor.

It seems that Thurber was bothered by his position in the literary pecking order. Kinney tells of his meetings with four major novelists—Hemingway, Faulkner, Fitzgerald and Thomas Wolfe—and notes that each went badly. Thurber appears not to have grasped that great books can be written by an inferior prose stylist like Wolfe. What he cared about most was the structure and effect of his sentences, and he aimed for perfection in six or seven pages. He often hit his target, but his artfully casual pieces did not amount to a work on the scale, say, of *The Sound and the Fury*. His brain was so used to conciseness, he complained once, that he lacked the ability to stretch out. That must have been frustrating for a creative spirit.

Thurber's life ended sadly. He was almost completely blind at 45, yet he lived for almost 20 more years. It is a testament to his character that he still got some work done, mostly through dictation, but he gradually became more irascible and less stable and wound up offending everybody at the *New Yorker* with his book about Harold Ross (*The Years with Ross*), which was criticized for its unfair treatment of the founder. The times were changing, too, and William Shawn, Ross's successor, was steering the magazine in a new direction, away from light humor toward weightier reporting. Thurber railed against it all and died of a massive brain tumor in 1961.

Kinney's book is not without its faults, of course, and its 1,238-page length is chief among them. The word "leisurely" would be a kind way to describe the pace at which the story unfolds. We have to endure 300 pages before Thurber even gets to New York. The author has a tendency, as well, to regard the *New Yorker* with the same sort of devotion a practicing Catholic might demonstrate for the Vatican. One wishes, too, that he'd been more selective and analytical; the childhood episode that cost Thurber an eye, for example, is dismissed in a single paragraph.

It was E. B. White who warned Kinney that Thurber would not be a simple subject for a biography—White figured the project would take about 125 years—and we are fortunate that Kinney didn't heed his advice. He has captured the essence of a sacred monster whose blindness has in it the seeds of a Greek tragedy, and we are left to ponder how a man so tortured by private demons could put together a body of work that rests so lightly on his readers and affords them so many comic pleasures.

*Los Angeles Times*, 1996

## *Sir Vidia's Shadow* by Paul Theroux

Few writers are as ambitious, hardworking and gifted as Paul Theroux. He published eight books before he was 30, often writing them in trying circumstances while living poor in Africa and Asia. They might not have been written at all without the encouragement of his former friend and mentor, V.S. Naipaul, if we are to accept Theroux's account in *Sir Vidia's Shadow*, a memoir that raises as many questions as it answers.

The memoir is a tricky business, and Theroux knows it. He begins *Sir Vidia* as a roman à clef, with the arrival of U.V. Pradesh—a brilliant but difficult Indian writer—at a university in Uganda, where a young American—a would-be writer—happens to be teaching.

The tone is comic, but Theroux drops the fiction in the second chapter and confesses that he's lying. "Wait, wait, wait," he says. "This is not a novel, it is a memory." It would be impossible to disguise V.S. Naipaul anyway, he adds, asking us to believe that he had no choice in the matter, issues of trust and privacy aside.

When the real Naipaul steps onstage in Kampala in 1966, he comes across as proud, arrogant, funny, mannered and cruel, locked into a sexless marriage to a devoted English wife. He reads palms and is sensitive to vibrations. A Brahmin, he regards the world from a lofty height and despises the African bush. Its people are "infies," or inferiors, as are the tutors on the university staff. At 34, Naipaul cares only about his writing. Two maxims guide him—from the Gita, "One must act"; and from his heart, "Tell the truth."

Theroux, 10 years younger, is dazzled. He shows his early poems to Vidia (short for Vidiadhar), who remarks, "Lots of libido." The older man offers support and shares his wisdom freely. He's also lonely, in need of a friend. He and Theroux walk the city streets and take trips to Kenya and Rwanda.

Naipaul can feel the jungle closing in; he predicts Uganda's demise. At the Gardenia, where Theroux picks up bar girls, Naipaul admits that he was once "a big prostitute man." Always precise, he praises a roadside sign, "Beware of Fallen Rocks," for its economy.

These African scenes are wonderfully detailed. Theroux writes with a bright flame, for keeps, as though striving to meet Naipaul's impeccable standards. He captures the drunken, ecstatic chaos of Uganda as the country falls apart, and his pulse still quickens when he describes his wild shack-ups with the Gardenia women.

There are moments of pure poetry, too, as in the village of Bundibugyo, where "One night after rain I went outside and found thirsty children licking raindrops off my car." With a single image, he sums up a continent.

It's hard on Theroux when Naipaul returns to England. Not only does he miss his friend, he starts to see Africa through Vidia's eyes, as dusty and flimsy. Soon he is on his way to London for a Christmas visit, during which Naipaul generously puts him up and introduces him to his literary circle.

But Vidia's mood has not improved. The writing goes slowly, a form of torture. He ridicules others and reduces his wife to tears, dislikes children and avoids strangers. He does enjoy dinner parties, though, but only if he's the guest of honor. His work merits such treatment, he feels.

In time, Theroux marries and settles in England himself. He continues to write books that don't earn him any money, including one on Naipaul, *V.S. Naipaul: An Introduction to His Work*. Their friendship changes gradually, becoming more distant. Both men travel a lot and keep in touch by mail. There are occasional lunches; Theroux always gets stuck with the check. When Theroux has a commercial hit with *The Great Railroad Bazaar*, Vidia seems envious. Vidia's own books are still highly regarded, but they're more hermetic and insular. His life is troubled.

Naipaul suffers a blow when his brother, Shiva, dies at an early age. The two have never made peace. He conducts a public affair with a woman from Argentina and considers moving somewhere else. New York? Montana? He is fond of snow, but only in the abstract. He dreams of having a million pounds in the bank. He builds an elaborate wine cellar, although he scarcely drinks, and accepts a knighthood. Through it all Theroux remains his shadow—his loyal squire—despite his own growing fame, but the position is increasingly uncomfortable. The balance of power is shifting and inevitably does.

When Vidia's wife succumbs to cancer in 1996, Vidia asks Theroux to write an obituary, and he complies. He is astounded when, two months later, his mentor remarries.

The bride, Nadira Alvi, is a Pakistani raised in Kenya, much younger than Naipaul. She is not worthy of him, Theroux thinks, and yet Vidia is smitten, even happy! He holds her hand and tells an interviewer, "I took writing far too seriously." It is a complete reversal, one that ultimately leaves Theroux out in the cold.

The new Lady Naipaul decides to clean house. When a few of Theroux's inscribed first editions turn up in a bookseller's catalog, he faxes the pages to Vidia to tweak him. There's no reply. Instead, he receives a fax from Nadira—childish, ungrammatical, insulting. It strikes him as a little crazy.

Again he importunes Vidia, and again the answer is silence. He is obsessed by the situation; he feels used, angry with himself for defending Naipaul and explaining away his flaws. Vidia isn't eccentric; he's mean, "mistaken about so much." Even the work begins to seem suspect.

Theroux has one last meeting with his mentor, by chance on a London street, and Naipaul delivers a final piece of advice: "Take it on the chin and move on." But his old apprentice has done the opposite and has chosen to put the 30-year experience between covers.

We do not doubt the extent of his hurt. *Sir Vidia's Shadow* is a brave, intelligent book, rich in anecdote and beautifully written, but it's also vengeful and damaging in places. It belongs to the literature of transgression, wherein an injured party—the betrayed—turns into a betrayer and bends the rules to settle a score.

It may well be that Naipaul is a holy monster, guilty as charged: a monomaniac. His behavior is surely tongue-in-cheek at times, but at others he's undeniably nasty. In the end he will get his wish, and only his books will matter—and matter they do.

Whether he truly betrayed Paul Theroux is moot, however, and subject to interpretation. But it does seem strange that Theroux couldn't take an ounce of pleasure in his friend's late-blooming romance or find more to admire in his character. In closing the book, a favorite admonition of Theroux's father comes to mind, one that he cites in the text, just two words, "Be kind."

*San Francisco Chronicle*, 1998

## *Kingsley Amis: A Biography* by Eric Jacobs

Beware the authorized biography that's written while its subject is still alive. The pitfalls are obvious, of course, but they don't seem to have daunted Eric Jacobs, a Fleet Street journalist, whose life of Kingsley Amis has the air of an "as-told-to" rather than a critical study or a clear-eyed historical account. That doesn't make for an unreadable book, just one that skates lightly over the negatives and finds positives where they may not exist.

Amis, who died in 1995, gave Jacobs access to his papers and his person in exchange for a chance to use a red pencil on the final text. He used it sparingly, Jacobs tells us, but he had no reason to do otherwise, since the book's tone is mostly chummy. Jacobs enjoyed Amis's company and drank "a great deal" with him at various pubs and clubs, rising (or sinking) to such a degree of intimacy that he learned how Amis's bowel movements could affect his mood.

Born in 1922, Amis was an old-fashioned man of letters, equally at home as a novelist, poet, essayist and reviewer. He attended Oxford on a scholarship, where he distinguished himself as a mimic, a literary wit and a toper of truly prodigious thirst. He also met his lifelong friend Philip Larkin at university. They shared a passion for booze, jazz, books and women, and their correspondence forms a primary source for Jacobs.

Both men, in youth, complained about how difficult it was to find sexual partners. After a stint in the army, Amis put things right by marrying Hilary Barnwell, who was pregnant with his first child. Yet the marriage didn't keep him from belatedly sowing his wild oats. Soon he was having affairs with his new wife's friends, a pattern of infidelity that went on for many years. What was Hilary to do? "Motherhood and lack of money narrowed her options," Jacobs writes. "Besides, she still loved him, still wanted to keep him." One wonders.

In 1949, to support his family, Amis took a job teaching at a college in Swansea, Wales. He'd published a volume of poetry by then, but writing fiction was his chief interest. Five years later, he scored big with his first novel, *Lucky Jim*, an anarchic comedy about academics that sold extremely well and made his reputation. "Humorous, self-mocking, hopeful and endearing," said a blurb on the book's jacket—words that can still be applied to Amis at his best. Critics thought he might be the next Evelyn Waugh or P.G. Wodehouse; later, they began to ask if he'd ever fulfill his early promise.

Fame followed, and Amis seems to have handled it no better than most. He drank more, screwed around more (once, when he fell asleep sunbathing, Hilary used her lipstick to write on his back, "I F—Anything") and accepted paying gigs that forced him to travel to places he never wanted to go. His taste in literature remained parochial, though, and he pushed the merits of such minor British writers as John Dickson Carr while trashing giants like D.H. Lawrence and James Joyce.

Still, he always put in his daily stint at the typewriter. He would produce more than 20 novels in all, along with a miscellany of other books, among them *The King's English*. He hoped it would be a companion to H.W. Fowler's *Modern English Usage*, but it is more eccentric and cantankerous. The contents do point up the attention Amis paid to the importance of style, however, and the little essays he provides on, say, the exact meaning of "pristine" are often enlightening. He loved the language and worked to keep it as pure as possible, and that in itself was a worthwhile goal.

At the time *Lucky Jim* was published, the British press tended to regard Amis as "a provincial philistine drunk, boor, Lefty, and all-purpose Angry Young Man." That image would be revised over the next two decades, until he came to stand for everything conservative and even right wing, a Colonel Blimp of the literary world. He would desert Hilary and his children for another woman, but that marriage ended badly, too. In his 50s he complained to Larkin that he'd lost any desire for sex, and he turned into a crusty old bachelor who sought out his thrills at the bar of the Garrick Club.

The last years were not kind to Amis. His single high point came when his novel *The Old Devils* (1986) won the coveted Booker Prize. But he also stood accused of misogyny, watched his fame drop away and seemed irritated by his son Martin's growing success. He liked to toss Martin's books across the room and claimed never to have finished one. He had a terrible fear of living alone, so Hilary, now married to her third husband, a politician, took him in, and he would remain in her extended family until his death.

There's something delicious about Amis collaborating on an authorized biography, especially after he'd already written and published his memoirs. The premise could serve as a plot for one of his comic novels, with the subject and his scribe toddling off to the Garrick to discuss his vagaries over another round. Although Jacobs doesn't go very deep, it's fair to say he's never boring—a standard Amis insisted upon. He recounts the approved story in a good-hearted way, and his book should be read in that spirit, preferably with a glass of Amis's preferred Macallan scotch nearby.

*San Francisco Chronicle*, 1998

## *My Racing Heart* by Nan Mooney/*Stud* by Kevin Conley

There's a belief around the racetrack that all of humanity can be divided into two groups: those who fall deeply in love with horses and those who don't. If you belong to the first group, you can't help regarding the second as flawed in some essential way. Passion is relative, of course, but we still reserve the right to pass judgment on it. When Mozart's Requiem moves someone to tears, we're inclined to be approving, while we're less sympathetic to the fellow caught weeping over "The Impossible Dream." A heart that fails to respond to the beauty of thoroughbreds, then, probably deserves our suspicion.

Fortunately, Nan Mooney and Kevin Conley both have big hearts and an urge to celebrate the fact that horses allow us into their orbit at all. Mooney is an insider who writes for an industry journal, *The Blood-Horse*, and she tells us in *My Racing Heart* that she was seduced by the world of racing when she was a little girl. Conley stumbled into the magical realm as a reporter for the *New Yorker,* who wanted to learn more about the breeding habits of stallions and mares. Though their books differ in tone and style, the authors share the blissful sort of awe you see on the faces of riders in Central Park as spring approaches and blood dulled by winter begins to beat with renewed energy.

Mooney's story revolves around the impressive figure of her grandmother, Mary Stuart Mooney, known as May-May because a cousin "couldn't get his mouth around the word Mary." As a blue-blooded graduate of the Hannah Moore finishing school, class of '06, May-May could have assumed a privileged spot in the social hierarchy of Baltimore, but she was a rebel and a budding feminist and chose to hang out at Pimlico Race Course. She had fantasies about becoming a jockey, even though women were barely tolerated in the grandstand at the time, and eventually she bought a pair of broken-down American saddlebreds, nursing them back to health and driving them in trotting races herself.

May-May passed on her affection for horses to her granddaughter, plunking Nan down in front of a television set at the age of 7, pouring her a glass of port, and introducing her to the Kentucky Derby. Mooney had a rebellious streak, as well, so the two formed a bond that centered on racing and lasted until May-May's death. That put an end to Mooney's enthusiasm for thoroughbreds, at least for the moment. As a young woman, she pursued a conventional career, only to find the old attachment welling up again around her 28th birthday. She missed the risk, the excitement, and the camaraderie of the racetrack, and longed for a different life that was "authentic and rich and full," so the horses seduced her once more.

Mooney's account of her relationship with May-May is the freshest, most touching aspect of her book, but she is an ambitious writer and aspires to more than a memoir. Her account sets up as a quest; she tries to investigate every angle of the sport, as if piecing together a puzzle. Here she's less successful. She delves into racing's history, chats with people around the barns, and ties it all together with a thread of autobiography. But her design has a by-the-numbers quality that feels forced. Her visits with famous tricksters like Bob Baffert and Angel Cordero, the hotheaded jockey, amount to no more than interviews and don't reveal much that's new, while her historical sections might seem overly familiar to anyone who's done some reading about the track.

She's far better when she tackles Clevie Raines, a groom at Gulfstream Park, who likes to watch an *Untouchables* rerun when he rises for work at 3:30 in the morning. There's a friendly intimacy to the scene that's lacking when Mooney's working to plan. Her portrait of Donna Barton, one of the first women jockeys to compete in major races, is equally sympathetic. In fact, her book serves as an excellent reminder that the track is only slightly less patriarchal and hard on a woman than it was in May-May's day. Mooney's chief virtue as a writer is her ardor. She wants us to care as much as she does, so we overlook the rough spots and applaud her attempt to make it all cohere.

\* \* \*

Kevin Conley's *Stud* is tighter and more focused, and it explores a smaller canvas. Conley has two gifts any reporter would envy: ceaseless curiosity and a great sense of humor. His touch is light, sure, and charming, and his style is clear and intelligent. He had luck going for him, too, when he stepped through the looking glass and entered the big, complicated business of breeding racehorses, where he encountered "the sexual act in all its mystery and brute mechanics." He hit on a story tailored to his gifts. What comes across most forcefully in his narrative is the sheer amount of fun he's having. It's positively shameless.

The fun starts in the first chapter when Conley journeys to Lexington, Kentucky, to meet Storm Cat, the world's No. 1 stud, at Overbrook Farm, a high-stakes breeding operation. Storm Cat earns $500,000 for each mare he covers in season, at the staggering pace—in our pathetic terms—of two a day. The price might sound excessive, but his yearlings sold for an average of $1.68 million apiece in 2001, providing a return on investment any day trader would relish. The stallion has hundreds of children by now and still has a productive decade or so ahead of him, barring injury, illness, anxiety, or ennui. It's not surprising to hear that Storm Cat has a strapping libido, but Conley also serves up clever celebrity-type gossip about him, describing what he prefers to eat (bluegrass, oats, and sweet feed) and what he does for fun (rolls around in a sand pile).

Indeed, Conley's ability to turn the horses he studies into believable characters is uncanny. They're drawn sympathetically as individuals, from the majestic Seattle Slew—he is recovering from an emergency spinal fusion and must undergo physical therapy—to the hapless Honcho, a teaser stallion consigned to arousing a mare before he's replaced by the stable's star for the final act. Forever searching for parallels between the species, Conley claims to identify with the teasers ("like it or not"), because they have a "knockaround, real-life quality." His travels teach us we have more in common with thoroughbreds than we might think. "We both bluff, exaggerate, ignore; maintain alliances, betray loyalties, reward courage, seek affection; we annoy one another out of boredom; we mock our betters; we respond to flattery; we punish and humiliate those we can, and with those we can't we cultivate appearances. We try to get along."

Conley tends to run out of steam a bit as his inquiry progresses. There are only so many ways to describe a stallion mounting a mare, after all. When he wanders into the farm country of New Mexico and California to talk to minor-league breeders, you feel he's padding out the original idea. That isn't to say he fails to entertain. He's always witty and informative, but the material loses its edge, and though his prose is wonderfully colloquial, he has a taste for pop similes that can be distracting. When he evokes the noise Storm Cat makes during an orgasm, for instance—"frightening and long and full of the inevitable"— the air goes out of the sentence when he adds "like the squeal of tires you know will end in shattering glass."

Horse lovers will discover lots to please them in both *Stud* and *My Racing Heart*, two first books displaying talent and grace. Conley arrives at the paddock in fine command of his medium, as frisky and playful as a colt, and he treats his readers to a lively ride. Mooney has passion on her side, and though the risks she takes on her initial outing don't pay off entirely, she never gives it less than her all and manages to cash her share of winning tickets.

*The New York Times*, 2002

## *The Horse God Built: The Untold Story of Secretariat*
## by Lawrence Scanlan

It takes a brave writer to tackle a subject as well documented as Secretariat, among the most popular racehorses ever. Already celebrated in two substantive biographies, Big Red, as he was called, was such a media darling that he has been commemorated on a United States postage stamp. As Lawrence Scanlan notes, Secretariat came of age during the corrupt Watergate era, and since he didn't cheat, lie or order any illegal wiretaps, he embodied the wholesome values Americans treasure. When his picture appeared on the cover of Time in 1973, many readers found it "refreshing" to see the front end of a horse in the space often reserved for politicians.

Scanlan's goal is "to paint a fresh portrait in words," and he approaches the task from the perspective of an avid horseman rather than a track insider. His quest sends him on a road trip through Kentucky, South Carolina and Florida as he digs for any scrap of information that might provide a new twist on the old story. A zealous researcher, he seems to have read everything about racing and even attends such mundane events as the unveiling of a bronze statue of Secretariat in hopes that it will yield some clues.

From the start, Secretariat had the look of a matinee idol. Born at the Meadow Stud in Virginia, he was a handsome chestnut—"bright as an orange, shiny as brass"—and the manager of the farm described him as a "big, strong-made foal with plenty of bone." Despite such assets, the colt was so clumsy when he first took to the track that he earned the nickname Ol' Hopa-long, and it would be months before he was comfortable with his magnificent physique. (His heart was twice the normal size, and his gait the most efficient ever measured, according to an M.I.T. equine specialist.) Under the tutelage of Lucien Laurin, his French Canadian trainer, he went on to astound the public, never more so than when he won the 1973 Belmont Stakes by 31 lengths.

It's unfortunate for Scanlan that Laurin is dead, as are other members of Secretariat's entourage. More than 30 years have passed since the horse's last race, and memories grow dim. Racetrack folks are notoriously tough nuts for an outsider to crack, too, pledged as they are to a peculiar code of omertà. When a jockey or an exercise rider does open up to Scanlan, the results are hardly revelatory. Secretariat was a wonderful horse, they all agree, and everybody loved him. It doesn't help matters when Scanlan consults the Internet and reproduces similarly bland sentiments from the fans.

Scanlan fares better with Edward (Shorty) Sweat, Secretariat's devoted groom, a flashy dresser who liked vodka, danced the boogaloo and fathered four children by three different women. Powerfully built, with massive forearms, Sweat joined the exodus of Southern black men who hired on as grooms because the job paid a halfway-decent wage and beat picking cotton. The son of a poor sharecropper, he was working steadily with horses at 14 and eventually landed at Laurin's Holly Hill Farm, the ticket that led him to the big time in New York.

Like Laurin, Sweat has been dead for years, so Scanlan must rely on the testimony of friends and relations. He locates Marvin Moorer, Sweat's son, and the groom's old cronies Gus Gray and Charlie Davis, among others. Again the comments he records are remarkably uniform. By all accounts, Sweat was kind and generous, with a habit of deference to whites and a gift for drawing out the best in a horse. He adored Secretariat and even slept on a cot outside his stall before important races. Their rapport was extraordinary. Moorer says Sweat talked constantly to his charge in a Creole patois known as Geechee, a centuries-old slave language, and Secretariat listened.

In the end, though, there's a fair degree of unsolved mystery about Sweat, who lost his house in Queens in a dispute over back taxes and died a pauper. Drink played a part, apparently, and he may not have been properly compensated for his efforts on behalf of Secretariat and Riva Ridge, another Derby winner, but grooms are a strange tribe and often contribute to their own misery. Scanlan rightly praises them as unsung heroes who deserve better pay and living conditions, yet they also resemble Melville's Bartleby, in that they "prefer not to." Shorty Sweat had the skills to be a trainer, for instance, but Moorer suggests he didn't want the responsibility.

A case can be made that Sweat's sad decline was a form of mourning for the horse he loved, and the celebrity that went with it, but it's also probable that Sweat knew how to do only one thing—be a groom—and it wore him down. Scanlan is a compassionate reporter, but he doesn't bring Sweat to life or explore his dark side, so the rough-and-tumble aspects of racing stay under wraps. Still, the author is an amiable companion on the road, and his portrait, though neither gritty nor entirely fresh, will satisfy those who can't get enough of Secretariat.

*The New York Times*, 2007

### *Black Meastro* by Joe Drape/*Man O' War* by Dorothy Ours

Hard as it is to imagine, horse racing used to be nearly as popular as baseball, so rich in prize money and the profits from fixed races that Babe Ruth once demanded the Red Sox pay him as much as a top jockey. The Babe's asking price was $15,000 for one season, or about five grand less than Winfield O'Connor, only 15, had earned as a contract rider in 1900. Dressed in a white vest with $5 gold pieces for buttons, Winnie relished the role of superstar and shared the spotlight with some famous African-American jockeys, none more extraordinary than Jimmy Winkfield, the subject of Joe Drape's *Black Maestro*.

Born to sharecroppers in the Kentucky Bluegrass in 1882, Winkfield caught the racing bug as a pint-size kid and began working as a groom and exercise rider not long after. Since the days of slavery, owners in the Deep South had trusted blacks with their horses. As a black stable hand put it, the track was one of two places on earth where all men were created equal—on the turf and under it. Still, Winkfield didn't have it easy. White riders banged him around, and the stewards hampered him. After his first race, in Chicago, he was suspended for a year over a questionable infraction.

Yet Winkfield survived, improved and won the Kentucky Derby twice, in 1901 and 1902. Along the way, he met a lot of eccentric characters, whom Drape captures in cameos—Father Bill Daly, for instance, a wooden-legged New York trainer and owner (but not a priest), who preyed on Irish street urchins, schooled them as jockeys and beat them if they rode badly; and the inimitable Winnie O'Connor, whose pasty face "was often black-and-blue from his third career as an amateur prizefighter." His second was as a competitive cyclist.

The success of black riders led to a backlash, especially in the East. When Winkfield tried to crack the New York circuit, he got nowhere because white jockeys had formed "an anti-colored union." The rides began to dry up in Kentucky, too, thanks to Jim Crow, so he headed to Russia, where he took the drastic step of signing on as a stable jockey to Gen. Michael Lazarev, an Armenian oil magnate. Winkfield was 21, stood five feet tall and couldn't speak a word of Russian.

Drape's impeccable research lends this aspect of the story scope and drama. In Moscow, Winkfield rode so brilliantly that he joined the city's elite and married Alexandra Yalovicina, a beautiful White Russian. In Poland, he won the Warsaw Derby and became known as the Black Maestro. Even when the war broke out in 1914 and his apartment turned into a halfway house for wounded soldiers, he stayed busy until he was forced to move to quieter Odessa, leaving behind his wife and child.

Ultimately, the Red Army reached Odessa, as well, and Winkfield joined Frederick Jurjevich, a Polish horseman, on an incredible mission—herding 262 horses to Warsaw, so they wouldn't be cannon fodder. Afterward, he set up shop in Paris as a jockey, married another Russian woman and began training, only to be uprooted again by World War II. He departed for the United States in 1941 with $9 in his pocket and started over as a

60-year-old groom in South Carolina, although his tale doesn't end there. (He died in France in 1974.)

Drape's narrative gallops along at a sprightly pace. *Black Maestro* reminds us how important black riders were in those early days, a fact that's often overlooked or forgotten. The author, who writes about horse racing and other sports for *The New York Times*, does justice to an amazing life, but jockeys don't typically keep journals or write revealing letters, so we're left with a portrait that lacks psychological depth. Perhaps that's as it should be for a man of action, and there's more than enough action to satisfy.

\* \* \*

Another legendary figure undergoes close scrutiny in Dorothy Ours's *Man O' War*. Arguably the greatest American racehorse, Man O' War burst onto the scene just when the sport needed some fresh blood to wake it from the doldrums of a nationwide anti-gambling crusade. In 1911, only Kentucky, Maryland and Virginia offered state-sanctioned races with betting. New York was a wasteland until August Belmont Jr., the chairman of the Jockey Club, revived racing that same year with a "legal compromise" that allowed bookies to take wagers, although only via oral agreements with hundreds of "friends."

Belmont bred Man O' War, named in honor of his own efforts as a wartime major. By Fair Play out of Mahubah, the foal, who later acquired the nickname Big Red, was a tall chestnut with an impressive girth, so crucial for heart and lung capacity.

Needing cash, Belmont took his yearling to the Fasig-Tipton Company's sale at Saratoga Springs in 1918. Though Man O' War acted high-strung and looked ragged from a recent bout of distemper, Sam and Elizabeth Riddle plunked down $5,000 for him on the advice of Lou Feustel, their trainer, and their friend Jim Maddux, who was thought to be "unexcelled as a judge of horseflesh."

When Man O' War proved to be a diamond in the rough, the principals all wanted some credit for spotting him, and Ours (who used to work at the National Museum of Racing and Hall of Fame) cleverly conveys their wrangling. Like Drape, she has a passion for research, although she seems to include every fact she's uncovered, not always for the better. She approaches each of Big Red's races in the same way, describing the track, the crowd, the weather and so on, and these passages become repetitive. But she's good at sketching characters quickly, as she does with Feustel, who looked "as if the sculptor who had molded him got distracted before giving him a final polish."

*Man O' War* is clearly a labor of love, and it certifies Big Red's claim to immortality. The colt won 20 of his 21 races, usually carrying lots of weight, and his only loss—to the aptly named Upset—may well have been the work of a crooked jockey. Indeed, Big Red was so feared that few owners would run against him. His final race was a match against Sir Barton, the first Triple Crown winner, at Kenilworth Park in Canada for a pot of $75,000. Man o' War left Sir Barton in the dust, but he came back to the barn with a bruised foreleg and was soon retired.

At the Riddles' Faraway Farm in Kentucky, Big Red became a major attraction. "Tourists ask first where they can find him and then where they can find the Mammoth Cave," the farm's manager said. When Man O' War died in 1947 after several heart attacks, his funeral ceremony, "including nine eulogies and a bugler playing 'Taps,'" was broadcast around the country. His story lives on, a treat for die-hard fans.

*The New York Times*, 2006

## *Horse Heaven* by Jane Smiley

Horses have a knack for arousing our passions, especially at the racetrack. The sight of a talented colt or filly entering the starting gate wakes us from our usual doldrums and reminds us that we, too, are intuitive creatures and just as subject to the laws of chance. In an instant, we're cut loose from our moorings and reintroduced to the uncertainty principle, at which point the adrenaline kicks in and the heart starts pumping for real. Beautiful and noble, complex and frustrating, thoroughbreds speak to us in a language all their own, but only those who listen with great care can interpret them as admirably as Jane Smiley does in her spirited new novel.

The track has many different levels, and Smiley chooses to concentrate on the upper reaches in Southern California, where big-money racing is the order of the day and the wealthy owners have a shot at getting to the Kentucky Derby or the Breeders' Cup. Her trainers are modern fellows who breathe the same rarefied air as top trainers like Bob Baffert and D. Wayne Lukas. They're businessmen by default, forced to cope with cell phones and fax machines while they tend to the wrapping of sore ankles. Some are as dignified and high-minded as Farley Jones, who follows the advice in *The Tibetan Book of Thoroughbred Training*, a laminated sheet of paper taped to his office door, and refuses to hanker after signs of progress or see any fault anywhere; but others are as wily as Buddy Crawford, a maniac, butcher, madman and jerk, who sometimes depends on crooked vets and illegal drugs to achieve a victory.

*Horse Heaven* is crammed with similarly colorful characters. Take Marvelous Martha, for instance, still an exercise rider at 53, who studies kundalini yoga as a sideline, or Elizabeth Zada, an animal communicator capable of reading the streaming thoughts of thoroughbreds and plucking hot tips from the flow. Jockeys, grooms, breeders and bloodstock agents, they all roll through the pages in pursuit of their fate, and their paths often cross in unexpected ways. That's in keeping with the nature of the track, where the magical is commonplace and anything can happen. It seems perfectly credible that Tiffany Morse should walk away from her Wal-Mart job to join the posse of Ho Ho Ice Chill (think M. C. Hammer), a rap star who has "a real instinct for knowing what people wanted just before they wanted it" and rewards Tiffany with a horse of her own.

Smiley opens the novel in 1997, with a brief prologue that centers on four of the major equine players, all yearlings. Residual and Froney's Sis are fillies, bred respectively in Kentucky and California, while Epic Steam is a Kentucky-bred colt. The most lackluster of the bunch, at least in terms of his pedigree, is an unnamed colt from Maryland, who'll later be called Limitless and will confound the odds by going to Paris to run in the prestigious Arc de Triomphe as a 3-year-old. At the start, each horse is a cipher, with its destiny still unknown, but they should already be considered successful, Smiley says, since they have "gotten conceived, gestated, born, nursed, weaned, halterbroken, shod, transported and taught some basic manners with some misadventure but nothing fatal." Such witty, energetic sentences are a hallmark of the novel.

What's remarkable about Smiley's handling of horses as characters is that she manages to bring it off at all—and more, she does it brilliantly. Through an amazing imaginative leap, she enters into their heads and lets us see the world as they do. Epic Steam is big, burly, hot-tempered and as black as night, and you can feel the resistance in him whenever he butts up against an obstacle to his freedom. These horses are intelligent, too, and as involved in self-discovery as their human companions. Froney's Sis, orphaned when a month old, isn't sure about her identity and proves to be too delicate for the harsh demands of racing. Residual, on the other hand, has a "meditative air" and the bearing of a princess. In time, all four animals become distinctive presences, so well developed that you can almost hear and smell them, but it's a lowly gelding who steals the show.

Justa Bob is a 5-year-old hard knocker. He's such a calm, experienced guy, with 39 races under his belt by 1998, that he takes it upon himself to tutor inexperienced jockeys. A joker at heart, he teases the bettors and tries never to win a race by more than a nose. He has a stall at Santa Anita in the early chapters, but his age soon works against him, and he embarks on an astonishing odyssey. No longer does Justa Bob compete in classy allowance company; instead, he is turned into a claiming horse, one that can be bought or sold by any licensed trainer or owner, and he descends from the lofty heights and travels north to the Bay Area and east to Colorado, consistently traded down the ladder until he lands in the barn of R. T. Favor, a stumblebum in and out of jail.

Smiley's two-legged characters face problems of their own. They love their horses desperately, but they're much more cautious when it comes to relationships with other human beings. Rosalind Maybrick, the wife of a rich industrialist, throws herself into a curious affair with a trainer who suffers from dread, simply because she has a sense of wanting something that she can't name; while Farley Jones has an unexpected romance with a younger woman, a horse fancier who doesn't know what she wants, only what she longs for. In fact, a longing for the ineffable seems to affect everybody who's been touched by a horse. Buddy Crawford yearns to be a better person, and even embraces Jesus (although it doesn't help), and Audrey Schmidt, a little girl who's lost her father, dreams about cashing enough tickets to own a thoroughbred someday.

The racetrack provides an ideal, multidimensional backdrop for all the plots and subplots Smiley puts in motion. Her research is exemplary, too. It's deeply satisfying to read a work of fiction so informed about its subject and so alive to every nuance and detail. From veterinary surgery to the riding tactics of jockeys, she has immersed herself in the anecdotes and the lore of the track, and that allows her to create some nifty set pieces, as when a horse doc encourages an overtaxed stallion to mount a mare by serving him a ration of gin. Only a writer dedicated to the fine points could have come up with Luciano, a horse masseur and amateur philosopher, whose answer to stress is to defeat it with a plate of gnocchi and a glass of wine.

In such a big, ambitious book, there are bound to be a few slow spots. With so many characters in action, it's inevitable that some stories will be more compelling than others. The quirkiness of the cast gets a little cute at times, and a couple of people could disappear and never be missed. Smiley has a much-appreciated gift for narrative, but her prose can be clunky in places. And the novel, as a whole, is so sunny that a realist, particularly a paranoid, might wish for a splash or two of darkness to even out the canvas.

But this is *Horse Heaven*, after all, and a heaven of any kind implies a happy ending. It's no surprise, then, when the bad dudes don't wind up paying for their sins. Buddy Crawford ought to be punished for doping Residual and giving her a life-threatening case of pleuropneumonia, but the filly battles back and survives. Epic Steam, banned from flat racing on account of his savagery, finds redemption as a jumper. Even Justa Bob is spared a trip to the knacker's yard, courtesy of a sympathetic trainer. There's a benign deity at the helm in Smiley's world. Her final chapters have a wonderful restorative quality, filled with grace notes and epiphanies that offer a fitting close to this smart, warmhearted, winning book.

*The New York Times*, 2000

*Every Time a Friend Succeeds Something Inside Me Dies:*
*The Life of Gore Vidal* **by Jary Parini**

Lonely, alcoholic, incontinent, arthritic, confined to a wheel-chair in the Hollywood Hills and listening tearfully to tapes of his dead partner, Howard Austen, croon Sinatra tunes is how it ends for Gore Vidal in Jay Parini's revealing new biography. What a sad last act for the former boy wonder who, at the age of 25, had already published five novels including *The City and The Pillar* (1948), a best-selling landmark in the history of gay literature. It takes some unravelling for Parini, a friend and fan, to get us from Point A to Point B.

Vidal had an unruly childhood. Born Eugene Vidal, he adopted his maternal grandfather's surname as his first, an homage to Senator Thomas Gore of Oklahoma. The senator's flamboyant daughter, Nina, was his mother. Her marriage to Vidal's father, a South Dakota farm boy and football star, was brief, and she soon embarked on a life of parties, affairs, and wealthy husbands. She "loved athletes, famous men, and booze, not necessarily in that order," her son remarked. They rarely spoke. "She didn't see me," he complained. "I wished I didn't see her."

In Parini's opinion, Nina's early defection caused Vidal's crippling narcissism. Her neglect led to his need to "inflate himself." Vidal might well take issue with that theory, much as he once distanced himself from the word homosexual. It's an adjective that describes a sexual act, he insisted, and not a person. Though he was a tireless cruiser who favoured cleancut youths, he refused to think of himself as gay; instead he was a "degenerate," a term he used ironically, who "messed around" with guys. He took pride in being a top, more "manly" than a submissive role. The sex he preferred was furtive, often anonymous.

In spite of his early success, Vidal encountered an unfortunate literary truth. The good reviews don't always translate into bank notes, so he turned to TV and the movies to fund an increasingly lavish lifestyle. His scripts earned him a small fortune and a slew of movie star pals like Paul Newman and Joanne Woodward. (Vidal was a world class name-dropper, a tendency Parini shares.) He bought an estate on the Hudson River, the first in a series of grand properties that culminated with a villa in Ravello, Italy, known as La Rondinaia or "swallow's nest" for its perch on a cliff overlooking the Gulf of Salerno.

Parini makes a case for Vidal's fiction, citing in particular the late historical novels that began with *Burr*, but it's the essays that matter. There's no one who writes so incisively or intelligently about the "United States of Amnesia" now. Vidal pulled it off with brio and wit, gleefully tackling the power brokers. He stood witness to his country's moral laxity. "The world, in his view, had fallen away from a beautiful moment at the inception of the American republic, when—briefly—the ideals of life and liberty seemed to prevail," writes Parini. Talk shows still courted writers back then, and Vidal made the most of it. "Never lose an opportunity to have sex or be on television," he quipped. He sparred with Mailer and Capote on *The Dick Cavett Show*, and jousted with William Buckley, the Republican arch conservative, in several explosive debates during the 1968 presidential conventions. (A new documentary, *Best of Enemies*, focuses on the debates.) When he accused his opponent of being a crypto-Nazi, Buckley called him a queer and threatened to punch him—heady stuff for prime time. It only added to Vidal's fame.

Vidal travelled widely and once, disgusted with the US, considered a move to Ireland. He had Irish ancestry on both sides, liked the tax angle, and looked into buying some property, dirt cheap at the time, in Dublin or Cork. "He had this fantasy of being some kind of Irish gentleman," Howard Austen, sounding exasperated, told Parini. "I think he was reading Trollope . . . I said, 'No way!' I wouldn't set foot in Ireland!"

Meanwhile, the list of Vidal's celebrity chums grew longer—Princess Margaret, Claire Bloom, Leonard Bernstein. He nicknamed his coterie "the Swirl."

At his core, Vidal remained a devoted writer, brave and fearless. Mailer, his ostensible antagonist—they actually had a lot in common—praised him in private for handling homosexual themes "modestly, soberly, and with instinctive good taste." His *United States: Essays 1952–1992*, a 1,300-page tome that should have come, notes Parini, with "a retractable handle and little wheels," won the National Book Award for criticism in 1993. His acceptance speech was predictably tart. "As you have already, I am sure, picked the wrong novelist and the wrong poet," one line went, "I am not so vain to think you got it right this time, either." Shades of Oscar Wilde.

Parini's book has a curious provenance. Initially Vidal, always controlling, invited Walter Clemons, a sympathetic reviewer, to write his biography, but Clemons never finished it. The project fell next to Fred Kaplan, who delivered a long, stolid work that displeased its subject. Vidal lobbied Parini to write another version, but Parini had his own obligations to fulfil. He suspected his mentor would drive him crazy, too, so he held off until Vidal exited stage left before seeing *Every Time* into print. His stated aim was to portray the "angel and monster alike."

To a fair degree he succeeded. Parini was fond of Vidal, so his tone is gently affectionate. He's content to relate the facts without digging too deeply. He could've done more with such sources as Anthony Burgess and Graham Greene; they're given short shrift. The book was written at intervals over decades, and it feels sketchy in places. But the diaries Parini kept offer valuable observations and insights, as well as some splendid set pieces—a liquid lunch in Amalfi with Bernstein, for instance, who shouts at the garrulous Gore, "I'm the fucking guest here! And I can't get a word in edgewise!"

For all his fame, Vidal died alone in Hollywood at age 86. He'd salted away a $37 million estate, but he didn't leave a dime to his closest relatives or the devoted Filipino cook/nurse who cared for him during his last years. He donated the money to Harvard instead, presumably for the prestige. That shouldn't come as a surprise. He seems never to have been beholden to anyone, except perhaps Howard Austen. He fashioned an empire of self, as Parini puts it, and from that there was no escape.

*Irish Times*, 2015

## *Dog Soldiers* by Robert Stone

With the death in January of Robert Stone, at the age of 77, the United States lost one of its grand masters, a novelist of keen intelligence and supreme integrity whose work never shied from addressing such daunting questions as the problem of faith in a godless age.

In Stone's books, as in Joseph Conrad's, the value of human life always hangs in the balance, and his characters, because of their frailty, confusion or plain mean-spiritedness, often serve to diminish it. That's certainly the case in *Dog Soldiers* (1974), a classic tale of the paranoia and duplicity of the Vietnam era, now reissued by Picador.

At the novel's centre is John Converse, a jaded freelancer based in Saigon, who gets involved in a drug deal to earn some easy money—or so he assumes. In exchange for arranging to smuggle three kilos of heroin into California for a former lover Converse will make a cool twenty grand. But he soon feels uneasy about the mission and wonders if that's because he finds it morally objectionable.

Moral objections can be slippery in Vietnam, however. Sometimes, as Converse has learned, they are overridden by "larger, more profound concerns."

He recalls an incident known as the Great Elephant Zap, when machine-gunners in US planes mowed down elephants (a true story) because they were "enemy agents" carrying supplies for the Viet Cong. The Zap left everyone disgusted, but the memory leads Converse, hyped on pot and Scotch, to a cock-eyed revelation. "And as for the dope, Converse thought, and the addicts—if the world is going to contain elephants pursued by flying men, people are just naturally going to want to get high."

So much for the moral objection. Converse has overridden it. As for his malaise, it's merely fear: "It was the medium through which he perceived his own soul, the formula through which he could confirm his own existence."

In this remarkable passage, with customary insight, Stone deconstructs the hapless logic that governed the United States' conduct in southeast Asia, showing how its ripple effect threatened to corrupt an entire society.

The bungled war grew into an obsession, one he came by honestly. After the success of his award-winning debut novel, *A Hall of Mirrors* (1967), set in the New Orleans of hipsters and hucksters, he moved to London and decided to see Vietnam up close—a duty, he felt, for an American writer of fiction. He obtained press credentials of a sort from *Ink*, an underground paper, and bought a plane ticket. He lasted six months and departed in a state of shock. The war "was this enormous, endless, boundless, topless, bottomless mistake." Stone told the *New York Times*, "something I was not used to seeing the United States do." His outrage colours every page of *Dog Soldiers*.

Converse's path to the big score quickly turns rocky. His partners in crime are equally unsuited to the task. His wife, Marge, a cashier at a sleazy San Francisco porn theatre, has a taste for opiates herself, and his courier, Ray Hicks, an old army buddy, is a probable psychopath who studies *The Portable Nietzsche* and "cultivates the art of self-defense."

Hicks, too, is uneasy about the job. Dealing smack is bad karma, he believes, but he agrees to deliver the stash to Marge. "Why not, he thought. There was nothing else going down. He felt the necessity of changing levels, a little adrenalin to clean the blood."

That "why not" echoes through the novel like a mantra. In the absence of moral objections it's possible to construe every act as permissible, even excusable, from slaughtering elephants to dropping napalm on innocent civilians.

Among the dark pleasures of *Dog Soldiers* is Stone's inimitable style. Few writers can match his range. He swings from baroque literary flourishes to down-and-dirty street talk, creating a rhetoric all his own. His dialogue is tart and blackly funny, one reason Hollywood latched on to his books as movie material. (Stone wrote the screenplays for *Dog Soldiers*, filmed in 1978 as *Who'll Stop the Rain*, with Nick Nolte, and for *A Hall of Mirrors*, filmed in 1970 as *W.U.S.A.*)

For Hicks the nightmare starts at Marge's place. She's strung out on Dilaudid and doesn't have the money he's owed on delivery. Worse still, two men break into the house while they're arguing. They claim to be feds; Hicks subdues them: "'You know these guys?' Marge shook her head. 'We're Federal Agents, lady,' the blond kid said. 'You're in plenty of trouble.' Marge looked at him for only a moment. 'Are they?' she asked Hicks. 'They're take-off artists,' Hicks said. 'That's who they are.'"

Whoever they are, they want the heroin. Hicks and Marge escape, hitting the road through southern California's low-life enclaves and attempting to unload the drugs. Converse, back home, falls victim to the phoney feds, who savagely beat him and drag him along as they track the fugitives. All the elements of a highbrow thriller are in play.

The chase ends at a commune near the Mexican border, where Hicks once basked in the hippy glow. That scene is now as dead as the Summer of Love, and the resident guru zones out on home-made rose-hip wine. Hicks and his pursuers engage in an apocalyptic shoot-out, and it's fair to say, without revealing the details, that no one is better off in its aftermath.

Converse and Marge, reunited again, are on the lam without the heroin, although scarcely a happy couple. "'Why does this shit happen to me?' he asked Marge. 'Do I like it?' 'You manage to handle it,' she said. 'Handle it?' He was outraged. 'One thing I hate,' he told her, 'is tough-mindedness. It repels me.' 'Sorry,' she said."

Some critics cite *Dog Soldiers* as Stone's best novel, but surely *A Flag for Sunrise* (1981), his Central American epic, or *Outerbridge Reach* (1992), about a solo sailor who betrays himself by cheating to win a race, are just as accomplished.

And for sheer enjoyment there's his memoir, *Prime Green: Remembering the Sixties* (2007), an account that begins aboard a naval transport ship in Antarctica and features his adventures with Ken Kesey and the Merry Pranksters. The title refers to the greening of the day on Manzanillo Bay in Mexico, where Kesey hid out for a while—primal, primary, primo.

Stone's short stories will also reward the reader, particularly the anthologists' favourite, *Helping*.

Robert Stone was a gentle, humble man, the child of a schizophrenic mother and an absentee father. For four years from the age of six he lived in an orphanage run by Marist brothers. Largely self-educated, he carried his learning lightly. Stone had a finely tuned sense of humour, qualified as a first-rate raconteur, and loved a drink and a good conversation.

When Stone was last in Dublin, some years ago, we talked about the world's ongoing miseries over a pint. Our only hope for the future, he suggested, was to imagine that we're better than we are. His characters usually fall short of the mark, but the books they inhabit will last a long, long time.

*Irish Times*, 2015